WOMEN

and

SOCIAL

POLICY

PRENTICE-HALL SERIES IN SOCIAL POLICY

Howard E. Freeman, Editor

Constantina Safilios-Rothschild

WOMEN
and
SOCIAL
POLICY

prentice-hall, inc.
englewood cliffs, new jersey

Library of Congress Cataloging in Publication Data

SAFILIOS-ROTHSCHILD, CONSTANTINA
  Women and social policy.

  (Prentice-Hall series in social policy)
  (Bibliography)
    1. Women in the United States.   2. Women's
Liberation Movement.   3. Woman—Rights of women.
I. Title.
HQ1426.S22   301.41'2'0973   73-12215
  ISBN 0-13-961698-5
  ISBN 0-13-961680-2 (pbk.)

HQ
1426
.S22

To all women and men who have the courage
to bring about in themselves and around them
the significant changes necessary
for liberation.

10   9   8   7   6   5   4   3   2   1

Printed in the United States of America

Prentice-Hall International, Inc., London
Prentice-Hall of Australia, Pty. Ltd., Sydney
Prentice-Hall of Canada, Ltd., Toronto
Prentice-Hall of India Private Limited, New Delhi
Prentice-Hall of Japan, Inc., Tokyo

CONTENTS

PREFACE

A large number of books about women and the liberation movement appeared in the late 60s and early 70s. Many of the early books were angry and polemical, and represent catharsis for women's long-repressed rage. Some books have been historical analyses of women's status, feminist women, and liberation efforts of earlier times. More recently some books have presented sophisticated sociological, psychological, or political analyses of sexism in different life sectors. Meanwhile there has been a proliferation of exciting, fascinating ideas related to sexism and liberation in all kinds of journals and professional, literary, and women's literature. Many professional and popular journals have had special issues on women. The Women's Liberation Movement seems to have set afire women's imagination and stimulated their creativity. Women are doing increasingly high quality, original research, and the findings often suggest significant reformulations and refinements for existing theories or creation of entirely new theories. Meanwhile organized formal groups or informal groups of women, or individual women, are involved in different types of social action aimed at changing sexist laws, policies, practices, and, to the extent possible, sexist values and attitudes.

But it is rather striking that despite all the abundance of literature, ideas, and research about sexism and women and women's active and relentless commitment and involvement in social action, there has been no book on social policy. It is exactly this vacuum that this book attempts to fill. The main purpose in writing it was to delineate the entire map of strategies, social action, policies, and laws necessary to effectively eradicate sexism from all aspects of our lives and from the entire society. In doing so, available facts, research findings, and experiences in practice of different strategies or social action, and in the implementation of laws and policies in American and other societies have been synthesized within the framework of a number of theoretical assumptions derived from sociological theories and the liberation ideology.

Because of the book's dual emphasis, on the one hand, on synthesis of available and relevant information, research, and theories, and, on the other hand, on the detailed description of the range of social action, social policy, and laws that can and should take place, it will have a wide audience. It is relevant not only for classes on "The Sociology of Women," "The Sociology of Sex Roles" or on "Women's Studies," but also for courses on the "Family," "Social Problems," "Social Policy," and "Contemporary American Society." Furthermore, it would be a very useful book for all women who as leaders or members of formal women's groups or as individuals are actively involved in social action to bring about liberation. Furthermore, officials in government, foundations, industries and corporations, unions, universities, and other large bureaucracies will find in this book a delineation of a platform of necessary short-range and long-range changes to eradicate sexism, and a rationale for these changes, as well as their implications. Finally, this book will also be valuable to all those women and men (particularly those men who are the recipients of women's individual or collective pressure for change) who cannot quite understand and are still asking, *"What do women want?"* This book will answer all the questions they have always wanted to ask but were afraid to hear the answers...

While writing this book many friends, colleagues, students, and my liberated husband collected very valuable articles and information for me and became increasingly aware of the high degree of sexism around us. I owe a great deal to all of them. In addition, I am very grateful to Jacques Dofny, Barbara Polk, and Pamela Roby who read the draft manuscript and made most valuable comments, criticisms, suggestions, and additions. I am particularly indebted to Jacques Dofny who not only read and commented on the many drafts and colected several articles and information from French journals and newspapers, but who also discussed several important issues with me and helped me grope for possible alternative answers.

Of course, I am basically thankful to Howard Freeman who invited me to contribute this book to the series on social policy that he is editing, to Ed Stanford for his cheerful and friendly support, and to Sheryl Fullerton who copy edited this book with enthusiasm and love, and who significantly contributed to its clarity.

Finally, as always I am most appreciative of my good friend Irene Zak who typed the many drafts of this book while raising her consciousness and that of her whole family considerably.

CONSTANTINA SAFILIOS-ROTHSCHILD

Chapter 1

THE THEORETICAL BACKGROUND OF SOCIAL POLICY AS RELATED TO WOMEN

Some Introductory Comments

Analysis of all social movements shows that their first stages usually focus on efforts and activities that help bring about new forms of consciousness and new groups of people with common ideals and goals. Thus we find that the Women's Liberation Movement in the middle and late 60s necessarily represented a concentrated effort toward making women and men aware of the disastrous effects of traditional sex roles upon their lives and upon their chances for growth, self-actualization, and happiness (Kontopoulos, 1972). All social action as well as most writings were directed toward unmasking women's oppression or both women's and men's oppression, all types of discriminatory practices against women, and women's unhappiness and lack of self-actualization due to both discrimination and the operation of traditional sex roles at the psychological level. While the women (and to a lesser extent men) were raising their consciousnesses by intensive and emotion-laden collective soul-searching in rap sessions, and as new followers were coming to the Movement, research regarding discrimination was also accumulating. And a new term, *sexism,* was coined to go hand-in-hand with racism—to refer to the *entire range of attitudes, beliefs, practices, policies, laws, and behaviors discriminating against women (or against men) on the basis of their gender.*

The intensive early focus of the Movement on consciousness-raising was a necessary beginning. As a result, large numbers of women (and a considerable number of men) became aware of gross discriminatory and oppressive policies, practices, behaviors, and beliefs, and, increasingly, of some of the subtler forms of sexism, regardless of whether or not they formally identified with the Movement. A new collectivity of people "enlightened" but differentially committed to the causes of the Movement has now emerged. Most of them agree on the nature of the problem and that something must be done to bring about change. But not all agree on *what* has priority and *how* changes should be accomplished, partially because the nature of the goals and the necessary strategies have never been clearly defined.

Analysis of social movements also indicates that once a new collectivity with a considerable degree of togetherness, rapport, collective activities, and esprit de corps has emerged, a well articulated ideology and an ideal image of the future, as well as specific delineation of their course of action, become necessary. Only then has a social movement become specific, crystallized, and only then has it ceased to be a "passing fad" (Kontopoulos, 1972). The articulation of the ideology started in the 60s together with consciousness-raising efforts, and there has come to be considerable agreement concerning not only basic ideological principles but also the features of the ideal sexism-free society and man-woman relationships of the future.

What is totally missing, however, is an integrated synthesis of the ideology, the research evidence on all types of sexism, and the required strategies, policies, and social action necessary to free women and men and the society from all types of sexism. The time is right in the Women's Liberation Movement's stage of evolution for such a synthesis. Sufficient evidence of all types of sexism has already been collected and a sufficiently large number of women (and at least some men) have become aware of and concerned with sexism. The collection and presentation of more evidence would not by itself serve any worthwhile purpose at this time. Those who still remain unconvinced cannot be convinced by factual evidence because their resistance is emotional. Not only are definite social action and strategies needed in order for significant social changes to occur, but delineation of appropriate and comprehensive social policy is also necessary at this point, since efforts, social changes, and policies must be well coordinated and focused, as well as mutually supportive and reinforcing.

The Basis for Social Policy Recommendations

First of all, recommendations for social policy made in this book will be based primarily upon the implications of the synthesis of research findings and factual evidence about sex roles and sexism with the basic ideology about the nature of sex roles, sexism, and the nature of "liberation." In addition, the recommended social policy and strategies will also be based upon, and benefit from, related strategies, social action, social policy, laws, and recommendations that have already taken place or that have been proposed by different groups of women and men or by officially appointed task forces. While relevant data from different countries will be discussed when available, most of the research and the social policy information relates to developed Western societies, especially the United States, Canada, Sweden, and some Eastern European countries.

Whenever the reactions to, difficulties encountered in the implementation of, or "undesirable" side effects of proposed legislation, strategies, social action, experiments, or policies are known, their evaluation has helped to pinpoint danger signals of and possible avoidable errors in the formulation of recommendations, in their implementation, or in the type of strategies to be followed for the acceptance and institutionalization of social changes. Also, the experience gained in related or similar social policies has often aided the formulation of possible safeguards or alternative or simultaneous courses of action.

Second, a basic assumption of the recommended social policies is that, in order to effectively bring about significant changes in the status of women, social policy directly affecting only women is not sufficient. A wide range of social policy and action affecting the status of men, the institution and structure of the family, as well as the entire society (that is, the language, the law, religion, etc.) are necessary too. The psychology of women as well as their social-structural position and the range of their options can only change proportionately to the extent that the psychology of men and their options change—as well as to the extent to which the different societal institutions are freed of sexism. Since changes in women's options and values cannot altogether take place in the absence of considerable change in men's options and values and in the structure and dynamics of all societal institutions, many of the social policy and action recommendations are overlapping.

Third, despite some rather spectacular short-range changes in social policy, the liberation of women and men, as well as of society, will require a considerable period of time, maybe two to three generations to be complete. Because of the long and tortuous road that liberation most probably will follow due to strong emotional and "vested interest" resistance, drastic transitional policies and actions are necessary in the immediate future. Three different major categories of transitional policies and actions are needed only during those years during which people, institutions, social structures, and actions will be slowly and painfully moving along the multidimensional "nonliberation-liberation" continuum:

1. Measures and policies that aim at increasing women's and men's awareness of different options previously considered to be sex-role inappropriate and hence "deviant" must be employed. In order for women and men to extend their spectrum of choices significantly, some of these transitional measures and policies will have to be compulsory, especially in relation to the options of children and adolescents. The main reason for such measures and policies is to safeguard the new generations from the lingering stereotyped sex-role appropriate values and beliefs of their parents, teachers, and other adults. Compulsory attendance in designated courses, athletic activities, etc., at an early age would assure that children and adolescents of both sexes are equally exposed to a wide range of subjects, interests, and skills and have the same chances to evaluate their potentials, abilities, and inclinations in a variety of areas.

2. Another category of necessary transitional measures, policies, and actions will include special inducement mechanisms such as economic, prestige, or other types of inducements to be built into previously sex-role inappropriate options. These measures and policies are necessary to help adults of all ages to overcome their reluctance to opt for previously unconsidered occupational, educational, or role-playing choices by rendering these choices more socially acceptable, desirable, and attractive. In this way many significant changes will be possible before liberation is complete for people and the entire society.

3. Finally, a third category of transitional measures, actions, and policies will have to actively and selectively aid women in order to eventually bring about a state of social equality between women and men. Because of the centuries-old discrimination against women, widespread underrepresentation in all power, prestigious, or high-paying occupations, positions, and roles has placed them at a disadvantage. This discrimination has created such a serious unbalance that the establishment of equal options, opportunities, rights, and privileges for women and men would not *in fact* help to bring about social equality. Before the same opportunities and options for everyone can guarantee social equality, existing inequalities have to be corrected. These kinds of corrective, transitional measures are necessary, on the one hand, to influence and change women's values, self-concepts, and attitudes that now prevent them from choosing what are presently considered deviant options. On the other hand, they are necessary to change the social-structural and institutional conditions that have been for a very long time discriminatory against women, as well as to alter the prevailing set of subtle built-in resistances to equality. Only when people, institutions, social structures, and policies have managed to become free of all sexist remnants and hang-ups, will there be no more need for compensatory or compulsive transitional measures and policies. Social equality between women and men will then be feasible.

Here it must be said that many people mistrust and question the necessity for or desirability of compensatory, transitional measures, mainly because of their possibly "adverse" side effects. Such often mentioned "adverse" side effects may include overemphasis on newly available (and previously "deviant") options and the "discrimination" against previously privileged groups (in this case, white men). Thus, many women and men fear that measures encouraging women to work even when they have infants, or to enter previously "masculine" occupations, or to have one or no children may lead to different degrees of social disapproval or stigmatization of women who decide to be mothers and housewives, or who enter "feminine" occupations, or who have many children. It is, of course, quite difficult to accurately predict the extent to which a certain devaluation of women taking the "traditional" options might take place during the transitional period. But most probably such a devaluation trend will be only temporary and will tend to lessen after liberation has been achieved to a considerable degree.

It must also be taken into consideration that, while being a full-time housewife or a home economics teacher or a nurse might tend to be devalued in the beginning of the transition in comparison to being a lawyer, or physician, or university professor, other mechanisms and processes will be operating at the same time that will tend to upgrade these options. Concerning the option of the full-time mother and housekeeper, for example, the fact that some men may choose these options for some years of their lives, together with the fact that women choosing the same options would by law have to be paid wages for their services by their husbands, could significantly upgrade this occupation's prestige. Furthermore, the increasing diminution of barriers to upward mobility for women will contribute to the promotion of many secretaries to administrative positions, whenever most of their work involves administrative duties and responsibilities. Nurses could also re-examine their role within medical settings and redefine their functions and relationships vis-à-vis physicians, who will more and more be women. Thus, depending upon the stage of the transitional process, traditional options for women will be influenced by a number of various devaluating and upgrading factors.

The second fear, that the previously privileged group—men—will be discriminated against as a result of transitional measures favoring the previously oppressed group—women—is a fear typical of groups resenting the loss of their monopoly on advantageous and desirable options. The transition, for example, from a monopoly on exclusivity of options for high-prestige and high-paying jobs to the necessity to compete with equally or better qualified women will be painful for men, especially mediocre and average men. But the stress of this transition will be eased by the fact that at the same time men will gain access to a number of other significant and desirable choices previously open only to women, such as the option to work part-time for several years and enjoy fatherhood, their relationship with their wife (or mate), and leisure; or the option to stay home for some years and be full-time fathers and housekeepers. Men, in addition, would then have the very important choice to assume only partial responsibility for the economic support of the family. Thus, what may temporarily seem to be discrimination against men will in the long run lead to equalization of opportunities and options for women and men.

Fourth, it must be clarified that while legislative reforms and specifications are necessary and helpful in officially institutionalizing social changes and in legitimizing or occasionally stimulating social action, passing laws cannot guarantee the liberation of individuals and society. For liberation cannot be offered, it must be won. That is, individuals must want to be liberated, must demand that changes come about, must pressure those entitled or empowered to change policy and action, and must be psychologically ready and eager to make the most of legislation. The American experience with the Feminist Movement and acquiring the vote for women early in this century has shown that such legal steps make little difference when the majority of women and men are not ready for liberation and when women have not developed a consciousness of themselves as women.

Furthermore, it must be pointed out that in Sweden and to some extent in all Scandinavian countries the legal equality of women and men and the widespread acceptance of the equalitarian ideology by men as well as by women has suppressed the development of an active and militant Women's Liberation Movement like the American one. A considerable number of people in power positions—politicians, administrators, educators and intellectuals—have endorsed the equalitarian sex role ideology due to its social (rather than intrinsic) desirability, and there is no significant Women's Movement to stimulate and bring about changes, to closely examine the implementation of policies, and to help raise the consciousness of women and men. Because of the above special conditions, operating simultaneously, the outcome is much more static than warranted by the progressive social policies that have been already passed or are presently being considered in Sweden.[1]

Thus, it seems to be extremely important that there exists a significantly large number of women (and at least some men) whose values and attitudes are as sexism-free as possible and who have become conscious of and sensitized to all forms of explicit or subtle expressions of sexism. But it is not necessary to change everybody's values and attitudes in order to succeed in bringing about important social change. With a significantly large and militant group of liberated women and men effectively and consistently acting as a pressure group, the behavior of persons in powerful key positions, such as politicians, high level administrators, big businessmen, large industrial and business firms, and those who control the distribution of money and other resources can be changed so that they act in an equalitarian way or so that they treat women preferentially, regardless of their own personal values, attitudes, and feelings.

Most probably many of these key people who are pressured or induced to treat women equally or preferentially, despite their stereotyped beliefs

---

[1] The radical "Group 8" is very small, but it still probably represents the only effective pressure that Swedish women are exerting upon their government for needed legislations or social change and for the enforcement of existing legislations.

about the "role of women," may, in order to diminish the stress they experience from the discrepancy between their values and beliefs and the behavior required from them, seek some kind of stress-reducing mechanism. Such cognitive dissonance is often relieved by finding tactical usefulness and value in the superimposed behavior and through a process of rationalizing and at least temporarily relinquishing the contradictory set of values and beliefs. In this way some powerful sexist men might slowly and painfully move toward a psychological liberation that would permit them to do what is required with less stress.

Similarly, many social policies and much legislation do not have to be enacted and implemented only after the beliefs and values of the majority of people have changed. In many instances it is necessary to establish legislation and social policies that will help change women's and men's images of and beliefs about women. Thus legislation and social policy should not only reflect ongoing changes but should also stimulate and further the direction of initiated social changes.

At this point it is important to define *liberation* as used in this book. Liberation of women and men requires that they and act according to their wishes, inclinations, potentials, abilities, and needs rather than according to the prevailing stereotypes about sex roles and sex-appropriate modes of thought and behavior. Liberation by no means implies a "reversal of roles" as envisioned by those threatened by ongoing changes in processes and discussions. Men will not behave as women did before liberation and women will not behave as men do now. Some women and some men night *choose* to behave according to their sex's stereotypic "feminine" and "masculine" patterns. But some women and some men may *choose,* if they are so inclined, to take options in some or all of the life sectors now limited to the opposite sex.

The liberation of society, as opposed to that of people, means that the different social institutions and the prevailing social-structural conditions will be such that they permit women and men to take options for which they are most inclined and best fit rather than make choices as sex-stereotyped roles dictate.

The Assumptions of the Theoretical Framework

This book and all its included recommended social policies and actions are based on some fundamental assumptions or axioms about social equality and the "nature" of women and men. First, whether certain categories of people are the same or different, all people have the same rights to social equality in all life sectors and behavioral expressions. While their actual differences may be self-acquired or genetically inherited, how the differences were come by does not alter a person's claims to social equality. This principle holds true for women, the poor, racial or ethnic minorities, and different types of disabled persons.

Second, valid evidence to the present has pointed only to substantial anatomical differences between women and men. The available research has failed significantly to connect sex-role appropriate attitudes and behaviors with consistent biological, hormonal, or genetic differences between women and men. The existence of these anatomical differences has, however, been very important since it has usually led to inferior status for women due to the nature of social values attached to these differences. The visible anatomical differences between women and men aided considerably in the establishment of a social stratification system based on gender in which all women were inferior to all men. It is interesting to note that in societies in which these anatomical differences have been and still are exaggerated (North African and Middle Eastern Arab societies or the traditional Mediterranean societies —Sicily, rural Greece, and Spain) women have as a result experienced very blatant oppression.[2] Lessening the visibility of these differences by means of "unisex"-type clothing seems to be related, if not helpful to, decreasing sex-related inhibitions and prohibitions that oppress women.

Although social stratification systems based on gender may be convenient and "efficient" as some American male theorists have been arguing, such systems cannot survive because they have consistently led to the oppression of women. It could of course be envisaged that in some societies the social stratification system based on the anatomical differences between sexes might be retained as a transitory or more or less permanent classification system, but the inferior social values would be attached to male rather than to female anatomy.

Third, "masculine" behavior and "feminine" behavior are not determined by anatomical differences or any other inherent biological or endocrinologic differences between women and men. But sex-related behavioral and attitudinal distinctions are socially and culturally induced through lifelong socialization and continuous reinforcement and can, therefore, be changed by means of altered socialization experiences. On the basis of such socially and culturally imposed differences between women and men, a wide range of rights, privileges, and opportunities have been denied to women (and fewer rights and options denied to men), sometimes because of their alleged "biological inferiority," sometimes because of their purported intellectual inferiority, and sometimes because of vague or nonexistent reasons.

It is, of course, true that under the present widespread sex-stereotyped socialization practices by parents and other adults, much research concern-

_____

2 Actually rural Greek men (and other Mediterranean and Middle Eastern men) with very traditional values often touch their covered genitals in public as if to remind the world of their "tangible" anatomical superiority while the corresponding gesture for women would be considered unthinkable, most disgusting, dishonoring, and an indication of immorality and looseness.

ing differences between women and men, even with infants, is of little
validity. Testing many hypotheses relating to sex-related distinctions is extremely difficult, perhaps impossible. There is, then, at least some possibility
that many years hence, when liberation from sexism is more or less achieved,
we will be able to investigate behavioral differences on the basis of gender.
We might find that there are some behavioral attributes that are sex-related.
But even if this possibility exists, the strong argument for the need for real
and total social equality in terms of options and opportunity-structures still
stands. After all, all that these few possible sex-related behavioral attributes
can do is to eliminate a few options for some people, because a woman or man
is truly not interested in them. But this possibility (*and not fact*) cannot
warrant a state of social inequality, even if the existence of some biologically
determined differences between women and men were to be positively established.

According to these three basic axioms, a central assumption of liberation is that women and men have the right to the same set of options, un-
restricted by sex-stereotypes. Of course, here it must be clarified that the set of
possible options in each life sector and subsector is limited to those which are
not harmful to other people, to the society at large, and to the individual.
While suicide or living on opium are to some extent options open to individuals, it can be argued that both options must be avoided and that considerable effort be spent in convincing people to shun them.

Having a wide set of options to choose from is an important characteristic of modern life, especially when the same wide set of options is open
to *all* people, regardless of categorical membership such as sex, race, age,
social class, etc. (Safilios-Rothschild, 1970a). This, of course, is a modern
ideal toward which societies are moving at different speeds and with varied
enthusiasm, depending upon the type of categorical membership; the political structure, orientation, and commitments; the degree of the discriminated
group's organization and intensity of protest; and a variety of other social,
cultural, and historical factors. Thus, Eastern European and Scandinavian
countries have concentrated on the equalization of options across social classes,
but the degree of success seems to remain quite mediocre. In the Scandinavian
countries, especially Sweden, policies focusing upon the equalization of
options for women and men still cannot be assessed, partly because it may
be rather early. In the United States efforts in achieving equality have with
some success mainly concentrated up to now on the equalization of options
for blacks (and whites) because of the intense protest, open conflict, and
considerable success of the Black Movement.

In general, it seems that whenever ideology has preceded action,
thoroughly permeating a society's entire political system, so as to minimize
conflict and protest on the part of the interested parties, the success of implementation of social policies has been less than when an active "watchdog"

or protesting group follows the progress and success of the implementation of legislation and social policies. This basic difference may, for example, explain why the American Black Movement has been more successful (despite the lack of an overall ideological agreement among politicians and administrators) than the Sex Role Debate in Sweden. There politicians' campaigns sound like speeches of leaders of the American Women's Liberation Movement. But in Sweden there is no powerful Women's Movement, except the very small radical "Group Eight."

Since the equalization of options across each type of categorical membership (age, sex, race, social class, etc.) follows a different rate according to a number of factors and mainly according to the style and intensity of protest on the part of the discriminated group, it is best not to combine their causes. The rationale is not only theoretical; it is primarily tactical. The Women's Movement should not attempt to carry on its shoulders all the burdens of needed social reform. Liberation from sexism implies the equalization of options between women and men with the same financial resources, of the same social class, at the same age, of the same race, with the same inherent abilities and potentials. This battle is hard and complicated enough and does not need the further complications of arguing for equalization across social class, or age, or other categorical memberships. Women and men over fifty (or over sixty, whichever is the appropriate age ceiling) could, for example, organize separately as an interest group to demand and bring about the equalization of options for persons regardless of their age. But this type of protest and organization goes beyond the movement to free women and men and the society from sexism.

There is also a clearly political debate among some segments of the Women's Liberation Movement centering around the relationship between capitalism and women's oppression. Some women claim that capitalism is closely linked with the patriarchal society and the oppression of women, and that total women's liberation cannot be accomplished under a capitalist system. But as Eva Moberg, a leading spokesman for change in traditional sex roles in Sweden, has said, a male dominated society cannot be considered a direct consequence of capitalism, and socialism does not represent "any guarantee whatsoever against sex discrimination..." She also stated that she believed that important social changes could take place in a country like Sweden without a revolution (Moberg, 1971, as quoted in Linner, 1971). Moberg's beliefs are supported by cross-cultural research evidence indicating that the liberation of women and men does not seem to be related to the type of prevailing political system (Safilios-Rothschild, 1971). After all, probably the most significant social Women's Liberation Movement is taking place in the United States, a capitalist country. Furthermore, as we shall see later, women's or men's liberation has by no means been achieved in the U.S.S.R. or the Eastern European countries. We shall assume, then, that social policies and social changes necessary to bring about women's and men's liberation can take place under most major political systems.

Another issue raised by some women active within some segments of the Women's Liberation Movement is the need for redefinition of many existing values and social roles. For example, some women would question the extreme value attached to achievement and competitiveness in America and other Western societies. Or they would like to see some social roles so redefined that people (women and men) would not be able to misuse their power and cause large numbers of people without power to suffer from their decisions. While these issues are extremely important and require careful examination and the possible eventual formulation of relevant proposals, they again are beyond the scope of this book. What may be lost in scope will hopefully be gained in focus on one central, crucial area—the equalization at all levels of all options and opportunities for women and men.

The Widening of Options: Some Theoretical Questions and Implications

Having a wide range of options means that all possible choices are equally socially acceptable and desirable for both sexes. Each choice, however, does carry a different set of social, sociopsychological, and psychological consequences for the individual. Furthermore, having many options does not necessarily mean that everyone would necessarily have them throughout life. Taking one option often restricts further choices open to the individual. But it is very important not only that a wide range of options be open when one is making significant life decisions, but also that the decision-making not be intruded upon by sex-stereotyped inhibitions and proscriptions. Only in this way does the individual have considerable freedom in choosing the particular option that is best suited to his (her) needs, wishes, abilities, potentials, inclinations, and expectations.

The fact, however, that many options are at a specific time available to both women and men does not mean that they will remain open forever, or that everyone will desire to keep them open. Most individuals will tend to choose one alternative at the exclusion of all others. Some will try to combine several choices as far as possible, especially in the case of relatively overlapping and not mutually exclusive options. Others will try to take different options at different stages of their lives, but always one at a time. Finally, a few women and men might want, and be able to cope with, a multiplicity of options at all times. This, of course, means that they do not make a substantial commitment to any type of option, thus trying as much as possible to keep "all options free." But it is questionnable whether they can in fact do it. They will most probably end up entirely closing out some options, while diminishing the degree of intensity, frequency, or quality of interaction in most others, the degree of involvement varying with their value hierarchies.

The existence of many options will in most cases require a new model of socialization that teaches people how to cope with a multiplicity of options. People will need to learn to perceive, evaluate, and choose among different alternatives. New models of socialization will not prepare women and men for *one,* preferred, and socially desirable set of options, but will instead enable them to perceive and carefully assess all possible sets, as well as to identify the one(s) that best suits them. As with all models of socialization, it can be expected that a number of women and men will be incompletely or inappropriately socialized. They will be unable to perceive or accurately evaluate the available options or their own needs and wishes, or to make the "right" kind of decision representing the "best" fit between the available options and their own needs, wishes, abilities, potentials, inclinations, and expectations. Furthermore, it can be expected that these socialization "failures" will be much more frequent during the transitional period, while people learn the meaning of liberation, how to cope with options, how to make decisions, and how to appropriately socialize the new generations.

Furthermore, the history of humanity indicates that people have always invented cognitive and value systems—religious, ethical, cultural, political, familial—that narrowed their options to a few acceptable ones. In this way decision-making was simplified at the expense of personal fulfillment and satisfaction. This human tendency throughout the ages and in most societies suggests that women and men will again find a way to simplify decision-making by relegating the evaluating and choosing to a benevolent and trusted authority, in this case, most probably science. Behavioral scientists will be asked to help women and men choose the appropriate option by assessing the different alternatives and their consequences, as well as the individual's wishes, needs, expectations, and abilities. Some people may rely entirely on behavioral scientists and behavioral practitioners for most decisions. Others will rely on them only for decisions in some areas where the assessment of options and self requires great skill and talent. They will be able to do most other types of decision-making themselves. Still others will feel more comfortable and will be better helped by the experiences and the decision-making process of other women and men who have faced similar sets of options and similar potential decisions. The exchange of ideas found in the introspective and analytical atmosphere of group therapy sessions, encounter groups, or similar exchange groups that stimulate self-examination and critical assessment could be the most beneficial type of interaction for many people as they try to find the most suitable and enjoyable options.

Actually, it is interesting to note that it is the already existing trend toward this type of therapeutic model that might become increasingly prevalent (Scheff, 1972). This trend does not represent the "Brave New World." Already as more options become open to women and men, it is becoming increasingly obvious that people are not only asking the advice and help of psychiatrists, psychologists, and sociologists, but are also exchanging experiences, decisions, and tactics with a variety of "similar" people. Their efforts are directed toward understanding and assessing the ongoing changes, their meaning, and the impact on their lives. People need help in making decisions in view of new and yet noninstitutionalized options for which norms have not yet been formulated.

As has been true for all other cognitive and value systems, the degree of reliance upon the advice of behavioral scientists and practitioners may be greatly influenced by a person's degree of intelligence, consciousness, and degree of belief and trust in scientific assessment and expertise or in similar people's experiences and insights. And it is obvious from the ways in which all past systems of social control have operated that the benefit of scientific assessment concerning options in important life sectors would reach all individuals through primary schools, high schools, and diagnostic centers in clinics, industries, universities, etc. Costs of all these services would normally be covered under medical insurance. Scientific help with basic life decisions concerning educational, occupational, and maybe also marital and familial options would be dispensed free (as it is already in much of the U.S. and in most developed nations). Or, as an alternative, exchange and experience-sharing discussion groups among people who have faced or are facing similar decisions and dilemmas could be organized within different educational, work, and residential settings. Such groups could possibly use professional advice and services at particular critical points or for specific problems.

Since such a guided narrowing of options in the lives of women and men will most probably necessarily occur, one can ask what is, then, the point of widening the range and the sets of options? And what is the advantage of doing away with the presently operating restriction of options on the basis of sex stereotypes if the resulting wide range of options is again going to be narrowed? What will have been gained for human happiness? The answer is that a great deal will have been gained for human happiness, for the basis of such tapering will not in each case be an option arbitrarily chosen on the basis of religious, moral, social, political, or cultural values. In each case the "desirable" and "appropriate" option will not be determined by "external" factors but rather on the basis of the individual's personality, potential, needs, and wishes. Instead of creating misfits and maladjusted persons by trying to fit everyone in *one* desirable model, everyone can be helped to find the model that represents the "best fit." The degree to which each individual finds the "best fit" option in every life sector and subsector will largely depend upon his (her) own ability to understand himself (herself) and to assess options as well as the quality of scientific help or "friendly advice" he receives. The quality of scientific help, on the other hand, will not only vary with the behavioral practitioner, but also with the progress made by the different behavioral sciences in accurately evaluating personality, potential, needs, wishes, and expectations, as well as the implications of the different sets of options.

While undoing restrictions in options on the basis of sex stereotypes can, as explained above, lead to greater human happiness, another very important question remains unanswered. How will this novel model of option selection and life decision-making influence the social structure and functioning of societies? What will the new reference system be for predicting human behavior when the existing prevalent trends disappear? How will social planning be guided when we will not be able to predict that most people will marry and have children, or that practically all men will work, or that all married couples will live in the same type of residential unit?

It is quite important to answer these questions because they represent the fears of many people, including social scientists, who tend to envisage a chaotic situation resulting from the abolition of traditional, sex-linked limitations in the potential options of women and men.

It can be questioned whether a high degree of predictability of human behavior is necessary for the efficient, well-organized, and smooth functioning of a society. It can be further questioned whether a smooth, or a dynamic, uneven but ever-changing functioning is most desirable. Possibly the requirement that a high degree of predictability concerning human behavior is necessary is a bias developed in Western societies in North America and Western Europe. Many developing and developed societies in Latin America, Africa, and Southern Europe have managed to function adequately with a relatively low degree of predictability. Quite often and in many sectors the only clue to prediction and social planning has been the fact that no predictions could be made and, hence, a considerable degree of flexibility had to be built into the system by means of informal, flexible interpretations of rules, regulations, policies, and laws.[3] Thus it may be that the high degree of predictability of behavior required for societal functioning is at least to some extent a construct of a Western origin sociology. Furthermore, most probably even with this novel model of and criteria for option-taking and decision-making, some definite and predictable patterns of possible choices will emerge. Studying such patterns will permit social planning. However, social planning will now have to be much more versatile to accommodate a wider variety of life styles and models.

A final issue that may be raised is the extent to which all the recom-

___

[3] Of course, it is true that in many developing countries and in many areas the lack of predictability is met with a total lack of planning and inaction, but this is not necessarily due to the lack of predictability but to a number of contributing social-structural conditions.

mendations in this book, the abolition of sex-linked constraints, and the widening of options is meaningful for all societies, regardless of level of economic development. The basic question is actually whether or not a certain level of economic development is necessary before it is possible to open up the range of options available to women and men.

It must first be pointed out that widening the options in many life sectors does not cost money. But it is true that expanding educational and occupational alternatives is tied to and depends upon the economic and industrial structure of the society. While the number of jobs in a nation at a low level of economic-industrial development may be limited, which persons take these jobs does not depend upon the level of development. The fact that usually only men are permitted to take the jobs is determined by prevailing traditional sex stereotypes and not by the level of economic development. Furthermore, in most developing nations only a small percentage of the total population (even males) has access to certain options in different life sectors. The large majority of the rural poor and urban slum population is involved in an everyday, completely absorbing struggle for survival that does not permit the luxury of considering options. The usual alternatives facing them are of the following type: to starve, or to steal, or to become a prostitute in order to eat. But what is interesting is that the available evidence clearly indicates that even under such deprived living conditions, women have even fewer options than men because of beliefs about the inferiority of women and the associated sex-linked proscriptions and constraints. For example, even when only 10 percent of urban slum children go to school, more boys have this option than girls (Safilios-Rothschild, 1971). In fact, while the degree of prevailing sexism in developed societies is not related to social class, in developing societies sexism varies inversely with social class. Liberation in developing societies implies that the given number of jobs or the existing educational facilities are equally distributed among all children, girls and boys, the criterion for selection not being sex membership but potential, ability, and interest.

Probably a more basic difficulty than the low level of economic/industrial development blocking the abolition of sex stereotypes and the expansion of options for women and men in developing nations may be the pervasive influence of all types of particularistic rather than universal standards and criteria. Sex stereotyping fits a particularistic mentality, according to which an individual is judged and evaluated on the basis of *who he is* rather than on the basis of *what he is* or *what he can do*. Judging and evaluating women and men on the basis of their potential, abilities, and interests rather than on the basis of their sex membership (and the accompanying stereotypes) would require an even more radical social change and collective psychological shift than that required for economic and industrial development.

It is, however, possible that the liberation of women in developing societies with different combinations of political, religious, ideological, historical, and cultural structures and beliefs might become justified on the basis of selective features of these existing beliefs and structures. In some developing societies the "modern" economic and social development philosophies requiring the use of all potential talent, effort, and energy of citizens might aid the educational and occupational liberation of women. Following this initial utilization, the now larger base of well-educated, economically independent, and occasionally powerful women might become the nucleus for more fundamental changes in the woman-man relationships as well as in all major social institutions. In other developing societies, such as Islamic or Catholic societies, no significant steps can be made unless the liberation of women can be justified through reinterpretations and modernization of the particular religion.

In some cases the first social policies and actions toward social equality between the sexes might have to be vested with and justified by existing traditional beliefs. In other developing societies, the first steps will have to be clearly labeled as "social change" and "modernization" breaking away from tradition and the status quo.

Chapter 2

SOCIAL POLICY
TO LIBERATE WOMEN

Most of the social policies needed in order to combat sexism affect not only women and men but also a variety of societal institutions. Because, however, of the different impact and consequences of sex stereotypes upon women and men, there are some social policies more crucial for the liberation of women and others more crucial for the liberation of men. A number of these liberating policies require legislative changes, others require only policy changes within large bureaucratic structures, and still others require only changes in values and attitudes. In general drastic changes in the values and attitudes held by a considerable number of women (and men) are necessary to stimulate, implement, and follow up the reactions to liberating legislative or policy changes. In some cases legislative and policy changes are needed to stimulate changes in images, beliefs, and values held by women and men.

It must also be clarified that the liberation of women in different important life sectors implies the establishment of a wide range of socially acceptable alternatives that permit women to choose the one most appropriate to their needs, preferences, talents, and abilities.

Strategies to Liberate Women and Children from the "Motherhood Cult"

The "Motherhood Cult" has throughout history enslaved women more than all other beliefs and values. The idea that only children brought up with twenty-four-hours-per-day care by their natural mothers can have a normal development has cut women off from a large number of educational, occupational, political, and social options. This belief must be changed and the practical problems involved must be effectively solved. But how?

The practical problems of child care can be solved rather easily and without great cost once the disposition and willingness are there to take care of them. Primarily a basic principle must be discussed and clarified. The functions and tasks that women have performed as housekeepers, child care workers, social secretaries, and lay psychotherapists for their families do represent quite important, expensive, and terribly time-consuming and painstaking activities that will require considerable effort and cost to replace, once women refuse to do them any more in exchange for room and board. But the solutions *can* be a range of different alternatives, some of which can be quite inexpensive and painless.

The organization of efficient, well-run, and well-staffed child care centers operating twenty-four hours a day and equipped to accept infants and even newborns or sick children represents a necessary but rather expensive solution. Cost, of course, has not stopped the establishment of elementary schools and should not stop the establishment of a sufficient number of child care centers of the type previously described. They already exist in Scandinavian countries, Russia, and Eastern European countries (Roby, 1973).

There is still considerable resistance, however, to the child care center solution, especially as it applies to very young infants. Such resistance is largely due to long-standing psychological and psychoanalytic theories that predict and attribute everything that can go wrong with a child to the mother's absence from its side, even for a few hours, during infancy. Of course, by now considerable research has destroyed many of the favorite myths; e.g., that women who stay home to take care of their children are the best and most devoted mothers. Actually it was found that full-time housewives spend an average of less than two hours a day in direct interaction with their children (Rossi, 1972). It was also found that women who stopped working because they felt it was their "duty" as good mothers to stay home and take care of their children but who would have liked to work had, in fact, difficulties being "good" mothers. They had greater problems with childrearing, more problems controlling their children, were

less satisfied with their relationships with their children, and had less confidence in their functioning as mothers than working women (Radke
Yarrow, *et al.,* 1962).

Despite this kind of evidence (as well as significant potential improvement of children's socialization by freeing specific mothers and children
from the mother's possible neurotic tendencies and conflicts, or from limited
educational, cultural, and time resources, as in the case of lower-class
mothers), the resistance is still considerable among men and some women.
The reluctant women are most often those over forty. Such women either
have had to take care of their own children, causing at least for some years
a sacrifice of their careers and ambitions, or they did not marry and/or
have children because of the impossible burden it represented to their
careers. This category of women frequently opposes the day-care center
solution, probably because they cannot see that younger women need not
undergo the sacrifices they made.

The establishment of child care centers offers greater freedom and more
advantages to mothers who can then become self-actualizing individuals,
stimulating wives, and better mothers to their children. And such a solution
offers distinct advantages to children in terms of intellectual stimulation,
equalization, and optimization of chances for "normal" development as well
as resulting in "children's liberation." Children have the chance both to
interact freely with a variety of other children and a number of adults and
to be "themselves among equals" instead of always being under the direct
supervision of their mothers (Safilios-Rothschild, 1973b).

Despite all these distinct advantages for mothers and children, during
the transitional period at least there will still be some psychological resistance to this solution. But besides this issue, it is preferable that a number of
alternatives for handling child care be available, so that each parent can
choose the one most appropriate to her and/or his needs and preferences.

Alice Rossi has suggested one alternative which, when tried on a small
scale and under a variety of modifications, has had very good results. In
this situation, high schools provide girls and boys with practical experience
in child care and family courses by sending them for a quarter to take care
of children in a family while the mother is away at various activities or
work. Probably two students should be assigned to a family so that one's
illness or inability to be there would not leave the mother without assistance
(Rossi, 1972). But girl-boy teams should be avoided in order to avert the
danger of sex-stereotyped behavior that requires the girl to do all the "dirty
work" while the boy watches and gives suggestions and orders.

Other alternatives would permit mothers to take care of their very
young infants without penalties to their jobs and careers. Others would,
through a social and psychological redefinition of parenthood, permit fathers
to play an active role in childrearing and, thus, contribute to their enrich-

ment as human beings. Such alternatives would have to be reflected in legislation and policies related to maternity leaves, legal responsibility for raising and educating children, custody laws concerning children, financial responsibility for children in case of divorce, pension laws, etc.

Two basic principles must guide all necessary reforms in related legislation and policies. First, both parents must have an equal social and economic responsibility toward their children. Both of them must be equally involved in their children's socialization and development. This principle implies that fathers are just as responsible for childrearing, and taking care of well and sick children, and are as important as mothers in their children's "normal" development. The principle also indicates that, in case of divorce, mothers as a class cannot be considered the most important and absolutely necessary parent in the development of the children involved. And fathers as a class cannot be considered the ones exclusively responsible for the economic support of children. Laws should not only allow for choice of the father or the mother as the "right" parent to be granted the custody of the children, but should also specify that both must share in the financial responsibility for them. A new responsibility like this for women might have (as is true in Sweden) a depressing effect upon women's fertility, more so than many other direct or indirect measures of birth control. Women might be highly motivated to have fewer children when they will have to be financially responsible for them.

The second basic principle concerns pregnancy and women's work. Many discriminatory policies about women's employment have been justified on the basis of the sanctity of motherhood. Since we have now begun to think in somewhat more secular terms about pregnancy and motherhood, it is time to change policies so that pregnant women and mothers of very young infants can choose whether to work, how much time they will spend with the infant, and whether to interrupt work careers.

These two principles that permit pregnant women and mothers of young infants to enjoy the same options as other human beings and which divide parental responsibility equally between both parents also suggest a number of alternatives.

Some fathers and mothers may wish to spend a considerable amount of their time, although not all of it, taking care of their children, especially when they are very young. This choice should be open to women and men without penalties to their careers and/or advancement. Thus:

1. It should become a regular policy adopted by all employers that *a woman or a man* should be able to stay home and take care of a sick child for a certain number of days per year. Probably a total of ten days after a year's employment and twenty days after two years' should be allotted to each parent. Adoption of such a policy would allow for care of sick children at home, and could relieve the society of the expansive responsi-

bility for equipping all child care centers to accept sick children. This type of policy is already a reality in Sweden. In 1969, 11 percent of fathers in Gothenburg stayed home to take care of a sick child (*Woman in Sweden in the Light of Statistics,* 1971).

2. The institutionalization of part-time work for women as well as for men while their children are young would also constitute an important step toward the equalization of parental responsibility, the liberation of men, and the upgrading of part-time work. In order for this to be realized some conditions must first be satisfied: (a) providing the same fringe benefits for part-time and full-time workers; (b) crediting years of part-time work toward seniority, promotion, tenure, and salary adjustments in the same way as years of full-time work; (c) encouraging sufficient numbers of men to work part-time; and (d) making an effort to establish the part-time work option in at least some high-prestige occupations. The Swedish model owes its growing success to the increasingly successful fulfillment of the above four conditions (*Social Benefits for Part-Time Employees,* 1970).

Some outstanding congressmen and other influential and prestigious upper and upper-middle-class men have contributed significantly to the success of this measure by their personal and active adoption of part-time work. It is interesting to note that this kind of recommendation was also made by Jacques Henripin, member of the Canadian Royal Commission on the Status of Women in 1970 (*Status of Women in Canada,* 1970). Also a new French law permits civil servants with children under age twelve to work part-time for a period up to nine years without loss of seniority or pension rights.

This type of social policy gives parents the opportunity to spend a considerable amount of time with their children and in some cases to completely or partially forego the use of child care centers, if they can arrange their schedules so that one parent is available always (or most of the time) to take care of the children. The establishment of this alternative cannot by any means be expected to replace child care centers but it can relieve the excessive demand for them and help satisfy the parenting needs of some women and men.

3. Shared parental responsibility and exclusive parenting preference of some women and men should be reflected in the possibility for voluntary (but not obligatory) parental (instead of *maternity*) leaves. Such leaves would give both parents the opportunity legitimately to take time off from work to enjoy and take care of their infant. Here again the Swedish parental leave provisions are probably the most sensible ones in operation. Pregnant women are entitled to a paid six-month leave upon the birth of their child and a further unpaid leave of six months. The paid six-month leave can be divided equally between the mother and the father, but the additional unpaid six-month leave can be granted only to the mother. And the cur-

rently proposed type of parental leave (presented to the Swedish Congress) could well serve as a model to all other countries. According to the proposed legislation, women and men at the birth of a child are entitled to a year's paid leave which may be taken entirely by the mother or the father, or by both of them in any ratio or formula. For example, the mother might opt to take the first six months and the father the other six months, or the mother may take half of the week as paid leave and the father the other half while they both work part-time. Such legislation, if adopted by all employers, would more than any other type of policy legitimize shared parental responsibility from the time of birth and would provide a viable and often desirable (for many parents) alternative for child care during the infant's first year of life.

Of course, this year-long paid leave of absence would have to be treated very much the same as sabbatical leaves. An employee could not be fired during this absence, and would be obliged to return and work for at least one year for the same employer. Also, during the paid leave of absence, the employee would receive appropriate health insurance and retirement benefits, as well as across-the-board salary or wage increases, and would be considered, without any discrimination, for promotion, tenure, or other equivalent advancement decisions.

It is important to note that at least one university, the City University of New York, has already adopted a model of parental leave that makes a significant step toward the one we recommend here. According to this new model, starting with fall, 1972, wives or husbands have equal rights to a paid parental leave of up to twenty days or an unpaid leave of six months that could be extended up to eighteen months by the president of the college. Furthermore, these leaves do not in any way jeopardize the recipient's chances for tenure or promotion (Spiegel, 1972).

4. Probably the most effective—but also the most difficult to implement—strategies are those aimed at changing prevailing values and attitudes not only among laymen but also among professionals, especially family sociologists, family life educators, child development specialists, psychologists, and psychiatrists. The goal should be a greater acceptance of the important role of both parents. Care of children of all ages and both sexes by fathers should be considered equivalent and equipotent with that administered by the mother. There should also be greater acceptance of the fact that children do not suffer, but, on the contrary, benefit from the care given them by three to four different people, as well as from early interaction with peers in child care centers.

These attitude changes would be partly influenced by the dissemination of research findings that show the beneficial effects of such alternative child care models upon children's development, personality, and attitudes, and partly by new messages projected by the mass media, especially television. Already different research studies in the United States and Europe have started investigating some of these issues. They are expected to become increasingly free of biases and stereotypes that could interfere with the design, style of analysis, and interpretation of findings.

As objective research data become more available about the equivalence of different child care and parental models in children's development, it is expected that the mass media might start reflecting these new directions in their messages. Here, however, is an area in which federal and local funding could play an important role. Research funds could be made available for research and awards given to novels, films, and T.V. shows (not necessarily educational ones) successfully depicting the equivalence of parental roles, as well as effective, multiple child care models. Sex education courses for parents, young adults, and expectant parents, as well as students, could also play a very important role in changing attitudes through incorporating relevant research findings and in redirecting parents toward a wider range of parental and child care options.

Strategies for Women's "Housekeeping" Liberation

Some of the strategies needed in this area are similar to those discussed above because they are based on a redefinition of "women's roles" and "men's roles." Housekeeping must cease to be women's exclusive responsibility and become the equal responsibility of women and men. This does not mean that husbands will "help" their wives with some tasks and chores, while the wives retain the main responsibility for them as well as for all household organization and planning. And it does not necessarily imply that wives and husbands will share tasks and chores equally. Since such equality in labor division is hard to achieve or to maintain, it is better to think in terms of some type of division of responsibility to plan, organize, and execute the housekeeping needs of the family. Thus, this redefinition of women's and men's roles means sharing housekeeping affairs so that each spouse (and child over a certain age) can have the responsibility of certain tasks. In this way, the division of labor is, in fact and not only in name, shared by family members.

In some middle- and upper-middle-class Swedish circles the redefinition of housekeeping roles has effectively taken part since husbands have taken over the cooking and/or serving of meals to their spouse and guests, and/or the feeding and sleeping schedules of young children, or the entire responsibility for breakfast and/or dinner. It was also found that 72 percent of the Swedish husbands share (not help with) "washing up" with their wives, 66 percent share cooking, and 63 percent share cleaning (*Woman in Sweden in the Light of Statistics*, 1971).

Here again the mass media, especially television, could play a very important role in presenting husbands as sharing the responsibility for major housekeeping tasks in "normal" families in soap operas, movies, and other programs. Also major political figures (under the pressure of the women's vote, if not because of ideological commitment) could render this redefinition of men's role in housekeeping prestigious and desirable by advertising their own assumption of responsibility in some typical areas.

One condition that would greatly aid housekeeping liberation would be changing residential as well as commercial establishment patterns from isolated, one-unit type arrangements to integrated housing and commercial facilities. Town and city planning could transform urban networks to give more options to working couples who also want to have children. Up to now the physical planning of American towns and cities has been oriented toward one "ideal" family life model: the husband works, the wife takes care of the social and expressive needs of the family, mothering, and housekeeping. Furthermore, since the vestiges of a "pioneer" mentality mixed with romantic nostalgia still exist in the hearts of Americans, they did not consider cities to be conducive to healthy or gracious living, especially when children were born. Hence the "flight to the suburbs" and the physical, psychological, and social alienation of women who, through this move, were effectively and finally sealed off from most educational and occupational options. Since maids have been typically hard to find and expensive, and since many people have felt uncomfortable in using their services, women have been left with the painstaking and extremely time-consuming job of caring for large houses as well as for children. In addition, the great distances between houses and shopping centers or other commercial and service centers have taken up a considerable part of those women's time who were also left with all the other responsibilities.

Urban planning that would make apartment houses with incorporated services and facilities available for all income levels would greatly aid in the redefinition of housekeeping. Couples with children living in apartments with three to four rooms within five to ten minutes from their place of work (both wives and husbands), from most educational and cultural centers, and from all necessary facilities and services would spend much less time housekeeping, shopping, and caring for the different needs of the house and family members. Wives and husbands would then be able to devote more time to their own self-fulfillment as well as to their children. Apartments could also have a number of in-service housekeepers, cooks, and other staff people whose services could be hired by the week, the day, or the hour.

Design of apartments should allow for more styles of family living than the traditional one-or-two bedrooms and large living room arrangement. Many dual-career couples may prefer two small study rooms instead of a large living room, with the option to rent one or two large living rooms on the first floor of the building which would be available for tenants' parties and receptions. Many women and men prefer to work at home and seldom have the benefit of a conducive setting there. Moreover, the availability of such study rooms would alleviate high rent expenses since this part of the rent would be tax-deductible. The Scandinavian countries, especially Sweden, have been moving in this direction, and similar trends have recently appeared in large American cities such as New York, Detroit, or Chicago.

Of course liberation from housekeeping may also be interpreted as the liberation of all family members from it by engagement of one or more specialized persons (not exclusively women) to take care of it. Such a style of liberation, although predominantly dependent on the family's income level, reflects people's personal dispositions, the ease with which they use such professionals, and societal structure and organization, not only in terms of availability of such an alternative, but also in terms of the cost of these services. In a society in which the different types of seasonal services could be carried out by professional agencies and routine work by specially trained workers (women and men), the old-fashioned, expensive, and often domineering full-time housekeeper would become an antiquated custom to be chosen only by the very rich. Welfare and other forms of minimum income subsidizations could, on the other hand, include the cost of purchasing basic housekeeping services.

But liberation from housekeeping presupposes to a considerable extent certain conducive attitudes and living conditions. That is, it presupposes a change in values and attitudes concerning who is the "right" person to do the housework, what is the "appropriate" amount of money to be invested in the performance of housekeeping, and what is to be the required level and quality of housekeeping. It would be necessary to change the image of "good" family life. In the present image the unemployed wife does all the housekeeping, even in large houses. An alternative could be professionally trained people doing the work efficiently. And perfect order and orderliness could be made to seem symbols of undesirable conformity, typification, and sterility.

Strategies to Broaden Women's Training and Educational Options

Sexism in education is still quite prevalent throughout the world, although the degree of explicitness varies widely from nation to nation, from educational institution to educational institution, and from educator to educator. In many developing nations the majority of women still remain illiterate, especially in rural areas and in the urban slums. Their rate of illiteracy is always significantly higher than that of men, regardless of the men's low level of literacy. This is due primarily to prevailing sex-stereotypes in those countries that attach very little importance to education for women. Young girls must also assume responsibility for younger siblings while the mother works in the fields or as a servant (Safilios-Rothschild and UNICEF Secretariat, 1971). In addition, the quality of education received by girls is usually quite inferior to that received by boys, especially in countries where schools are not coeducational (Chabaud, 1970). It has been found that even when schools are coeducational a variety of discriminatory practices and attitudes results in girls showing poorer performance and a lower level of learning (Safilios-Rothschild and UNICEF Secretariat, 1971b), but the overall education of girls in sex-segregated schools is even lower.

Furthermore, girls and women are denied the acquisition of a salable trade in most developing (and developed) nations, including agricultural trades. Instead, girls and women are most often trained (when training schemes are present) in household and child care skills, sewing and embroidery. They are thus prepared to be housewives but not working women, as evidenced by the high unemployment rates of "trained" women who seek employment in all developing nations (Chabaud, 1970). Because of these conditions, these women who need to work to support or help support their families often are forced to become prostitutes or to work at the most unskilled, unstable, and poorly paid jobs because they lack necessary skills.

In most developed countries sexism has generally become more covert and subtle in recent years, with the notable exception of France where some professional colleges have only recently admitted women. In general, women are still officially or unofficially excluded from most types of professional military and religious training and from many "hardcore masculine" skills, trades, and professions, such as most building trades, many engineering specialties, as well as from being professional pilots. In addition to such educational and training fields, women are still quite effectively barred from many other fields stereotyped as "masculine" by means of adverse social pressure, discouragement, or downright refusal. They are psychologically discouraged on the basis of incompatibility between "masculine" or scientific fields and "femininity." The arguments, "After all, who wants to marry a woman engineer?" or "Why spend ten or eleven years getting a medical degree when you'll just marry and have children and stay home?" are still prevalent.

Even in countries like Sweden where equality of educational opportunities has supposedly been long established, analysis of school textbooks undertaken in the middle and late 60s showed that those used in all subjects and at all levels were permeated with sexism. In arithmetic books, only men drew up budgets, negotiated loans, bought land, or built houses. In history textbooks, the status and significance of women was often left out. (Westman Berg, 1969). Women were portrayed most often in domestic roles, and young girls were shown doing house chores (Fredriksson, 1969).

Similar findings have been reported in Dermark, Norway, and Finland (as reported by Westman Berg, 1969).

In educational options and opportunities, socialist countries like the U.S.S.R., Poland, Hungary, and Czechoslovakia seem to have considerably less sexist practices than all other countries. Women are trained at all levels for many trades, skills, and professions traditionally labeled "masculine" (Safilios-Rothschild, 1971). But as we shall see later in this chapter, women in socialist societies suffer as much as American or Swedish women from sexist practices in the occupational sphere. They too are greatly discriminated against in terms of promotions, advancement, power, control, and remuneration (Sokolowska, 1965). Furthermore, there is some evidence that in the U.S.S.R. males are preferentially admitted over female applicants to the science faculties of universities (Dodge, 1966).

Since the onset of the Women's Liberation Movement in the United States, a series of analyses, studies, and documents have appeared in the late 60s and early 70s that show quite clearly the extent of discrimination, as well as the techniques by which girls are effectively restrained within a very narrow range of training and education that is considered to be "feminine." Within the educational system the following factors are important: the textbooks used at all levels; the teaching style of teachers and their own sets of sex stereotypes; the sex-stereotyped games played and the sex-appropriate sports and hobbies in which boys and girls are encouraged to participate; the sex-stereotyped social life promoted by schools at all levels; the advice of vocational counselors; the sex-typing of fields, courses, and levels of achievement in them; and the *de facto,* if not official, exclusion of girls and women from several types of vocational training and professional education.

STRATEGIES TO COMBAT SEXISM AT THE ELEMENTARY AND HIGH SCHOOL LEVEL

We can now examine more in detail each of the areas in which women have been discriminated, as well as the strategies that could lead to the weakening of the sexist trends throughout the entire educational process, that is, at the elementary and high school level.

Sexism in Textbooks. The textbooks for all subjects and levels have been found to abound with and to be characterized by rigid sex-stereotyped roles and behaviors portrayed for men and women. A recent investigation in the Ann Arbor Public Schools has clearly shown that representative textbooks used in mathematics, history, or social studies portray only men in diversified occupational pursuits, high positions, and active roles. Women, on the other hand, are shown as predominantly occupied with housekeeping and mothering activities and only rarely in "feminine" occupations such as nursing, salesladies, waitresses, and maids. Women, and girls, are never portrayed in important, dominating, or very active roles but always as secondary, passive, and subservient to men. Men are shown as making important decisions and bringing about significant social changes while women follow and obey these decisions and prepare the men's meals. These trends are consistent both in the text and in the accompanying pictures (Federbush, 1971). Similar trends have been found in analyses of children's books (Weitzman, 1972), as well as in textbooks used in Canadian public schools (*The Status of Women in Canada,* 1970). The findings of a committee of forty-six teachers, historians, and school administrators who reviewed twenty-five social studies textbooks for grammar and high school for the Michigan Department of Education are also similar. They concluded that although some of these textbooks had somewhat improved in their treatment of blacks over the textbooks available in 1968, they remained sexist, and women were barely mentioned in history books (Salpukas, 1973).

Protesting letters directed to the publishers of these textbooks have been rather favorably received. These publishers proclaimed their eagerness to rid their textbooks of sexism (Federbush, 1971). Probably their knowledge of the women-dominated teaching professoins coupled with the potential significant loss of income from rejection of traditional textbooks are making them more sympathetic and sensitive to such protests than other institutions.

In addition to the publishers three other sets of involved parties must agree before a significant change in textbooks can come about: the teachers, the authors, and the educators who approve the use of textbooks for schools. Despite the fact that most teachers, especially at the elementary school level, are women, considerable consciousness-raising must occur among these women before they become aware of the situation and become motivated to change it. Women's liberation groups such as NOW could play a vital role in organizing consciousness-raising groups for teachers as well as for parents separately and/or jointly according to the starting point and the stage of consciousness reached by each of the two groups. Pressures that liberated teachers and/or parents could bring to bear upon schools and school systems would be quite effective in hastening the appropriate changes not only in textbooks but also in many of the other discriminatory features of the school system.

Concerning authors of textbooks, the most effective strategy for change would be the establishment of high prestige awards for textbooks in all fields and on levels judged to have the most sex-stereotype-free text and illustrations. Such awards established at the city, county, state, and federal levels could motivate authors to examine and analyze their own sex stereotypes and to become aware and sensitive to the extent that they avoid them in their writings.

Finally, a recommended strategy for the selection of nonsexist textbooks for use in public schools would be the appointment of a liberated educator (woman or man) as a sort of ombudsman in the selection process and in the replacement of sexist textbooks with nonsexist ones. Slipups in the implementation of this ideal either at the selection or the use level would be thoroughly investigated and speedily corrected by the ombudsperson.

Sexism in the Teaching Process. There is considerable evidence that teachers at both the elementary and high school levels tend to be quite biased in their treatment of students by sex-appropriate stereotypes. This seems to be true both for women and men teachers. Hopefully at least some of the women teachers, through experiencing a greater consciousness of the artificiality and arbitrariness of traditional sex roles, might become less biased in the future. The bias is demonstrated by teachers paying much greater attention to their male rather than their female students by disapproving them, punishing them as well as praising them, helping them, and following their progress more closely (Meyer and Thompson 1956 and 1963; Maccoby, 1966). Furthermore, a recent study of Canadian elementary school teachers showed that they punished boys much more often than girls for aggression and poor academic performance, and that they assigned housekeeping chores to the students entirely according to traditional sex stereotypes (Mulawka, 1972).

In addition, many teachers hold firm stereotypic notions about what subjects girls and boys can be interested in, and actively interfere with boys' or girls' desires to enter a course traditionally stereotyped as appropriate for the other sex (Federbush, 1971). Girls' attempts to take a traditionally "masculine" course are, then, seriously questioned by teachers and usually dismissed as not being "serious" educational aspirations but rather as a desire to "be with the boys" (Federbush, 1971).

There are, of course, other manifestations of such bias on the part of teachers in their treatment of the content of textbooks (reinforcing the included stereotypes), in their everyday classroom discussions of relevant themes, as well as the occasional more private talks with individual students. And there is evidence that teachers actively and effectively transmit and reinforce the traditional sex stereotypes by clearly delineating sex differences through separate seating arrangements, assignments of boys and girls to sex-appropriate activities, roles, games, and sports. Their reinforcement of traditional "feminine" and "masculine" behavior and choices through ridicule, high scholastic expectations and other types of pressure (Federbush, 1971) is also evidence of bias.

It has been reported, on the other hand, that teachers in some Detroit schools are categorically told by the principals of the schools that they must teach the traditional sex roles to the students—no Women's Liberation "nonsense"—or they will be fired. There is no reason to believe that the Detroit schools are atypical in most of the United States and in many of the developed nations such as Canada, Holland, Germany, or France. Under such deliberately sexist policies and pressures, teachers need a very active, supportive, and powerful group of protesting women and parents to go against them.

Very often individual liberated teachers and parents underestimate the extent of pressure and power they can exert, if they are determined and if they are knowledgeable about appropriate procedures. A very good example of individual initiative and effectiveness was recently provided by one of my students in a seminar on "The Sociology of Women." She studied, through available data as well as interviews with teachers and administrators, the public school system of Grosse Pointe, an upper-class suburb of Detroit, Michigan. As a result of her realization of prevailing sexist practices and attitudes, she is now trying to raise the upper-and upper-middle-class parents' level of consciousness and to organize them into a powerful and influential group.

She sent copies of her findings to the president of the Grosse Pointe Board of Education, the only woman member of the Board of Education, the Superintendents of Schools, the Assistant Superintendent of Personnel, the Head Counselor, the Education Chairperson of the Junior League of Detroit, the President of Grosse Point Citizens for Education, and to other leaders of important civic and educational clubs and associations. The result up to now has been that her report has been placed on the executive meeting agenda of the Grosse Point Board of Education, as well as on their public meeting agenda. The Assistant Superintendent of Personnel is setting a meeting between superintendents, the board of Education and the initiating woman, Eva Fillion. The Superintendent of Instruction plans to use her study to train elementary school teachers for new social studies units which attack bias through attention to values and decision-making. And all other organizations are studying her report in order to establish what social action they can initiate to bring about significant change (Fillion, 1972 and 1972a). This effort on the part of one determined woman effectively illustrates how much one person can accomplish single-handedly. Many more individuals or groups of women could replicate her efforts in different areas where changes are desperately needed.

Several strategies must be simultaneously put into action for the educational situation to be corrected, if we wish to provide equality of opportunity to all people and to tap and develop everyone's potential to the maximum. Thus the training of teachers must be changed to include good solid courses about sex roles and training students in a sex-stereotype free way. New curricula must be devised for educating teachers as well as students that would treat all subjects without sex stereotypes and would educate teachers concerning the "compensating" strategies necessary during the transition to a liberated society. Here the federal government can play an important role by allocating research funds in education to create new sexism-free curricula. In addition, the continuous availability of special training funds for practicing teachers to attend summer workshops on "Teaching without Sexism" would greatly assist the evolution of already trained teachers.[1] Of course, great attention should be paid to the people who organize and teach these workshops so that the right orientation is given. Sociologists, psychologists and educators who have been involved in teaching courses on women would be excellent choices for teachers in these workshops.

The already mentioned consciousness-raising efforts by women's organizations and the appointment of school ombudswomen who would follow up the implementation of policies and process complaints about sexist incidents would help both in the continuous evolution of teachers and administrators and in the consistent enforcement of appropriate strategies. For liberation from sexism is not a definite state that, when reached, is free of backsliding and regression. On the contrary, those who try to bring about and enforce the liberation of an institution from sexism will at first be faced with difficulties, doubts, conflicts, and retrogression at every step. This type of liberation in the educational process cannot be expected to be smooth or easy. For a long time to come both teachers and students, regardless of their degree of liberation, would be inclined to act according to sex stereotypes rather than according to their wishes and inclinations. That is why teachers, even after appropriate training and consciousness-raising sessions, would have to continuously check their behavior, attitudes, and values in order to assess the extent to which they may be still influenced by sex stereotypes. They must also assist and encourage students to choose and to act according to their abilities, talents, and wishes rather than on the basis of deeply ingrained sex stereotypes. The process will be slow and difficult and there will be much regression. Only continuous introspection and reassessment can achieve the desired goals.

Sexism in Vocational Counseling. There is also considerable documentation that vocational counselors are equally, if not more consistently, biased by traditional sex stereotypes than classroom teachers. Vocational Counselors

---

[1] It is interesting to note that such a short summer workshop for teachers at all levels was organized in July, 1972, by Dr. Nancy Schlossberg and Dr. John Pietrofessa, professors at the Department of Guidance and Counseling, School of Education, Wayne State University. Dr. Elizabeth Douvan and the author presented findings about sexism in education. The teachers and counselors involved were required to come back after three months and present evidence of concrete steps they had taken to diminish sexism in their school systems, the style of teaching, the curriculum, and the values and orientation guiding vocational school counselors. On the basis of these reports of implemented action, they were given credit for the training workshop. This represents an interesting model for a training workshop that could be funded by the National Institute of Education and other foundations. It would be more helpful, of course, if the teachers, administrators, and counselor trainees could have access to consultation by policy-makers, lawyers, and social scientists where the consultation fees were provided by the training grant.

have been found to hold definite sex stereotypes about girls' and boys' occupational choices that result in an extremely narrow range of appropriate occupations for women. Women vocational counselors seem to be guided by sex stereotypes as much as men counselors and to be equally and frequently discouraging to women wishing to enter a "masculine" occupation (Pietrofessa and Schlossberg, 1972; Thomas and Stewart, 1971). Many of the so-called objective scientific tests and criteria they use in determining girls' and boys' occupational aptitudes and in assigning the most appropriate types of occupations have been proved to be permeated by sexist biases. For example, the test most commonly used to measure vocational aptitudes, the Strong Vocational Interest Blank, is so biased that it classifies people with the same vocational aptitudes as potential physicians, if they are boys, and as potential nurses, if they are girls. Actually, this test discriminates against women in two ways: First it lists different occupations for each sex; second it sets different scoring requirements for an occupation listed for both sexes. For example, many more women can make a high score in the occupation of physician on the men's form, and less than half of them can do as well on the women's form (Schlossberg and Goodman, 1972). Also the recent biographies of young women have consistently showed how vocational counselors in high school strongly discouraged them from "deviant" occupational choices, that is, from any type of occupation stereotypically considered to be incompatible with women's "nature" and "destiny." It is interesting to note that some definite action has been already taken by the American Personnel and Guidance Association on this matter. It has passed a resolution stating that (1) the Strong Vocational Interest Blank clearly discriminates against women, and (2) that a commission of the Association in cooperation with the test publisher set a deadline for new sexism-free forms to be published and distributed ("American Personnel and Guidance Association Cites Vocational Test for Sex Bias," 1972).

The same strategies that hold for elementary and high school teachers also hold for the liberation of vocational counselors. An additional strategy is needed, however, in order to free the psychological tests and theories of sexist bias. Research funds should be made available for the specific task of revising psychological tests so that they become free of lingering sex stereotypes, as well as for rethinking and reformulating existing psychological theories. The availability of research funds for these types of activities would facilitate the implementation of important work by ideologically committed psychologists and vocational counselors, in addition to the opportunistic attempts of those who always tailor their interests according to the ever-changing funding trends.

It is important to note that the October, 1972, issue of *The Personnel and Guidance Journal* was a special issue on "Women and Counselors," and included a number of articles by women vocational counselors attempting to establish new models and principles for sexism-free vocational counseling.

Actually, throughout the period of transition to liberation, vocational counselors will have to make sure that children from an early age are exposed to a wide range of occupational alternatives so that their eventual decision on "what to be" represents a true choice. Often they may have to intervene by representing different successful examples of sex-inappropriate occupational choices and models.

Sexism in Curriculum. General educational directives are needed for the "integration" of girls' and boys' courses so that all children *have* to take the *same* courses related to home economics, industrial arts, child care, and all prevocational courses (architectural drawing, electronics, etc.). The *compulsory* attendance of boys and girls in traditionally "sex-inappropriate" courses would play an important role in breaking down to a considerable extent the prevailing occupational and sex-role stereotypes. Requisite attendance is necessary at the transition stage until the entire society has made significant steps toward liberation, and then the free choice of courses can be restored without fear of sex-stereotyped choices. During the transition students (as well as teachers and counselors) will not be consistently able to make stereotype-free decisions because of internalized values, beliefs, and inhibitions. The liberation process has to be aided by compulsory regulations, if it is to be achieved at all. Only such compulsory measures can help break the very powerful barriers that presently prohibit women and men from making choices inappropriate to their sex role. The implementation of several types of compulsory measures will actually tend to increase rather than to diminish the freedom of choice for women and men because they will allow everyone to be exposed to alternatives previously excluded from her or his experience. Thus, during the transitional stage, some types of compulsory measures are not only warranted but also strongly recommended, since instead of restricting freedom of choice they tend to significantly enlarge it by broadening the variety and number of educational, occupational, or interpersonal options open to women and men. It is also interesting to note that such a policy, requiring boys and girls to take "sex-inappropriate" courses at the elementary school level (such as home economics, sewing, and child care for boys and modern manual handicraft and other "masculine" skills for girls), has been in existence in Sweden since 1962 (Linner, 1971).

Quite a different type of policy has been suggested by Dr. Barbara Polk, a sociologist at Wayne State University, that might help in breaking down the stereotyped masculine and feminine images. From the time that girls and boys start going to nursery school they could be required to wear the same type of "uniforms," consisting of blue jeans and shirts, that would enable little girls to move freely and to escape the physical limitations and all the implications of wearing a skirt or a dress. This type of "uniform" could be made compulsory throughout school; it represents more than symbolism. After all, the black uniforms with white collars that European children have been wearing for long years were supposed to minimize social class differences (which they did with varying degrees of success).

Sexism in School Athletics. General directives are also needed in the extension of all athletic options to girls and boys, as well as in the opportunity to be directed and trained by the same high-caliber coaches. The participation of girls in all types of competitive sports must be assured, and the organization of "mixed-sex" athletic teams must be seriously studied and attempted until the appropriate formula is found for effective functioning. Only through the establishment of such mixed-sex teams will separate boys' and girls' teams (and the hard-core discrimination against women in most competitive games) cease to exist. In order for these changes to occur, not only must physical education teachers and athletic coaches receive training in sex roles and undergo consciousness-raising sessions from time to time, but the architectural and interior design and equipment of buildings and spaces designed for sports and gymnastics must also be adapted for use by both sexes. Most probably the entire philosophy of competitive sports will have to be redefined somewhat so that it becomes free of stereotyped masculine "roughness and toughness." It will also have to encompass a wider range of rewarded and appropriate behavior on the part of the players.[2] Extremely severe punishment for ice hockey players for beating each other could, for example, totally eliminate this altogether unnecessary and nonsport-linked but institutionalized brutal behavior.

Furthermore, since the world of sport has been dominated by men, professional women athletes, even in more "feminine" sports like tennis, were assigned a second-class, marginal role "in terms of prestige, prize money, and the attitudes of the press and the public" ("Tennis: A Triumph for Women's Lob," 1972). However, already in 1971 ongoing changes in the image of women were helpful in that a professional tennis player like Billie Jean King earned more than twice as much prize money as she did in 1969. Her earnings were just approaching those of equivalent male players ("Tennis: A Triumph for Women's Lob," 1972). Different companies and businesses (such as Virginia Slims) have started offering prize money for women's tennis tournaments. This new tendency can be extremely helpful in getting professional women athletes an equal acceptance with men, especially if prize money is given for women's tournaments in "masculine" sports or for mixed matches.

Sexism in Vocational Training. Equality of educational opportunity for school drop-outs as well as for pregnant married or unmarried girls

---

[2] Although, of course, anyone who has watched the roller skating derby would seriously doubt whether any change in necessary, since women in this sport show as much, if not more, brutality than men.

must be assured. Most of the mass media campaigns and special educational programs aimed at informing, assisting, and providing dropouts with alternative educational opportunities and salable skills have focused upon boys. The vocational education opportunities available to girls have been quite limited and predominantly in "feminine" areas that usually prepare them for low-paying, low-prestige, limited advancement jobs such as typists, secretaries, beauticians, dressmakers, and hairdressers. In addition, many of the very well-paying semiskilled jobs such as construction work and jobs at the assembly line have often been closed to women for a variety of sex stereotypes referring to women's "weak" physique and biological limitations.

For these reasons, it is very important that public school or specially funded youth centers counsel drop-out girls or girls drifting away from school in the wide range of trades and vocations that are open to them. Not merely the availability of but also the compulsory attendance in courses in industrial arts and a variety of prevocational subjects would help familiarize girls with a wide variety of trades and skills and would, in many cases, create a concrete interest in one of them. Simultaneously, a study should be made of the policies concerning such options and teaching procedures affecting the equal treatment of girls and boys. Such a study would aid in implementing the appropriate strategies so that equality is guaranteed and safeguarded. At this point, special attention must be paid so that the acceptance of girls into all types of vocational training on an equal basis with boys does not have as a side-effect the splitting of offered programs and curricula into two (or more) types, one of which is of lesser importance and is made especially attractive to girls.

The availability of adequate training stipends from federally supported programs for training drop-out girls in traditionally "masculine" skills, such as electronics, car mechanics, plumbing, industrial drawing, etc., could serve as a very attractive stimulus for these girls, and would make choices of these options acceptable and socially desirable in the eyes of their parents, peers, and teachers. Again, the active support of and encouragement in these vocational choices, essentially, tangible proof of the official societal approval, is needed in order to transform these "deviant" choices into "normal," socially acceptable ones.

Pregnant girls, as well as mothers, on the other hand, have often been very discriminated against in public high schools in a variety of ways. While in some schools it is still virtually impossible for pregnant girls or mothers to attend, in other schools the peers' as well as the teachers' and administrators' attitudes and behavior are such that attendance is psychologically painful and scholastic achievement considerably blocked. Pregnancy and motherhood are especially stigmatized, if they have occurred without marriage, but in all instances either status tends to lead to great stigmatization of the woman. Teachers and administrators do not expect any significant achievements from pregnant girls or mothers, even if they are quite bright and previously good students—as if the experience of pregnancy and motherhood has a deteriorating effect upon a woman's intelligence and potential. Of course, it is true that very often pregnant girls and mothers are not able to function at a high level or at their previous level because of social and psychological pressures and stress they are undergoing and because the entire high school educational process is not favorable or accommodating to their special status.

Although special attention must be paid so that pregnant girls or mothers are not socially, physically, and psychologically isolated from the entire student body and otherwise discriminated against through assigning them a "special" status or a "special" program, some special facilities, such as child care centers, must be made available. They should be treated in exactly the same way as other students, but be provided with whatever facilities or other special assistance they require in order to be able to "normalize" and receive the same educational opportunities as all other students.

Furthermore, special provisions must be made for adequate training facilities and stipends for low-income girls with illegitimate children that will permit them to support themselves and their children and have access to subsidized or free child care centers while finishing high school or while learning a salable skill. Special job placement policies and procedures might also be needed to insure successful placement in jobs and access to child care facilities while they work.

Sexism in the Sex Ratio Composition of Teachers. Finally, recruitment strategies are needed to balance the sex ratio composition of teachers and administrators. At present, elementary school teachers are overwhelmingly female, while there are many more men than women high school teachers and hardly any women administrators, especially at the top. Corrective recruitment would add qualified men teachers at the elementary school level and qualified women teachers at the high school administrative level. Here it must be clarified that recruitment of male teachers at the elementary school level (especially in the lower grades) is not recommended to provide boys with a "masculine model" but to make this option open and socially acceptable to men who would like to take it.

Strategies should also involve special attention to the training and hiring of female and male teachers in "sex-inappropriate" subjects, such as men teachers for courses on history, English, social sciences, family, child care, or nutrition, and female teachers for mathematics, science, or prevocational courses. Fellowships available to women and men for training as teachers in sex-inappropriate subjects would make more of them available and would enlarge the educational options of both sexes. This policy of preferentially hiring teachers for sex-inappropriate subjects would also help break down children's stereotypic images of women and men in different specializations.

Of all these corrective recruitment policies probably the most important and urgent is that relating to the hiring and appointment of women educators to administrative positions, especially at the top. Its importance lies in the fact that only then will women possess the necessary decision-making, reinforcement, and implementation power to bring about all the changes needed to free the entire educational system from sexism. Besides, this particular corrective strategy is relatively easier to implement since there is already a considerable number of women educators available who are both highly qualified and competent as well as interested in assuming significant administrative responsibilities.

SEXISM IN COLLEGE AND UNIVERSITY EDUCATION

The educational process at the college level suffers from most of the same biases and sexist beliefs and practices as the educational system at the elementary and high school level. In addition, however, even more sexist beliefs and practices abound at the college level, many of which are quite explicit. Some of these practices were formal policy until very recently. The University College of Arts and Sciences at Charlottesville, N.C., for example, did not admit women until recent legal action forced them to do so (*A Matter of Simple Justice,* 1970). In other cases discrimination against women was not formally included in the rules and statutes of the college or department, but the prevailing sexist beliefs and attitudes were so potent and so systematically applied to entrance screenings that the exclusion of women was practically total.

Of course, the occasional unusually brilliant girl who is clearly superior to all male applicants has always been accepted, even in the most prestigious graduate programs or professional schools. No administrator wanted to lose an unusually brilliant candidate (even a woman), and she also served an important purpose: He could brag about his "liberal" views and opinions that would permit him to admit a competent "female." This explains why in the past one (and very rarely two) girls were often admitted to medical or law schools or graduate departments of chemistry, physics, or mathematics. That is why so few women were admitted, despite the fact that many more qualified women must have been available. According to the Office of Education women tend to do better than men on tests for admission given by medical and law schools (*A Matter of Simple Justice,* 1970).

Recent reports of the investigations of committees on the status of university women (students and faculty) from different universities have specifically documented all the tactics used in explicitly or subtly discriminating against women. Some chairmen (acting as advisors and professors) openly discourage women from applying for admission to the graduate or undergraduate program of their departments. While feelings run much higher at the graduate level, some physical science, engineering, and biology departments are not sympathetic to admittance of women even at the undergraduate level. The beliefs, often verbalized and used as a basis for their reluctance to accept women, indicate that women are not usually "serious" in the pursuit of these fields; they will not work after marriage and motherhood and hence will waste all their training; and, since even the few women who work almost never make outstanding achievements, they will not add prestige to the department. Because of these opinions, as well as the basic belief that women are intellectually inferior to men, girls are actively discouraged from pursuing academic studies, becoming good scholars, or developing high professional aspirations. Coeds are also often pressured to transfer to less prestigious, "feminine" fields despite their aptitudes, talents, and interests, and are not aided by professors along the different steps of professional socialization and development in their specialization (*Report of the Subcommittee on the Status of Academic Women on the Berkeley Campus,* 1970).

In the area of financial aid, existing evidence varies according to field, availability of funds, and the competence level of women. In humanities where many girls are admitted, where their level of competence varies, and where there are virtually no research funds or federal support, girls seem to be more often discriminated against than in other areas, with regard to their chances for receiving a teaching assistantship. There are also some fellowships in all fields that are restricted to men. Furthermore, married women students (especially mothers) seem to be often discriminated against in terms of fellowship awards, especially if their husbands have relatively well-paying full-time jobs. The implication here is that their husbands should assume the financial burden of their education, an assumption that not only precludes such education for many married women, but also creates unnecessary serious marital conflicts and even break-ups. Men, however, are not excluded from fellowships, even when their wives hold a well-paying full-time job. (*Report of the Subcommittee on the Status of Academic Women on the Berkeley Campus,* 1970). Furthermore, in many universities a woman would not be hired as research assistant if she was found to be pregnant at the time of the required medical examination, a policy clearly discriminating against young married women of childbearing age.

Although it is true that in the early 70s formal discriminatory policies against women in terms of fellowships granted, admissions, and pregnancy-related restrictions had to be eliminated from most universities, subtle forms of discrimination against women at all levels persist, and have in some cases intensified. Granting fellowships to women still depends upon the level of the husband's income, thus rendering them economically dependent upon their husbands. Women are still subtly but effectively discouraged from engineering, physics, or chemistry by both faculty and peers.

The important question here is how can all these different types of discrimination against women at the college and university level be removed? The most formal and explicit types of discrimination can be rather easily controlled and eradicated. All colleges and universities can become "integrated" by federal order. The admission of all qualified and interested girls in all departments and professional schools can be enacted by special nondiscrimination acts such as the Comprehensive Health Manpower Act and the Nurse Training Act of 1971 which forbid sex discrimination in admission to schools receiving federal grants, together with the requirement of a quota system admitting women to law and medical schools and departments of engineering, chemistry, physics, mathematics, economics, business, etc.

Establishment of gradually increasing quota systems is only necessary during a transitional period during which the existing administrators' and professors' beliefs about women and their "place" in these fields are being changed. The function of the quota is multifold. First, it would encourage college and university administrators to recruit girls for all fields controlled by such regulations by actively interesting and encouraging freshmen women during the orientation week and by helping academic advisors and vocational counselors to consider the suitability of fields previously labeled "deviant" or "masculine" for women. Second, it would serve to implement nondiscriminatory legislation which could otherwise remain "dead" laws through: (1) the very subtle discouragement and "cooling off" treatment; (2) the lack of sufficient women candidates due to ongoing "cold war" activities and lack of women being actively oriented toward these previously "forbidden" and nonexistent educational options; and (3) the discriminatory treatment of girls in schools which lead to a higher rate of failure and lower percentage of awarded degrees because of the higher standard of excellence demanded of women and the more severe evaluation and judgment process. The last type of discriminatory process can be avoided only if the quota of graduating women are also established on the basis of the usual rate of failure for the particular department or professional school.

The third function of the quota system, the establishment of both admission and graduation quotas for women, will motivate universities, foundations and government institutes to establish a considerable number of fellowships for women entering the regulated fields. The availability of financial aid for training in "masculine" fields would constitute a significant motivation for women and an important guarantee that a sufficient number of qualified women will become available to meet the quota requirements.

Effecting such admission and graduation quota systems for women in fields previously considered "masculine," in addition to enacting specific nondiscriminatory acts, is necessary. However, their success in carrying colleges and universities, as well as professors and students, through the stress of transition to liberated higher education can be enhanced by means of a number of supplementary strategies.

First, the introduction of courses of a general nature such as the "Sociology of Women" or "The Sociology of Sex Roles" must be established as a requirement for all undergraduate students, women and men, including students in professional schools who have not had such a course during their undergraduate training.

Second, there must be courses such as "Women and the Law," "Sex Roles and Biology," "Sex Roles in Medicine," "The Economics of Sex Roles," "Sex Roles and Property, Savings, Investments, and Wealth," "Sex Roles in Business and Trade," etc., in the regular curricula of law and medical schools, as well as in departments of biology, economics, business, etc.[3]

Federally funded summer workshops should also be accessible for college and university professors in different fields; a great number of training followships for them should be available. Some workshops would be for professors of anthropology, sociology, psychology, education, political science, and social work; others for physical scientists; others for physicians and biologists, and so on. It would be advisable to make the professors' participation, attendance, and thorough examinations compulsory. Penalties for noncompliance should include publicity concerning their behavior and denial of a variety of academic rewards. Failure in the examinations would require that the professor repeat the workshop. Of course it is not expected that all professors would change their beliefs and values radically, but a sufficient number may become motivated enough to modify their discriminatory behavior toward women.

The following two strategies in this area would also aid considerably in the modification of their behavior. The first would help raise their awareness and, in some cases, change their values, the other would motivate them to examine their behavior closely and act in a nondiscriminatory way, regardless of their persisting sexist values and beliefs.

---

[3] The first two strategies are necessarily short-range and transitional to the time when the content of all courses offered at the college and university level are no longer sexist. The main goal is of course the liberation of all academic subjects. Since, however, this goal may not be totally achieved for at least some years, specific courses on women and sex roles are needed to raise students' scientific consciousness and to stimulate relevant research. Also students exposed to such courses can exert considerable pressure on sexist professors and help bring about significant changes in the content of all courses.

The organization of frequent consciousness-raising discussions, lectures, and meetings, stimulated and organized by women's organizations on campus and sponsored throughout the year by all departments, faculties, and professional schools, and attended by administrators, faculty, and students, would be a fourth supplemental strategy. During these meetings and discussions different relevant practices, beliefs, and actual behavior would be reported, analyzed, and criticized as to the extent to which they were discriminatory and determined by traditional sex stereotypes. Such continuous critical examination is necessary throughout the transition to true liberation.

Together with critical examination of everyone's beliefs and actual behavior regarding sexism, administrators and professors would be singled out who are unwilling to change and who continue the "cold war" on women through a variety of subtle but effective techniques aimed at discouraging them, or at least increasing the number of difficulties they encounter not only in their studies but also in their later occupational success. Such administrators and professors could then be penalized by being socially stigmatized by unfavorable publicity in the campus and community mass media. Thus, students would be warned about the orientation and biases of these professors and could accordingly make decisions as to whether or not to take their courses. Persistently "sexist" professors could be further penalized according to the degree and severity of their demonstrated sexism by "freezing" their salary, or by postponing promotion, or, in some very serious cases, by not granting tenure.

In addition, a campus women's body such as the University Commission on the Status of Women or a special ombudswoman could function as a clearinghouse for complaints and reports of sexist behavior on the part of professors, administrators, and staff. Such a group could become the official grievance handling body empowered to investigate, sanction, and intervene. After some preliminary investigation concerning the nature and circumstances of sexist acts, the women's commission could intervene to correct and/or to sanction in these cases on the campus. If, however, the women's commission takes appropriate action to correct the situation, first through the existing administrative channels and within the limits of its entrusted power, but is ineffective, a greater amount of external pressure may be necessary. Alternative action may be appeals to state and national women's organizations, HEW, AAUP and other state and federal organizations.

The need for the establishment of institutionalized channels within commissions on the status of women (for reporting, assessment, publicity, and handling of sexist incidents) exists because sexist incidents take place even after equalitarian social policies are adopted. It has been reported (but cannot be documented), for example, that some professional schools and academic departments that have accepted gradual admission quotas for women used dubious screening techniques that result in the overrepresentation of less qualified women. Well-qualified women are screened out and have to compete with qualified men, while quota requirements are filled from among the less qualified women.

Sixth, the employment of considerable numbers of women faculty members and administrators at all levels and in all fields would have a considerable impact upon lessening discriminatory practices against women. Such a policy would give women and men students not only role-models of successful and respected academic women, but would also provide women students with sympathetic and encouraging professors and advisors. It seems that in the past the few women university professors suffered from the "Queen Bee Syndrome" and tended to be quite unsympathetic, uncooperative, and even hostile to women students. Moreover, they often held a double standard of academic excellence (usually much stiffer expectations for women than for men), and often more so than their male colleagues. Their overidentification with men made them feel quite threatened when they had to come in contact with the "untouchables"—the women (*Women in the University of Chicago,* 1970).

There are, however, many indications that this situation has already changed considerably. Academic women (at least in the social sciences, especially sociology, but also in law, history, modern languages), as a result of raised consciousness, identification with other women rather than with male colleagues, and a higher self-esteem and esteem for other women have generally ceased to be hostile toward each other. They have started to help each other; to invite each other to meetings and symposia; to ask each other to write chapters in their books, or articles in the special issues of journals they edit; to nominate each other for important professional committees; to inform each other of job opportunities, the availability of research funds, travel grants, and other professional opportunities. In addition there is evidence that women students and young professionals are now being "sponsored" by more established women and aided in their professional careers as men protegés of established scholars have always been able to advance in their fields (Safilios-Rothschild, 1972b). On the basis of these current indications concerning improving professional relations among women, it seems that the employment of greater numbers of women faculty members and administrators would significantly contribute to the liberation of higher education from sexism and would encourage women to take many presently more or less barred educational options.

It must be noted that some departments in several American universities have, up to now, given only lip service to a policy of hiring of women faculty; others have not gone beyond tokenism. This tokenism is interestingly enough represented by schools hiring a young and supercompetent woman Ph.D. at the beginning assistant professor level or engaging a woman chairman (especially in sociology), since this is a highly undesirable position for men who prefer to pursue a regular academic career. Recent data collected by the National Center for Educational Statistics show that the percentage of women faculty at colleges and universities has increased slightly over the corresponding figures for 1962–63, with the largest gain at the instructor's level ("Survey Indicates That Colleges Have Increased Hiring Women but Still Pay Less," 1973). Such detailed data must be collected and widely publicized in order to further raise the consciousness of academic women and stimulate more effective organization and protest. Here again the establishment of definite goals for hiring as many women as possible, especially in top faculty and administrative positions, over a period of three to five years can be the only social policy that will break through present tokenism and assorted resistance.

Another strategy, the establishment of a woman recruitment representative, usually a student in each specific professional field, would ensure that more competent women are recruited to satisfy established admissions quotas. The law school of Wayne State University, as a result of demands by the women law students' organization, sends a woman law student with the usual recruiters on all recruitment trips and contacts with potential candidates. The result of this practice was the admission of seventy-five highly qualified women in 1972–73, a number representing a spectacular change from the two to three women usually admitted in previous years.

Finally, special professional committees made up of outstanding women who are known to hold nonsexist beliefs must be appointed by the different national institutes or other foundations funding research to examine currently used textbooks in all fields for the degree of sexism permeating their findings, theories, and discussions. These committees would be charged with selecting textbooks free of sexism that can be used, specifying the type of revision to be made in textbooks requiring minor revisions, determining the textbooks that must be withdrawn from the market because of their high degree of sexism, and recommending authors who are scientifically competent and of a sexism-free orientation. Probably special programs within the National Institute of Health and other similar institutions will be necessary for funding and organizing such committees.

This activity should have high priority since considerable time is re-required to organize, to evaluate currently used college textbooks in all fields and at all levels, and to revise and rewrite textbooks. The proposed legislation currently under consideration, the Women's Education Act, if passed would authorize the secretary of H.E.W. to approve grants to develop nonsexist texts and tests, nondiscriminatory vocational education and career counseling, sports education, and other educational programs and activities. Meanwhile, the different foundations could also endorse similar programs.

Most of the strategies discussed in connection with the equalization

of educational opportunity for women and men are short-range and compensatory. They are necessary to smooth the difficult transitional path to
liberation during the 70s and possibly the early 80s. Gradually many of
these strategies will no longer be necessary. But at present it is an illusion
to think that sexism within the educational institution can be stamped out
without a considerable array of compensatory mechanisms.

Strategies toward the Economic and Employment Liberation of Women

THE DISCRIMINATION AGAINST WOMEN
IN EMPLOYMENT AND SALARIES
AND THE ECONOMICALLY DEPENDENT STATUS OF WOMEN

Historically and cross-culturally, women's social inferiority and sub-
servience has been partly due to their economic dependence upon men.
Men have always held the purse strings, and because of this claimed power
and authority have had all women under their jurisdiction. The importance
of economic independence becomes quite clear when one considers the
remarkable educational, employment, political, sexual, and psychological
emancipation that upper-class women have always had, even in the most
traditional and sexist societies. There is considerable documentation that
upper- and upper-middle-class Mediterranean women have always been
sexually and psychologically emancipated, despite the prevailing rigid sexual
double standard and the great importance placed upon honor (Safilios-
Rothschild, 1972c). Furthermore, Mediterranean as well as Latin American,
African, and Asian upper-class (and to some extent upper-middle-class)
women have always been politically, educationally, and occupationally
emancipated in that they have enjoyed a wide range of options, have
been able to reach high positions, and have enjoyed prestige, power, and high
salaries. Thus, despite the fact that the societies in which these women lived
were very traditional and sexist, they could escape all the barriers and limitations imposed upon women in the name of religion, cultural tradition, and
"morality." The high social status and the economic independence these
women inherited from their fathers (or their husbands in the case of widow-
hood) exempted them from all the prevailing stereotyped sex-related proscriptions and permitted them to take many options in many life sectors
traditionally open only to men.

Women and men of high social status have always been permitted a
wider range of behavior, including what could be considered "deviant"
behavior in terms of the standards of the majority of the population.
"Deviant" upper-class women and men have always been tolerated, partly
because their deviance did not spread to the rest of the population, and

partly because families and individuals could still maintain the appearance of "normality." In the case of these upper-class women their emancipation was clearly due to their high social class and their economic independence. It is a matter of fact that most of these upper-class or upper-middle-class women have seldom identified with the womankind in their countries or attempted to facilitate the emancipation or liberation of all women. They have usually behaved in the same way as men of their status in regard to women. The phenomenon of their emancipation was attributed to their "exceptionality," which would be very difficult to duplicate, except perhaps in their daughters, sisters, or cousins. Because of this explanation men of high status were not threatened by these high-achieving, freed women. Instead they supported them, collaborated with them, and were flattered to marry them, or to associate with them.

While this type of inherited economic independence explains the few highly emancipated women in traditional societies, the large majority of women around the world have been and are kept economically dependent upon men, first upon their fathers and brothers, then upon their husbands and sons. Such economic dependence is ensured by the fact that they are not given the chance to obtain salable skills. Most employers (including civil service) are not willing to give jobs to women above a very low level and are not willing to pay them equally with men, even when they perform exactly the same type of work.

In addition, the laws in most countries (including the United States) not only assume but also promote and reinforce (and occasionally force) women's economic dependence upon men. Recent work and training provisions for welfare families, for example in the U.S., definitely emphasize and foster women's economic dependence upon their husbands by in fact providing low-income women with the doubtful "choice" "between lack of economic opportunity options and an enforced homework female "caretaker role" (Levin and Vergata, 1971).

The overall trends are the same for developing and developed nations. The only difference is that oppression of women is much more striking in developing nations because it is stronger, more prevalent, and more open. In developed nations such as the United States, Canada, or Sweden, the economic oppression of women tends to be somewhat more subtle, although equally effective. American, Canadian, and Swedish women have been trained for "feminine" occupations, most of which have low prestige and low salaries. They have not been permitted to engage in higher prestige and high income professions and occupations such as medicine, law, dentistry, business, architecture, or upper level administration, because, as it has often been said, "When women come in, the prestige of the occupation goes down and people are no longer willing to pay high fees for services rendered."

In all countries and times the implication of this statement has been that any kind of work that women are able to do successfully cannot be very important, hence it cannot enjoy a great amount of prestige and it cannot pay well. Women's work has always come cheap. As a matter of fact, as Bernard rightly points out, woman's work has been traditionally defined as unpaid work performed out of love and/or duty (Bernard, 1971). Thus domestic work performed by housewives has always been expected to be performed for no special fee (except room and board) for the benefit of husbands and children, legally as a duty and informally as an expression of love and a demonstration of women's self-fulfillment.

Millions of rural and urban women around the world are supposed to help their husbands with farm chores or with their businesses (restaurants, coffee shops, grocery stores, etc.), not as equal partners in the overall decision-making process and in profits-made, but as subservient and unpaid workers. They work long hours, cannot take vacations, have no fringe benefits and no claim on any profit sharing, except that which their husbands are willing to give them (Klein, 1965). As a matter of fact, it is interesting to note that two of the most popular so-called "feminine" professions in the United States, social work and nursing, originated as services rendered free by wealthy and public "welfare-oriented women." This type of origin of some of the "feminine" occupations may be one of the explanations for the low salaries paid in them today. Also, there is a cross-cultural trend for women to enter and dominate either new and marginal occupations entailing considerable risk in terms of employment stability and/or remuneration, or established occupations abandoned by men for more prestigious and profitable ones. Thus we find that while men are involved in secretarial and service jobs or elementary school teaching in societies of low social and economic development, at later stages of development, as many more training and occupational options become available to men, they tend to shift to more prestigious and profitable occupations. At that point these earlier masculine occupations lose much of the prestige they had and women are permitted to enter. This general trend explains why women were the first sociologists and psychologists in some countries like Greece where it was problematic, if not impossible, to find permanent and self-supporting positions (Safilios-Rothschild, 1968).

Furthermore, it is interesting to note that even when a considerable number of women are allowed to enter "masculine" occupations as in the U.S.S.R., women tend to be employed at low-pay, low-status jobs and to do the hard physical labor involved in blue collar work while men supervise and operate machinery (Power Goldberg, 1972). The same is true for other "masculine" professions. Thus in the U.S.S.R., while 42 percent of scientists are women, only 2 of the 204 members of the Soviet Academy of scientists are women. It is interesting to note that medicine is a low-status occupation in the U.S.S.R.; a doctor earns two-thirds of the wage of a skilled worker. Russian women dominate medicine but not engineering—the profession with the highest prestige and pay (Power Goldberg, 1972).

The discrimination against women in employment and salaries is undoubtedly the best-documented area of discrimination (Bernard, 1971; "Columbia Women's Liberation," 1970; *A Matter of Simple Justice*, 1970). Furthermore, the overall disparities between women's and men's salaries and wages, as well as the disparities between them at each educational, income, and employment level, seem to be the most sensitive indicators of the degree of discrimination against women. In Japan where women have been greatly and openly discriminated against, the overall average discrepancy between women's and men's wages was 58.6 percent in 1957 (Koyama, 1959). In the United States, the same discrepancy in 1957 was 36.2 percent and in 1970 41.6 percent (U.S. Department of Labor, 1971), while in Sweden it was 34 percent in 1970 (*The Structure of Incomes in Sweden*, 1970); and 36 percent in France in 1966 (Les disparités entre salaires masculins et feminins, 1972).

More specifically, a recent Swedish Royal Commission on Low Incomes reported that (a) 9 percent of males and 41 percent of the females working full-time had lower aggregate incomes than 15,000 kronor, which in Sweden may be considered as the ceiling below which people are considered to have low incomes; (b) 2.8 percent of fully employed males and 13.4 percent of fully employed females have maximum annual earnings of 10,000 kronor; (c) 18 percent of males and 53 percent of females, employed full-time, earn an hourly rate of less han 7.50 kronor (that is, the lowest hourly pay rate); (d) 23 percent of men and only 4 percent of the fully employed women earn more than 30,000 kronor (that is, a high income); and (e) the median income difference between full-time working women and men is 34 percent for men, but the median income differences are considerably larger at the highest (48 percent) and lowest (41 percent) levels of income and smaller at the medium range (*The Structure of Incomes in Sweden*, 1970). The fact that such a wide gap exists between the salaries and wages of women and men in Sweden, despite a widespread ideology and tradition of equality between women and men, as well as some laws against discrimination, illustrates how difficult and complex it is to break the vicious circle of *existing* inequality.

Recent American data show very similar trends in that (a) 12.2 percent of full-time working women and 5.1 percent of full-time working men earned less than $3,000 in 1970; (b) 32.5 percent of women and 8.8 percent of men, working full-time, earned between $3,000 and $4,999; (c) that 5.9 percent of women and 26.5 percent of men earned $10,000–$14,999, and 1.1 percent of women and 13.5 percent of men earned $15,000 and over. Furthermore, it was found that the least disparity between salaries existed between women and men with five or more years of college, while the greatest difference was among those with eight grades or one to three years of high school (U.S. Department of Labor, 1971).

Interestingly enough the wide discrepancies in salaries between women and men are equally well documented and just as prevalent in a socialist country like Poland as in a capitalist society such as the United States. Available statistical information indicates that while in 1960 in the United States about six times more men than women workers had high incomes, the ratio in Poland was even higher, that is, twenty to one. Substantial income discrepancies between Polish women and men hold true even when type of occupation, type of post held, and the level of education and work experience are the same for the women and men being compared. In addition, however, to the overall discrimination in women's remuneration for any work performed, the overall striking discrepancies between women's and men's earnings tend also to reflect the fact that very few Polish women are promoted or allowed to reach top executive posts in management and administration, even in fields in which large numbers of women are employed (Sokolowska, 1965).

There is no question that the key to women's economic independence is employment. Strategies and social policy aiming at the abolition of sexism in this area are, therefore, of utmost importance. Some of these strategies have been already outlined in the earlier section on the educational liberation of women. Once sufficient numbers of women have been trained in high-paying skills and professions, their chance of substantial economic independence will improve considerably, as will their prestige and standing in the family and the society. It is for this reason that, in addition to the educational strategies, a number of other specific strategies are required to assure a wide range of options in life styles, as well as in economic sectors.

RECRUITMENT STRATEGIES

First, one set of strategies has to be directed toward the use of already trained women in jobs that best utilize their skills, talents, and experience. In many fields there is a considerable number of highly qualified, competent women with significant achievements. Their potential is by no means being fully tapped, and they will not be able to have any kind of impact on society and the upcoming generations because of a lack of adequate visibility and recognition. Due to the preferential recruitment systems traditionally dominated by white male networks, women, regardless of their level of prominence, competence, and talent, have been consistently left out— unless some prominent man chose to "support" them, because of selfish, idiosyncratic, sexual, particularistic motivations rather than on the basis of professional universalistic criteria.

Strategies that would break the closed, male-dominated recruitment circle are needed desperately. HEW's requirement that public colleges and universities plan definite affirmative action to represent more women more equitably within a number of years in all fields, under the "threat" of withdrawal of federal funds, is certainly an appropriate and praiseworthy strategy. But even HEW's supposedly "tough" line is not quite effective because it is just not tough enough. The threat of withdrawal of federal funds has been actualized only rarely and for very short time periods, despite the lack of sufficient, tangible changes brought about by the universities in question. One real limitation has been, of course, the lack of a large enough HEW staff to both follow up actively the progress of different departments and universities and to enforce minor and major sanctions (Bazell, 1970; Shapley, 1972). The overburdening of the HEW staff is to some extent due to the expected "crank" complaints by more or less incompetent women who opportunistically or neurotically use "sex discrimination" as a cover for their real limitations and failures, which are only occasionally or marginally due to real sex discrimination. In addition to the fact that the HEW contract compliance staff is too small, few of them have academic backgrounds. Thus, unless they are given special "sensitivity" training, they have great difficulty in detecting the less obvious forms of sexism or in understanding the subtleties of discrimination in academia.[4]

It would also be more helpful if HEW could use a variety of sanctions that are less total and injuring than the withdrawal of funds from the entire university. For example, if a department or school continues to show sexism, it could be deprived of research funds. Or a professor who is sexist could be barred from applying for federal funds or from becoming appointed to a HEW review or advisory committee. Furthermore, members of the HEW review or advisory committees who show evidence of sexism in their judgements and opinions or who behave in a sexist way in their academic lives could be relieved of their duties. Such a diversification of penalties would permit HEW to be much more specific and effective in punishing the sexist departments or schools within a university, and not entire universities that include a large number of innocent students and faculty.

Here it is interesting to note the reaction of "male chauvinistic" male and female faculty, students, and administrators to the affirmative action requirements for the establishment of specific goals and timetables for hiring of women and minorities. The most frequently verbalized basic fears and objections are:

1. Despite the official reassurance repeatedly provided by HEW offi-

---

[4] From a letter from Rachel Kahn-Hut, Executive Vice-President, Sociologists for Women in Society, to Mr. A.J. Weiss of the Anti-Defamation League, on September 14, 1972.

cials, complying university presidents, deans, and university commissions on the status of women that affirmative action and the establishment of specific, numeric hiring goals do not represent rigid quotas, many such "chauvinistic" persons insist and persist in believing that the goals are in fact *quota* requirements in disguise. J. Stanley Pottinger, Director of the Office for Civil Rights for the U.S. Department of Health, Education, and Welfare, has clearly explained the difference between goals and quota.

> Quotas are.... numerical levels of employment that must be met if the employer is not to be found in violation of the law. They are rigid requirements and their effect is to compel employment decisions to fulfill them, regardless of qualifications, regardless of a good faith effort to fulfill them, and regardless of the availability of capable applicants. Goals, on the other hand, signify a different concept and employment practice.... By establishing goals, the employer commits himself to a good faith effort that is most likely to produce results. Unlike quotas, goals are not the sole or even primary measurement of a university's compliance...If a university falls short of its goals, that in itself does not result in noncompliance; a good faith effort to achieve these goals remains the test.[5]

Despite similar explanations and reassurances issued by complying university presidents, sexist faculty and administrators continue to perceive goals as quotas and to talk about "reverse discriminatoin" against white males. Furthermore, even though affirmative action implies open recruitment providing women with equal access to openings in the institutions, many sexist faculty women and men claim that there is no need for change. Recruitment has always been "open." By "open" recruitment they refer to the actually closed network that has always existed between men at different prestige universities and from which women have as a rule been excluded. Many sexist faculty members still argue that the few telephone calls to male "star" colleagues (and maybe also to one woman "star") for potential candidates constituted open and fair recruitment procedures.

2. In spite of hiring goals that are flexible—to be filled over a period of years—and based realistically upon the current availability of qualified women in the field, sexist arguments persist that the establishment of hiring goals will necessarily result in lowering academic standards of excellence used to hire new faculty members. The assumption on which this fear is based is that there are not enough qualified and competent women around to satisfy the goals. And the unstated assumption, on the part of hard-core sexists, is that it is impossible that so many highly qualified and competent women could ever exist because of their inherent intellectual inferiority and biologically determined limitations. This fear is twice wrong. First, in a number of fields there are sufficiently qualified and competent women who,

---

[5] J. Stanley Pottinger, quoted in *Women Today*, Vol. II, No. 9 (May 1, 1972), 2.

because of the widespread discrimination against them, often hold marginal positions in obscure colleges or community colleges, or who have nontenured jobs, such as research associateships. But even in the fields from which women have been actively excluded, and consequently where only a small number of qualified women is available, there is evidence that a considerable number of women chemists and physicists, for example, are either unemployed (11 percent with Ph.D.'s, in physics) or are employed in small colleges, in unsatisfactory positions, and at lower salary levels ("Discrimination Against Women in Physics," 1972; "AIC Survey Shows Many Women Chemists Feel $$ Discrimination But Less So in Education; 153 Respond," 1971; and "A Woman Professor Replies," 1971). Hiring goals have the necessary flexibility to take the scarcity of women in "masculine" fields into consideration. They are proportionate to the current supply of women in each field and become progressively larger as universities train more women in these areas.

Despite the unsubstantiated hearsay-type "evidence" offered by Seabury (1972), the HEW official guidelines, as well as the above-quoted statement by Pottinger, clearly indicate that the set hiring goals must not be filled blindly, that is, with less-qualified women. Furthermore, the final test of compliance is not meeting goals but evidence of open recruitment and honest efforts to hire qualified women.

Here it must be noted that since affirmative action for women in this area is linked closely with the affirmative action for minorities, especially blacks, the frequent scarcity of available and qualified black scholars for academic posts is used as an argument in support of the absurdity of all affirmative action efforts. Qualified women, however, in contrast to black males, are available in most fields if an employer is earnestly motivated to locate them.

3. Another fear that reluctant faculty members, administrators, and a few selected students present in attempting to resist the preferential hiring of *qualified* women faculty members is the alleged resulting "reverse discrimination" against white males (Seabury, 1972; Etzioni, 1971). Curiously enough, women and men, who had never been bothered by the continuous discrimination against qualified minority men and minority and white women, seem to be very sensitive and justice-oriented when they think that white males may be losing their long monopoly on power, prestigious occupations, and control of the occupational world. It is quite clear to anyone who can still think objectively that requirements that 10, 15, 20, 25, or 30 percent of faculties must be gradually made up of women do not constitute discrimination against white males.

Some current debates of the affirmative action policy in faculty meetings of several departments and universities actually indicate that the most threatened males are the average or below-average white males (and their sponsors). Their fears may be well-founded to some extent since they are losing the male prerogative that has allowed them in the past to be hired and promoted over even the most competent women or so treated only because many competent women were eliminated from the competition at an early stage. Competent white males have nothing to fear from competition with women, but mediocre males know that, should equality be enforced, they may be justly replaced by more competent women. And, should equality be truly practiced in recruitment, they will not only have to face overwhelming competition with outstanding and better-qualified women, but they will also have to compete on an equal basis with average or below-average women like themselves.

Up to now only a few outstanding women were permitted to survive in any professional field; their excellent performance was the only reason their "deviance" was tolerated. There was absolutely no way that an average woman could exist, especially in a professional field. But as the working and career involvement of women becomes normalized and glaring educational discrimination subsides, average and below-average women will appear to match the men at these levels. It has to be honestly faced that outstanding as well as average professional women are threatening to *average white men*, who in the past could do well only because women were eliminated from the battle. This fact should reassure university faculty and administrators who are worried over the possibility that the required affirmative action will lower academic standards of qualification and excellence. Most probably the enforcement of affirmative action goals concerning the hiring and promotion of women will have exactly the opposite effect. Well-qualified and competent women will replace average and below-average white males who in the past were often hired and promoted because there was no competition from more competent people. Furthermore, the establishment of goals and timetables will for the first time allow the average woman, not just the outstanding one, to have the same chances for employment as the average white man. And this is the unspoken crux of the problem: The average white man is afraid of the competition and is "copping out" by screaming "discrimination"!

Despite all these unfounded fears, affirmative action is necessary during the transition period to advance the employment of qualified women at all levels and fields beyond tokenism. It is the only compensatory mechanism that can combat tokenism and break the white, male-dominated recruitment circle.

Executive Order 11246, as amended by 11375 of October 13, 1972, requires all employers who receive contracts of $50,000 or more, and who have fifty or more employees to have affirmative action plans, including numerical goals and timetables ("Federal Laws and Regulations Concerning Sex Discrimination in Educational Institutions," 1972). How are universities and large companies reacting to this executive order?

Up to now the government has approved thirty-five affirmative action plans proposed by universities, including those submitted by Harvard, Wisconsin, and Michigan. HEW is currently negotiating with a large number of universities concerning the development of similar plans. Meanwhile about $23 million in federal contracts have been delayed in being awarded to a dozen universities because the administration is dragging its feet and is openly reluctant to comply with the executive order.

But the most important question is: How are the affirmative action plans implemented? Do they make any difference in the hiring of women at universities? Of course, it is unfortunate that all these efforts to stop occupational discrimination against women are taking place at the least economically opportune period when universities must continuously retrench and cut their budgets. But regardless of the more or less equally shared financial restrictions and the small number of openings, some universities are doing a much better job in hiring women than others. Stanford, for example, in 1972–73 hired twenty-five women, out of ninety new faculty appointments, while Columbia University hired only one tenured woman professor ("Faculty Backlash," 1972). In general, very few women have been hired at the associate professor level, even fewer at the full professor level, which entails tenure. In some universities, however, such as the University of Wisconsin, a few women managed to become tenured as associate or full professors after many years of delay (Bleier, 1971). And in several universities, some women's salaries have been adjusted; at others similar salary adjustments are under way. Up to now 100 women at the University of Michigan (Women in Michigan: Academic Sexism under Siege, 1972), 350 women at the Universtiy of Wisconsin (Bleier, 1971), and increasing number of women at several universities have received such salary corrections. These equity adjustments, however, correct only one type of gross economic discrimination against women. Many other types of discrimination remain untouched. For example, an outstandingly competent woman is often kept at the associate professor level much longer than her degree of competence and productivity would warrant. She may, therefore, appear to be the best paid associate professor on the faculty while in fact she is doubly discriminated against in terms of promotion and remuneration (since she is in fact the lowest paid person among professors of equal competence and productivity). The institutionalization of equity procedures that would consider and correct subtle types of discrimination against women are necessary if salary equality between women and men is ever to be achieved.

Recent national data clearly indicate that competent women who are allowed to become full professors are paid, on the average, about $3,000 less than male full professors at American universities. In lower ranks the discrepancy is smaller—on the order of $600–800 ("Survey Indicates That Colleges Have Increased Hiring Women but Still Pay Them Less," 1973). The large discrepancy in the salaries of women and men full professors is

of course partly due to the fact that there are very few women full professors at the prestigious universities that tend to pay much higher salaries.
Also women are seldom distinguished professors, positions which enjoy very
high salaries and other benefits.

Despite sporadic gains and encouraging results, many universities and
departments are still dead-set against any type of affirmative action plan
that would increase the number of women faculty. Instead, they attack and
accuse HEW of "reverse discrimination" against white males, and they enter
into endless arguments, battles, and bickering. HEW is currently investigating fifteen allegations of discrimination against white male faculty members
in order to quiet once and for all such sexist fears. Other university admin-
istrations at the highest or the middle levels officially comply with an affirmative action plan, but in practice they devise all types of subterfuges to
avoid hiring interviewed or invited women (Peterson, 1972). Great resistance, procrastinating mechanisms, and avoidance techniques still exist at
all levels. They are used by many university administrators and faculty
members to counter efforts and policies that aim to fight prevailing sexism
in academia.

Many sexist persons still like to delude themselves by saying that "All
this can't last; after all it cannot be legal, what we are asked to do," or
"It will backfire," and are in fact hoping that one nice day they will wake
up and everything will have disappeared like a bad dream. And it is rather
ironic that unless all these "dreamers" and procrastinators are able to rid
themselves of their favorite delusions and to face the reality of the changes
necessary to combat sexism, definite quotas and more rigid enforcement
techniques will have to be imposed. For sexism in academia, as well as in
all work settings, cannot go on. In this way their worst fears might be
realized, and it will be all their own doing.

Actually HEW itself must, as a large employer, bring about significant
changes not only in the sex ratio of advisory boards and committees but
also in the sex ratio of top appointive and mid-level positions for which
women have been rarely selected (*Report of Women's Action Program,*
1972).

Furthermore, although there has been pressure for change in the
discriminatory employment patterns of women in professional and administrative positions in state hospitals, training schools, state rehabilitation
centers, state welfare, and other state and city institutions, most of these
institutions receiving federal funds will have to adopt affirmative action
plans. Similarly, city and state commissions will be also adopting such plans.
The Detroit City Plan Commission, for example, recently adopted an affirmative action plan, according to which 50 percent of the future supervisory
positions would be filled with women until women make up 45 percent of
persons in such positions. The outstanding features of this affirmative action

plan are: (1) the fact that the present overrepresentation of women in clerical positions is not used to cover up the serious underrepresentation of women in high-level positions (a common practice among many employers); and (2) the provision of academic and on-the-job training for women to qualify them for high-level supervisory positions (*Affirmative Action Plan to Improve Employment Opportunities for Minority Groups and Women,* 1972).

The Association of American University Professors has, however, yet to play an active role in castigating sexism, as it has with racism. Departments and universities have been blacklisted for racism and their stigmatization received wide publicity and disapproval. It is time that AAUP does the same with sexist departments, schools, colleges, and universities.

The financial control that the federal government can have upon universities by means of the distribution of federal funds cannot directly regulate employment of women in private business, except in large business concerns that enjoy the benefits of government contracts of $50,000 and over and have fifty or more employees. Since last spring about 250,000 government contractors (practically all of them companies) filed affirmative action plans for women at all job levels. Already IBM has increased its roster of women managers by 18 percent (to a total of 560). Different companies are reported to be recruiting more women with business or management majors on several campuses. But many of the affirmative action programs filed were never meant to be followed, and so hundreds of interviews with women result in few job offers. A common avoidance tactic is to set demanded credentials at such a level that very few women can meet them because of earlier discriminatory practices ("Room at the Top?" 1972), a tactic often used by universities in their reluctance to appoint women deans, vice presidents, or presidents.[6]

In some private businesses pressures exerted by clients as well as the overall change in the climate of opinion seem to be quite influential, since several concerns have carried their employment of women in high positions beyond tokenism. Publishers of books have, for example, for the first time appointed women as editors and saleswomen; private companies have hired several women as managers; and several banks have appointed women as managers (Bender, 1971 and 1972a). Recently women have also started to be hired as saleswomen for magazines and cars, and to score a great success in their new careers ("Sales Liberation," 1972).

Many businesses have, however, restricted their compliance with the Affirmative Executive Order to the worst kind of tokenism. Such compliance meant in many cases the appointment of only one woman in a high

---

[6] From private communication and comments on the second draft of the book, by Pamela Roby on October 23, 1972.

position, then procedures to redefine this previously "high" position so it loses all incumbent power, prestige, and even high salary (Bender, 1972c). In these settings the only types of governmental control that can be exercised are that equal pay be given for the same type of services rendered by men and women, and that there be nondiscriminatory advancement for women. Beyond this only pressure exerted by clients can be effective in bringing about significant changes. The perennial preoccupation with public image can serve as potent motivation when the climate of opinion is such that a "male chauvinist" image would tend to diminish popularity and sales. Recently, however, and as a direct result of the government-issued Revised Order 4, which required federal contractors to begin affirmative action programs, "business anxiety has mounted." While few companies are genuinely concerned with setting and implementing significant affirmative action plans for women, the demand for "experts" is already great enough that two experienced women have set up a consulting firm in New York "specializing in affirmative action programs for women" in industry. Similar consultant services are appearing in large industrial centers such as Detroit. Several big companies such as Mobil Oil, Dow Chemical, and Norton Simon have availed themselves of their services (Bender, 1972b).

STRATEGIES TO INSURE
THE FULL UTILIZATION OF
EMPLOYED WOMEN'S TALENTS

A number of auxiliary and to some extent compensatory strategies are needed to aid the increased and nondiscriminatory employment of women in jobs commensurate with their skills and training. Such strategies would include the abolition of nepotism-type rules from all city, state, and federal types of employment, as well as from all colleges, universities, and other institutions receiving federal funds. Such an abolition would cover all types of present rules concerning nepotism. A husband and a wife would be able to be employed by the same employer, university, faculty, and department, even when the wife must be hired at a higher grade or rank than her husband. The present restriction that either spouse must not be hired in a supervisory position directly over the other spouse must be also abolished as unfair. Why in the past have we permitted men to have secretaries, assistants, or associates who were their mistresses, with everybody knowingly tolerating these potentially particularistic work relationships? If anything, spouses can apply more universalistic criteria when it comes to their spouse or children than when it comes to their mistresses or lovers. And the retaliation effects after a break-up are still less frequent among married couples than among lovers.

Actually it is interesting to note that the Universities of Maine, Michigan, and Minnesota, as well as Stanford and Oberlin, have recently revised or abolished their nepotism rules so that both the husband and the wife can work in the same department—if one does not make employment decisions about the other (Sandler, 1972).

Another type of strategy in the same category would go much further. The active preferential recruitment of dual-career couples over husband-career only couples would allow colleges and universities to give preference among equally qualified candidates to hiring those whose spouse also pursued an academic career, next consideration to those whose spouse also pursued a career but not an academic one, their consideration only as a third choice to those whose wife did not work. The same type of preferential hiring system could be also followed at all levels by private business, although there could be no enforcement system unless the employer was a federal contractor. The only hopeful sign seems to be that business leaders have started realizing that hiring husband-wife teams for managerial positions tends to be beneficial to the company, both in terms of each spouse's level of productivity and the stability of their affiliation with the company (Bender, 1971).

Such preferential hiring of dual-career couples, especially in the same or similar fields, is necessary during the early stages of transition so that all types of existing stereotypes about such couples are overcome and women's employment and advancement are not curtailed by a seriously handicapped geographic mobility. This strategy has a particularly crucial importance for professional women in high-prestige (previously stereotyped as "masculine") occupations who most often tend to marry men in the same occupations.

Furthermore, a number of strategies must be carried out by working women themselves. Women within each work unit must be organized and hold regular meetings during which ongoing processes regarding equal employment and pay for women are closely scrutinized, and strategies are developed for coping with setbacks. Thus a variety of mechanisms and subterfuges used by employers that permit them to continue discriminating against women with little fear of punishment could be detected, identified, made public, and corrected. Techniques could be devised to counteract the various subtle or not-so-subtle forms of sex discrimination. Furthermore, women within each major work unit could elect an executive committee of women (possibly including some clearly supportive and liberated men) to represent them and to carry out different types of action. Different executive committees of working women should be linked with each other and with a state or federal action committee empowered with evaluative and enforcement power in case of different issues and situations.

In order to ensure that women will be able to develop their talents and potentials, and not be employed only at the lowest levels, a set of strategies related to different types of retraining or further training for adult women under a variety of circumstances, regardless of their marital status, number of children, or husband's income, are greatly needed. Despite the still very conservative estimates of women's unemployment, due to their frequent classification (self-classification or assignation) as housewives rather than as unemployed, recent data have shown that the unemployment rate for women sixteen to twenty-four years old has risen from 1947 to 1968, while young men's unemployment rate during the same years declined. Furthermore, there is evidence that only 31.7 percent of the trainees in on-the-job training programs conducted under the Manpower and Training Act were women. Only 24 percent of those hired under the JOBS (Job Opportunities in the Business Sector) program were women. JOBS is a program for the employment of the disadvantaged. Poor women without suitable employment were not considered to be disadvantaged, unless they happened to be school dropouts, black, forty-five or over (or under twenty-two), or handicapped. Being female did not count as a minority status, despite plentiful evidence that it has definitely acted as such in terms of women's educational and employment opportunities (*A Matter of Simple Justice,* 1970).

At present and during the following ten to fifteen years of transition, a considerable number of women in their late thirties, early or middle forties, or even early fifties would like to enter the labor force with obsolescent skills or without salable skills. Free vocational counseling services should be available for these women at different specially established centers in colleges and universities. The quality of counseling should be such that it adequately examines the woman's potential and makes her aware of the entire range of training and occupational options. In addition, a large number of federally and state funded training grants should be made available to all unemployed women, women in danger of unemployment and in need of a change in skills and qualifications, or for housewives who need to obtain skills before they qualify for a well-paying job.[7] A great number of high-stipend training grants should be there to women interested in receiving training for jobs and occupations previously stereotyped as "masculine." Granting of such training fellowships should not be based upon need, as determined by the husband's income, so that women are independent of their husbands for their training and do not undergo severe psychological

---

[7] It is interesting to note that such training grants have existed in Sweden for several years and have permitted women to live decently (even when they had small children) while receiving training (Bernheim, 1968). These training grants are available to women over twenty who are unemployed or in danger of becoming unemployed, or to housewives who want to reenter the labor market. The grants are made to the trainees not only for their own maintenance, but also for that of their families. Half of the basic allowance (about $115) is always paid regardless of the husband's income, and from there on the amount varies with the husband's income, and the level of remuneration of the job for which the woman is trained (Seear, 1971). The entire stipend is tax-free.

stress. When husbands are required to pay for all their wife's educational expenses, plus child care (and in the middle- and upper-middle-classes for a regular or occasional housekeeper), it is rather difficult to get them to give their consent or to be enthusiastic and supportive of such an expensive undertaking. Furthermore, when training grants are available not to women as individuals but rather to wives (of husbands with a certain income), the "deviance" of these women's behavior and the lack of institutional supports is underlined, symbolically and actually.

Blue-Collar Women. Training blue-collar women for skills stereotyped as "masculine," such as electronics; drafting; machine repair and maintenance; new photographic techniques used in printing; precision skills; checking, maintenance, installation, and repair of new machinery (from aircraft and automobile to household appliances and gadgets), becomes more and more necessary to help women to continue to work in blue-collar occupations. Recent ongoing and projected changes and trends in industrial automation and modernization and occupational restructuring indicate that the jobs of about 2.5 million women workers will be in serious jeopardy. These women are now working at strenuous, dull, nerve-wrecking, dead-end jobs that pay them very low wages. They are employed mainly in clothing, food, textile, footwear, plastics, toys, costume jewelry, and notions industrial concerns that have modernized very little, because enough unskilled and semiskilled women have been and are willing to work at such low wages. However, once modernization occurs, as is continuously happening, it is quite possible that most of these women workers may be displaced. The new types of jobs created in automated or modern industries tend to have higher prestige and pay and become labeled "men's work."

This large number of women blue-collar workers must be protected through agreements between the employers and the unions guaranteeing them job continuity after "modernization" and training for the new upgraded jobs. Such a strategy has already been adopted by the German textile workers' union, whose members are mostly women (Buber Agassi, 1972).

Training and Upgrading Women on Welfare and in Lower Level Jobs. In general, in the United States all work and training policies relating to welfare women have been a failure. With each new legislation welfare women have been plunged deeper and deeper into the vicious cycle of poverty, economic dependence, social deviance, and alienation. Recent legislation is forcing them to accept dead-end, unskilled work at wages below the minimum hourly rate ($1.60/hour), and is depriving them of the ability to make elementary decisions and to control self-determination ("Welfare Rights: The Plight of Welfare Mothers," 1972; Levin and Vergatta, 1971). Legal reforms are urgently needed to permit low-income women to improve their skills through vocational or on-the-job training while their families are supported. Employment in satisfactorily paid jobs would help them break away from the vicious poverty cycle and stand on their own feet.

Also, because in the past even well-qualified women were often mired in dead-end, routine, boring jobs such as different types of clerical jobs, it is very important that, either through further training or through recognition of abilities and talents shown on the job, competent women are promoted according to their potential. Of course in some cases women are already performing higher-level jobs. Then it merely becomes a matter of actual recognition in terms of prestige, title, and pay. The creation of distinct advancement possibilities for women in all types of jobs is crucial, since for a very long time most women have been "kept down" by means of a variety of mechanisms and their alienation vis-à-vis work is deep, and it permeates their entire lives.

Flexible Work Schedules. Finally, a number of strategies aimed at increasing occupational flexibility without penalties for those who opt for less rigidly scheduled work hours must be established. But in promoting and legislating such changes, great attention must be paid so that these new options are equally available and are granted to men as well as to women. Women alone should never be granted any greater occupational flexibility; such privileges in the short- and the long-run create a climate of prejudice and lead to discriminatory practices. The Equal Rights Amendment will, of course, safeguard against such situations to a considerable extent.

Strategies should establish and promote part-time or three-fourths-time work for both women and men. All the benefits of full-time work, such as pension, seniority, vacations, insurance, etc., as well as promotion, job security, of leaves absence, and right to training and retraining, must be assured. The right to part-time work might be extended to fifteen years per person as in Sweden, or nine years as in France, or to any number of years to permit people who wish to work part-time or three-fourths-time throughout life to do so.

Other strategies could involve (1) granting longer leaves of absence (without pay) for both women and men; (2) working some months full-time, or more than full-time to be able to take longer paid vacations; (3) taking educational leaves (paid or unpaid) ; and (4) considering alternative retirement schemes. Women and men in all types of jobs should have the option to take off up to five years from work (no longer than one-year periods at a time) at reduced pay equaling the amount of pension they could receive on the basis of years worked. Then they should be able to work for five years after sixty-five or sixty, depending on the established retirement age. Such an option would permit men and women to enjoy leisure, travel, educational pursuits, artistic inclinations, etc., while they were still young without being occupationally penalized. And it would help to prolong active and meaningful lives, reducing the problematic years of "old-age."

STRATEGIES TO INCREASE
WOMEN'S ECONOMIC INDEPENDENCE

In addition to strategies directly related to women's employment, some other strategies to increase women's economic independence are needed. Laws, such as those already passed in the United States concerning equal pay between women and men for the same type of work, are necessary, but by no means sufficient, since even they can be countered by assigning women to a slightly different type of work that becomes low-paying. Ombudswomen paid by the federal government could, within different work settings, make sure that the legislation on equal pay is in fact enforced, and that that the employer does not attempt to beat the law, or to engage in uneven promotion practices that again relegate women to low wages and salaries and economic dependence.

Furthermore, the existence of several laws originally intended to economically and physically protect women presently tend to constitute serious blocks to women's liberation. Social security laws, life insurance policies, alimony, pension laws, as well as restrictions concerning overtime work, are examples. Most states have, for example, restrictive laws concerning the total number of hours that women can work per week, and thus restrict or totally eliminate for women a very profitable well-paid option. While compulsory overtime is unfair for men, the elimination or restriction of the option to work more hours is also extremely unfair to women. It is untenable anymore to "protect" and act paternalistically toward women; such restrictions seriously interfere with their right to economic independence, especially when many black and white women in the lower classes are family heads and must support their families.

Breaking Women's Institutionalized Economic Dependence on Men. In addition to the sex-stereotyped values and the discriminatory practices that have made all women's (and particularly married women's) economic independence problematic, such dependence is further fostered by institutionalized discriminatory policies in alimony, insurance, and all types of pensions. Some of these pension policies are in fact so discriminatory that a woman cannot establish her economic independence after retirement, even if she has worked all her life.

It is totally anachronistic to accept the fact that it is the man who is responsible for the economic support of a woman he marries while he is married to her, after he has divorced her (through alimony), or even after he has died (through his generous life insurance policy). During the transition period, divorced women with no salable skills could have the benefit of one year of training, with living expenses paid, instead of alimony (Safilios-Rothschild, 1972b). From there on, if they want to continue their training they would have to compete with other women for available training fellowships (as described earlier). In this way women would not be encouraged to live off their ex-husbands, but to face their life responsibilities. The only clear-cut exception should be women who helped their husbands receive their education by getting a job, by either totally or partially supporting the family. In this case, women should be entitled to financial support, while receiving some type of training or education, for as long a period as they had supported or helped their husband.

Similarly, life insurance policies taken out by husbands should only cover the living and educational expenses of children, and the living and training expenses of wives, who need to improve their education and skills at the time of their husbands' death. Or, in the case of working women, they should provide a part of child care costs and housekeeper's wages, but in no case stipulate a flat sum of money for the wives' support throughout life. It is high time that women are no longer considered appendages to men, but are seen as individuals who can face life and all its different types of responsibilities, including economic.

On the other hand, it is extremely unfair for the husbands and children of working women to be unable to enjoy the same rewards from the accumulated benefits of their wives and mothers that the wives and children of working men enjoy. The present social security and pension laws discriminate severely against working women. Couples where both spouses have worked now receive fewer benefits than those where the husband worked and contributed the same monthly amount. In general, women who have worked and contributed regularly for many years do not usually receive any benefits in addition to those they would have received on the basis of their husband's contributions, had they not worked at all. (*A Matter of Simple Justice*, 1970). Thus present social security policies do not in fact treat women's work and monthly contributions in the same manner as men's. Women have to be economically dependent on their husbands when they retire—even when they have worked all their lives. This is an area of discrimination that can be easily amended through federal decrees; it must be changed immediately.

In the same vein, pension systems seriously discriminate against women: the pensions of deceased women cannot be transferred to their husbands and children as men's pensions can, unless it can be proven that the husband or the children were supported primarily by the wife (*The Status of Women in Canada*, 1970; *A Matter of Simple Justice*, 1970). Such criterion, however, of the economic dependency of husbands and children is at the present time discriminatory, since women have a right to their husbands' pensions, regardless of their own income, and so do children, regardless of the extent to which they were supported by their deceased fathers. Since a working woman's pension is earned on exactly the same basis as a man's, it should carry exactly the same types of benefits to the same types of beneficiaries—that is, to husbands and children, regardless of economic need.

It has been ascertained that the Teachers Insurance and Annuity Association (TIAA) and the College Retirement Equities Fund (CREF) retirement systems available to members of teaching professions have also been discriminatory to women. Because life expectancy tables for all women in the United States show that, on the average, they live seven years longer than men, women were given less pension every month after retirement. The Commission on the Status of Women at Wayne State University, chaired by Dr. Nancy Schlossberg, figured that retired women professors received a monthly pension 16 percent less than retired male professors with equal contributions toward retirement. The longevity of women rationale used by these retirement plans is false because:

1. The cost of living after retirement is the same for women and men; therefore, women's economic independence after retirement is seriously jeopardized by lower payments, despite equal yearly contributions.

2. It is well known that married women and men have a different life expectancy than single women and men. Also, on the average, black women and men have, up to now, had very different life expectancies than white women and men. But the amount of pension granted to all of these groups after retirement has not been calculated on these differentials in life expectancy. Women are the only group that has been singled out and discriminated against on the basis of their longer life expectancy.

3. It is highly questionable whether working women and, especially career women, have in fact a longer life expectancy than men in the same type of work. It is very doubtful, for example, that women teachers and professors, the people covered by TIAA and CREF, do, on the average, live longer than men teachers and professors. Most probably there are no significant differences between the life expectancy of career women and men, or if any difference exists, it may well be in the opposite direction. That is, it is possible that, on the average, men tend to live longer than working women simply because up to now working women have had to carry the triple role of worker, mother, and housekeeper, while men faced fewer conflicting roles.

    It is impossible to answer these questions at present since we do not yet have reliable and valid nationwide data on the relative life expectancies of men and women in the same occupational groups.[8]

Strategies to combat this type of discrimination entail pressure from the women involved, legal action against TIAA and CREF, and complete

---

[8] A recent brochure of TIAA–CREF claims that the analysis of the 1965–1970 mortality data among all female annuitants aged sixty-five and over showed that "the mortality rates were virtually the same at all ages, regardless of whether the women had entered upon their annuities as retired staff members or as wives of retired staff members." ("Recent Longevity Studies," 1972). The studied women, however, represent past generations of women who worked only for some years of their lives rather than throughout life as is increasingly the case with academic women in all fields. Thus, the presented evidence is by no means very convincing or conclusive.

availability of research findings concerning the relative life expectancies of women and men teachers and professors. Demography students would do a great service to the abolition of sexism by doing this kind of research for their Ph.D. dissertations. They would provide the most powerful weapon against this argument: facts. It must be made clear, however, that even when research data become available, whatever the findings are, TIAA and CREF will either have to consistently use differential life expectancy tables for all groups or for none. They cannot single out women. It is interesting to note that some university Commissions on women have actually proceeded to sue TIAA and CREF for discrimination against women. Recently the American Nurses Association filed sex discrimination charges against TIAA for violation of Title VII of the Civil Rights Act of 1964 and Guidelines 1604.9(e) and (f) on Discrimination Because of Sex ("American Nurses Association Files Sex Discrimination Charges Against TIAA," 1973).

Changing Women's Saving and Investment Behaviors. In addition to the built-in discriminatory features of different types of pensions for women, there are some attitudes on the part of women themselves that must be changed so that they can enjoy greater economic independence before and after retirement. A recent doctoral dissertation by a woman economist showed that women, regardless of education, do not invest wisely, and because of a great degree of conservatism (partly reflecting their total lack of knowledge about finances, investment, and economic principles), end up with very little money, especially after retirement. Despite considerable differences in the sums of money earned, women tend to prefer savings accounts, annuities, and other fixed assets, all of which are quite vulnerable to inflation and other economic vicissitudes (Erb, 1969).

These findings suggest that there is a great need to educate women concerning basic economic principles and to acquaint them with the different types of investment, as well as with the advisability of each type of investment for different economic conditions and situations. First, a required high school course in basic economic principles and information should encourage girls and boys to think about investment or to actually invest a small, collectively owned amount of money. Second, different women's groups, associations of church women, etc., should organize short courses on the subject to be offered free or at a small fee, depending upon the economic status of the "pupils." And following this course, women should be encouraged to establish their own small investment groups to be guided and counseled by some knowledgeable person. Third, women in all work settings should be encouraged by the Commission on the Status of Women to participate in short informative lectures and discussions, and to establish and participate in an investment club that enjoys the counseling services of an investment expert.

Strategies to Psychologically and
Sexually Liberate Women

Traditional stereotypes concerning appropriate "feminine" behavior dictate passivity, gentleness, sensitivity, emotionality, sweetness, and submission. Women are paradoxically free to express their emotions, weaknesses, and fears and at the same time are supposed to be unable to control their many and uneven emotions, and to be weak, fearful, and defenseless. In short, the "weaker" sex is inherently and by necessity dependent upon the "strong" males for protection. It is this dependence upon men that dictates submission to them as the "protectors." Women, according to the same stereotypes, are therefore not supposed to be aggressive, rough, independent, self-assertive, or ambitious. Furthermore, a large number of social controls built in to the educational process, employment, and the entire society help to guarantee that women will restrict themselves to the roles for which they were socialized, and that they will behave according to the appropriate "feminine" norms. Thus, even when women were educated for professional or "masculine" fields such as medicine, law, or engineering, they often felt compelled to behave in a "feminine" manner by choosing pediatrics rather than surgery, domestic rather than criminal law. They had to also avoid any display of roughness, competitiveness, or aggressiveness if they wanted to escape being labeled "bitches" or "castrating females." And they were not only encouraged but also rewarded for behaving in this way and for accepting the fact that men have to occupy all the top positions.

Strategies that help to free educational institutions and educators from sexism, as well as strategies that promote nondiscriminatory employment, economic independence, and the equalization of opportunity for success and achievement for women also tend indirectly to liberate women psychologically and sexually. Women who are allowed to compete, aspire to high statuses and positions, achieve, and become successful in their undertakings will come to realize that they are just as desirable, warm, attractive human beings for doing so. And as men and the entire society at the same time become more liberated, independent women with high personal achievements in terms of social status, prestige, money, or fame will be sought out as desirable marital and sexual partners. Only when a woman's success makes her more attractive than other women (as is now true for men) will she feel comfortable to compete, to aspire, and to achieve. It is possible, however, that future changes in the prevailing value structures may help decrease the present overemphasis upon achievement and increase the importance of desirable personality traits.

Up to now women's fears of success and achievement have been largely due to their anxiety that such accomplishments would render them "unfeminine" and unattractive to desirable males, or would threaten husbands and lovers enough to seriously upset or sever relationships. The sex-role stereotypes themselves have been behind the association of personal success with failure "as a woman." Only the increasing association of women's success with attractiveness and happiness can reverse such a trend among women.

Women's economic independence and the possibility for effectively controlling reproductive functions of their bodies through contraception and abortion help women to become sexually liberated. After all, the basis of the sexual double standard was the economic dependence of women, which became acute in pregnancy, since they could not provide financially for their children. There can be no more reasons or rationalizations for the sexual double standard.

It is interesting to note that in the Scandinavian countries, and to a considerable extent in England (at least among the young), the sexual double standard was practically abolished (attitudinally and behaviorally) even before the achievement of widespread economic independence for women (Luckey and Nass, 1969; Christensen and Gregg, 1970). But Scandinavian countries, especially Sweden, have given women the knowledge and the means to control reproduction, despite the fact that abortion is not available on demand.

In addition, economic independence and the possibility of achieving according to desire and capability frees women from using sex as an instrument in acquiring status or money or other desirable goods. In the past the only means of achieving economic security and status has been through association with males, notably through marriage. Toward this end, sex has been a powerful weapon to be carefully controlled, wisely distributed, and cleverly manipulated. Sexual intercourse has thus been an instrument used to gain a particular goal; only rarely has it been a goal in itself. By using sex, women were able to diminish the social distance between important, rich, or powerful men and themselves, and to obtain desirable goods such as economic security and social status through marriage, or a desirable job or promotion through sexual relations with an influential man.[9] Thus enjoyment of the sexual act was not important, but the attainment of the goal through sex was. Because of this, relatively less importance was placed on males' physical attractiveness than on females'. All the available data on mate selection in the United States and other Western nations clearly

[9] Actually it has been quite questionable whether women did in fact obtain economic security through marriage, or desirable occupational advancement in exchange for sexual favors. In the latter case, most often adulterous men, for a variety of motivations (including guilt and fear that their infidelity will be suspected or known), have not returned favors or have done very little. Others have simply not honored the existence of any self-understood or implicit contract of exchange of favors. There are, however, even at present a few outstanding examples of professional women, businesswomen, and artists whose occupational success is largely due to a powerful male with whom they have a long-standing and open relationship.

indicate that the man's social status, income (or potential for social status and income), as well as occupation (present or future), are much more decisive characteristics in a woman's choice of a marital partner than his physical attractiveness or pleasant personality, while the reverse holds true for a man's choice of a mate. Since men's social status or economic security has not depended upon the economic or high-prestige achievements of their wives, they have been able to choose mates who were physically attractive and/or have possessed a "nice" personality (that is, sweet, gentle, and having other "feminine" traits) (Kephart, 1967; Prince and Baggaley, 1963; Combs and Kenkel, 1966).

It must be noted, of course, that the only way women were able to successfully perform sexually with men to whom they were not physically attracted was through the appropriately feminine passive role in sexual intercourse, and by their ability to feign orgasm to flatter their partner's male ego. Once liberation requires that women play an equally active role in sexual relations, acting may become a little more difficult and require more "talent."

Liberated women who are psychologically as free as men to achieve and live in a liberated society would not have to use sex as a salable commodity to be exchanged for money and status. They will be able to acquire money, status, or fame on their own merit, and enjoy sex as an end in itself. They will not have to use and manipulate the men they choose as sexual or marital partners, but will be better able to enjoy them as lovers, friends, and interesting people. This set of changes will also free women to have sexual relations with men they find physically or personally attractive and desirable, rather than with "stable, reliable breadwinners," or with men on their way up or already successful whom they despise, or whom they find dull and unattractive.

Actually there are already some indications that as some women become increasingly economically and sexually liberated, they will begin to view sex less as an instrument, and instead to value it for its intrinsic pleasures. This will place increasingly greater importance on the quality of the man's sexual performance and on the amount of pleasure derived. Also standards for men's sexual performance become increasingly higher and more sophisticated as women have more sexual experience with different partners, and thus have a wider base of comparison (Valabrègue, 1968). Some psychiatrists are claiming that this liberation of women is threatening to men who feel anxious about meeting high standards for sexual performance, and frequently find this leads to impotence (Ginsberg *et al.,* 1971).

The sexual liberation of women would be greatly aided by social policies that increase women's and men's knowledge of the *facts,* rather than the stereotypes, of women's and men's sexuality. Sex education courses at all levels as well as treatment of human sexuality in different types of textbooks and manuals are most important. Gynecology, psychology, psychiatry, family sociology, and textbooks allied to these fields must be rewritten so they integrate recent (and not-so-recent) knowledge and research findings about women's and men's sexuality, sexual potential, and its development with age. A systematic content analysis of currently used gynecology textbooks showed that Kinsey's and Masters and Johnson's research findings concerning female sexuality were entirely omitted, and the traditional stereotypes about female sexuality and personality persisted. The myths of vaginal orgasm, women's lesser sexual desire and potential, and rapid decrease in sexuality with age—in contrast to the everlasting male sexual potency and urges—are still perpetuated and taught to new gynecologists, who will have to practice among and advise increasingly liberated women and men (Scully and Bart, 1973). In addition to the urgent need to incorporate facts about female sexuality into scientific textbooks that treat the subject, there is an equally urgent need for the publication of popular "How to..." manuals that will aid in spreading the facts about female sexuality, and will help women, men, and couples to reach sexual liberation.

Furthermore, through liberation in economic, occupational, and personal achievement, women may tend to become increasingly liberated in another important area, namely, in self-assurance so that they can marry men much younger than themselves. There is actually some cross-cultural evidence that there is a significantly high correlation between the percentage of women marrying younger men and the percentage of women active in the labor force (Safilios-Rothschild, 1971). Before women in their late thirties and forties (or older) can feel secure in marrying husbands in their twenties or thirties, they would have to be able to achieve significantly in position and prestige, as well as in income, so that they feel totally independent and self-reliant. Only then could they feel that they could afford to marry a younger man, who would most probably not be professionally established, with limited economic means or occupational prestige. Instead of acquiring status and economic security through their husbands, these women would instead be bestowing both of these desirable goods on their younger husbands.

It is, of course, true that only those women who are famous, powerful, rich, or quite prestigious in their mature age are able to attract the admiration and the interest of younger men. Younger women have for centuries been exchanging their youth and beauty for the desirable assets and achievements of the older men they married. Up to now mature women have very rarely had such attractions for younger men, except through inherited money. But even then, they were unable to establish, maintain, and enjoy rich, meaningful, and stable relationships, partly because the money attraction is the least reliable and solid, and partly because they lacked the necessary psychological liberation.

Such psychological liberation is very important in that it presupposes liberation in many areas. Women will not only have to be free of the stereotypes about continuous physical attractiveness and perfection and the fears of loss of attractiveness with age, but will also have to accept and enjoy their stable, high sexual potential, even with advanced age. Furthermore, they will have to be able to free themselves of the "hangup" that the man they love, or marry, must be "superior" to them. They will need to feel comfortable and happy in being occupationally, educationally, and economically "superior" to their men. Being the objects of admiration on the part of their lovers or husbands will help them to learn to appreciate their men for properties, qualities, and talents outside those related only to achievement. That is, women will be able to enjoy men as lovers, as friends, as entertaining and stimulating companions, as compassionate idealists, as thinkers, as fathers, as cooks, as housekeepers, and as public relations men.

This complex type of women's liberation is hard to achieve, especially because women resist emotionally accepting, loving and admiring men they judge to be "inferior" to them. Even the most liberated women have great difficulties in reaching this level of liberation. Some facilitating strategies are necessary, but it is quite difficult to devise and implement them.

One such strategy would be to change the image of marriages between older and/or achievement-wise "superior" women to younger and/or achievement-wise "inferior" men as it now exists in all types of mass media. Since the federal or state governments in the United Staets cannot exercise direct control over the content of movies and other programs shown on T.V. (as is true in many other countries), or novels written, or articles and stories published in journals and newspapers, indirect influence techniques can be used. Special, high-prestige literary and film prizes could be established by the government (directly or indirectly by granting money to foundations) or by different foundations for novels, movies, short films, and different types of television programs that present sex-stereotype free themes and new images of man-women relationships. Thus the awarding committee could reward the presentation of new themes in man-woman relationships as particularly innovative, "liberated," very prizeworthy.

Some of the changes in the mass media images, however, may also come about by other means:

1. As more women hold positions of power in the management and direction of the different mass media, it is expected that they will change the content of many programs considerably by excluding sexist films, programs, advertisements, or commentaries. Thus, different authors and script writers can be expected to become increasingly motivated to write nonsexist and innovative articles, not necessarily because they have become "liberated" or are striving to change the images of women and men, but because they want to minimize the probability of rejection.

2. It is also expected that a larger number of men in responsible positions in the mass media will gradually become liberated to a sufficient degree so that they are bothered by clearly sexist content in articles, films, movies, programs, and advertisements, and will try to eliminate them. But even totally "male chauvinistic" managers, directors, editors, etc., of the different mass media are expected to yield slowly to pressures from listeners, viewers, or readers, as well as to their concern over the "image" of their station, journal, or publishing house with respect to "sexism." They too will help to bring about "desirable" changes, despite their "best judgment." No T.V. or radio station or journal or publisher would like to be labeled "sexist"; such a label would tend to diminish popularity and profit.

3. Through a similar process to that described in number 2, many businessmen and advertisement producers and consultants would also gradually change, partly because of pressures brought about by consumer women, and partly because of their desire to maintain or establish a "liberal" as well as "sympathetic" image toward women. Thus some T.V. programs which are extremely striking in terms of their "sexist" content may be publicly boycotted by women, as well as the products that support it. Or a journal containing particularly sexist articles and stories could receive disapproving letters from women as well as cancellations of subscriptions. This type of "cold war" by consumer women could be quite effective in changing the content of the different mass media, regardless of the degree of the directors', managers', and editors' change of values and attitudes. There is no time to change everybody's value system, especially all the men's value systems, before proceeding with social change. The main strategy is to bring about the necessary societal and structural changes, while at the same time exerting continuous and effective social and consumer pressure. Psychological liberation may take place after two or three generations, but social-structural changes and social pressure must take place immediately.

The economic emancipation of women and the perfect social acceptance of high-achievement women would also tend to free women from the sex-stereotyped range of expressions of feelings. Women would be able, partly because of the structural requirements of new types of jobs, partly because of the self-assurance that comes from economic independence, and partly because of the changing climate of opinion around them, to behave aggressively, roughly, to be independent and ambitious, to assert themselves, and to exercise their power whenever appropriate and necessary. But they will be equally able to show tenderness, softness, sweetness, affection, love, even dependence, whenever such behavior, in their judgment, is appropriate and/or necessary. And they will be able to liberate themselves sexually, since they will be expected to be able to refuse men's sexual advances, even those of quite powerful and traditional men, who in retaliation will try to punish them in some subtle way. Strong, economically independent women would be able to take the option of refusing without any serious consequences, and could then effectively dismiss the "threatened" male. Such women would be better able to separate sex from love and friendship, and to equally enjoy each in the same or parallel relationships.

But total sexual liberation cannot be achieved before *all* women can *at all times* have perfect control of the reproductive implications of sexual intercourse. This perfect control cannot really be achieved before a pill or an injection is invented that renders women infecund—without any ill effects on the health of any women—and another type of pill or injection that renders them fecund for a brief period of time whenever they wish to bear a child. Another alternative type of perfect control may be the development of a chemical compound that women could take orally during the first weeks of pregnancy to stop the development of the embryo without any health complications.

Since, however, at present and most probably for the next five to ten years neither of these two types of perfect birth control techniques will be made available for mass use, and since a great number of women cannot use the existing "safe" contraceptives for a variety of health reasons, the liberalization of abortion laws is an absolute necessity. The U.S. has given a good example to other societies by recently establishing abortion as the legal right of women. Similar legislative decisions are needed in all societies until the time when a variety of cheap, safe, socially and psychologically acceptable contraceptives have been developed. Furthermore, abortion must be made inexpensive through health insurance coverage and free of charge to low-income women not covered by health insurance. The legal and financial accessibility of abortion to all women can give them the option to have an abortion, regardless of economic means and without psychological and health penalties (sometimes as drastic as their lives). Without this option, only a part of womankind can become sexually liberated—those who happen to live in the "right" country, those who can afford relatively expensive abortions or can afford travel to the "right" countries where abortion is possible, and those whose current health status or anatomy permits them to use the pill or IUD. The rest of the women (probably still the large majority of women) are *forced* to have children, whether they want them or not, and must learn to love them, to adjust their lives and make their plans around them.

Chapter 3

SOCIAL POLICY
TO LIBERATE MEN

The different types of social policies which aim to liberate women and which we discussed in the previous chapter will also have a significant direct, or indirect, impact upon the liberation of men. For example the greater the number of employed women in all settings, the less men will be able to hire only sexually attractive women, and the more they will have to interact with "unattractive" women. The implication for men's liberation is that men will be forced to relate to different types of women in a variety of roles as colleagues, collaborators, or competitors on an equal basis rather than as sex objects, or inferiors. So men may be able to discover the wealth of experience that friendship with women can offer them, and may slowly learn to enjoy and value such friendships.

The more women have the option to achieve according to their desires and capabilities, the more their husbands and sons will have the option to achieve very highly, or only to some extent, or not at all, without serious psychological pressures from the women in their lives, and without the implied threat of rejection and love withdrawal should they not wish to achieve. And as more women are able to reach high positions in different fields, more men will be supervised, directed, controlled, hired, and fired by women bosses, and thus eventually overcome their psychological "hang-up" concerning the necessity of superiority over women in all types of relationships. They will sooner or later be able to feel comfortable, to even enjoy working for some women, to accept their authority, superior skills, and knowledge, and to learn from them. This in turn is expected to significantly promote the psychological liberation of men, because they will be able to love and marry women "superior" to them in terms of prestige, income, education, and/or achievement, who are occasionally older than themselves, and be able to admire and love them.

An important net gain, therefore, from women's liberation for men is that they might be helped to overcome their sexual hangups concerning the nature and proof of masculinity, one of which is a tendency to treat women as sexual objects to be conquered. They must gradually learn to see and enjoy women as equal human beings with whom a variety of relationships are possible and interesting. Then sexual relationships may be relegated to the status of alternative options or parts of relationships, rather than the central and unique purpose of any relationship with a woman. This change would significantly enrich the lives of men.

The economic independence of women would free men from the moral, social, and legal obligation to support all the "dependent" women and children in their lives. This is a particularly important type of liberation for men who, up to now, have not had the option not to work, to work part-time, or occasionally, to underachieve, or to fail occupationally and/or economically. Of course, there have been "deviant" men in American society who, because of social-structural, social-psychological, or idiosyncratic reasons, have been "failures." Lower-class unskilled men, especially blacks, have had such difficulties in holding regular full-time jobs and in achieving, due to a combination of adverse socialization experiences and social-structural conditions, that such "deviance" is almost imposed upon them. And despite the overall achievement-oriented socialization of boys in the United States, Canada, Sweden, and other Western societies, some of them grow up to be lazy, unambitious, and unmotivated to succeed. Others have low intelligence and are generally incompetent, but in many cases they manage to achieve and even succeed despite their shortcomings, because of the widespread societal protection and even promotion of incompetent people. Nobody is threatened by an incompetent person, so everybody is more willing to help him, but most people are quite threatened by competent persons and tend, therefore, to "keep them down" as long as possible.

"Deviant," unsuccessful, underachieving men have generally been despised in American culture, divorced by their dissatisfied wives, or at least eternally nagged and blamed for their failure, and considered to be "less of a man." Sharing economic responsibility for the family (extended and nuclear) with wives, or having the wife completely take over familial economic responsibility would free men from this stigma of deviance and from the compulsive neurosis to succeed and achieve. Men would become less anxious about economic success and be freer to enjoy life, to think, to be human beings, and to express all types of feelings and ideas. And men would be able to take the jobs they like rather than those that are secure, well paying, and dull.

But in addition to the significant, beneficial side effects of social policies which aim to liberate women upon the liberation of men, a number of corresponding or different specific social policies are needed to facilitate and reinforce the liberation of men (and reciprocally and indirectly the liberation of women).

Social Policy to Liberate Fathers

It is quite interesting to note and realize that the same policies that are crucial for the liberation of mothers are also vital for the liberation of fathers. Men should become increasingly conscious that they must also benefit from social policies that liberate women as mothers as well as individuals. The official, social, and legal recognition of the importance of the role of the father in socialization of a child and the interchangeability of parents in the care and "normal" development of children would allow men to spend more time with their children and to develop and enjoy meaningful relationships with them.

Social policy that would permit men to stay home and take care of sick children and to take off some months, or weeks per month, or days per week for a year after the birth of the child would allow fathers to officially declare their desire to spend time with their children and to actually take care of them, interact and relate with them, and play a more significant role in their development. These types of social policies, together with the possibility of working part-time for several years without any kind of penalty, allow fathers to actively play the paternal role without jeopardizing the occupational role, that function which up to now has been the main *raison d'être* for fathers. Furthermore, because exactly the same set of social policies officially liberates mothers from the exclusivity of the parental role, women would be much more willing to allow their husbands to take a more active role as fathers, contrary to what has been happening (Safilios-Rothschild, 1972a).

Besides a common set of social policies aiming to liberate both mothers and fathers to play their parental roles, some specific social policies are needed to further advance men's (and indirectly women's) liberation as parents.

First, the most badly needed policies are radical legal reforms concerning the child custody and visitation rights in case of divorce. It is true that the ratification of the Equal Rights Amendment will make unconstitutional the present practice of unilaterally granting custody of children to the mother (except when she is demonstrably mentally, physically, or morally unfit). Great attention must be paid to the legal interpretation of equality and to the establishment of the premise that both parents are equally important in the "normal" development of children. The actual implementation of the law must not continue to result in unilateral decisions that almost automatically grant children to mothers. New principles of parental fitness should be established based upon the new prevailing trends in life styles for divorced and remarrying women and men.

The basic assumption that men in general have less time for their children and do not know how or are not interested in coping with their problems must be eliminated, not only from public opinion but also from legal thought before divorced fathers can *in fact* obtain equal rights to their children. For there is considerable evidence that men have been consistently and cruelly discriminated against in this area, and that they are suffering from this discrimination, since many of them do not want and cannot stand to separate from their children. Despite the existing prevailing deemphasis of the father role and the social acceptance of a considerable affective disengagement of fathers from their children as long as they continue to carry the economic responsibility, many fathers have been reported to be so emotionally attached to their children that they go through endless legal battles to obtain reasonable visitation rights or the right to spend one month of vacation per year with them (Bart, 1970b).

It is, of course, possible that the legal redefinition of both parents' equal, shared economic responsibility for children may have a number of interesting side effects. Many women may become more enthusiastic about the option not to have children or to have only one child. Some working divorced mothers may neglect to consistently or adequately pay their share of the children's support—if the custody of the children has been granted to the father, and the mother rarely sees her children because she has to move to a distant state to get a better job. This type of maternal neglect may become even more accentuated in cases where divorced mothers remarry and have another child. For it is possible that a part of the documented economic neglect of children and their fathers' overall reluctance to support them may be a function of the imposed affective disengagement through the courts' granting custody to the mother (*The Equal Rights Amendment and Alimony and Child Support Laws,* 1972).

A second policy concerns research in family sociology which focuses upon the father's role and the nature of the father-child relationship upon the child's development and socialization. Priority funding or funding from a specially established subcommittee should allot money to research on the little-studied role of fathers and husbands (Le Masters, 1970). Because interviewing married men requires a much longer time period, as well as expense (on the average, three to four times more expensive than the wife's average interview), researchers have systematically avoided interviewing husbands, thus creating a "wives' family sociology" (Safilios-Rothschild, 1969). And the widely held notion that fathers are relatively less salient and important in families has greatly facilitated the omission of data on them from the study of the parent-child relationship. Focusing research on fathers and father-child relationships (and not just on father-son relationships that, due to the psychoanalytic theories, have been to some extent studied) would provide us with factual information about the impact of the father's role. Such information would be extremely useful in revising family sociology and child development textbooks, and in slowly changing the father's image in scientific literature, as well as in therapy, the different mass media, and overall public opinion.

Mass media in particular could play an extremely important part in establishing the vital importance of "father's love" on the same level as "mother's love," and the equal significance of the father's understanding and support with that provided by the mother. Probably some kind of institutionalized, societal recognition and reward of effective fatherhood would also be quite helpful in underlining the crucial contributions of fathers to their children. Cities, states, and different types of civic organizations (including women's organizations) could set up special prizes for the outstanding "fathers of the year." The establishment and award of these prizes to fathers, the ensuing publicity concerning the exceptional quality of the father-children relationship in the selected families, and the outstanding fathering accomplishments would considerably help to psychologically liberate fathers vis-à-vis their children.

Social Policy for the "Housekeeping" Liberation of Men

Cooking, washing, cleaning, and other household chores and responsibilities have been considered for centuries and in most countries to be women's work. Men have claimed to feel less "masculine" and respectable when they lower themselves to doing such work. As we have already seen in Chapter 2, it can be theorized that the low prestige attached to these housekeeping activities and responsibilities can be attributed to the fact that they were (and are) services rendered free by wives, mothers, daughters, or other female relatives as a duty attached to their role and in exchange for economic support.

When, however, the family income and the availability of domestic servants permitted hiring servants to do this work, their gender often depended upon the societal level of development and the rate of unemployment for males in the society. Thus in most developing African and Southeast Asian countries with high rates of male unemployment, men (or entire families) are employed more often than women as domestics. In the case of entire families of servants, some kind of sex labeling of housekeeping activities and responsibilities usually takes place that is not consistent and is not carried over to their own familial division of labor. When, however, the rate of male unemployment (especially for unskilled males) tends to diminish, men leave the underpaid, low-prestige, and low-security domestic jobs, which are then taken over entirely by women.

In developed countries male domestics tend to be very highly skilled, prestigious, and well-paid cooks or valets. Lately, however, in the United States and Canada, another type of highly professionalized and specialized male domestic service is making its appearance: the small business enterprise, such as a group of "professional" window cleaners, rug cleaners, etc. When, in developed societies, men carry out any type of domestic activity, they do so in a highly professional manner that guarantees them satisfactory pay for their services, specifically defined duties, and relatively high prestige.

Women, however, have never managed to have any prestige, pay, or recognition for housekeeping services that have been always considered an obligatory part of their familial roles. Some people have suggested that a regular salary be paid to wives (by their husbands) commensurate with the amount and quality of services rendered and the price of these services, based on what the expenses would be if they were rendered by a hired helper. If such a policy were incorporated in the family law, it could have very important repercussions for the "housekeeping" liberation of both women and men.

First, the housekeeping activities and responsibilities would gain higher prestige. Second, men would become considerably more motivated to take over several housekeeping activities and responsibilities, since, on the one hand, this would save them money that they would otherwise have to pay their wives (or hired helpers), and, on the other hand, because housekeeping would have become a more prestigious activity. Third, it would decrease the usual resistance on the part of American and Anglo-Saxon men to hire domestic help. The wages of a domestic helper could be shared equally with their working wives, and would, therefore, be cheaper than paying the entire wage to their wives (and even cheaper yet, since the wages of a hired helper do not include all the services and diffuse responsibilities performed by wives). Implications of this practice would be particularly important for many women who at present have few saleable skills, regardless of their level of education, and who are "trapped" at home because they must find a job that can pay the wages of a housekeeper, and the increase in income tax, the cost of a second car, and all other expenses before they can go out and work.

A final repercussion is that men would start having more reasonable expectations concerning the appearance and cleanliness of the house, and would tend to favor smaller dwellings and apartments that require less care and housework. They would, in general, become more aware of the drudgery and the great demands housework has on one's time, and would become much more appreciative for those services rendered by their wives.

Another social policy that could help in the housekeeping liberation of men would be the incorporation of equal housekeeping responsibilities for men and women in the family law. Thus a wife could sue a husband for divorce who refused to share household and housekeeping responsibilities equally, or to hire help to take over these responsibilities.

A changed image of men in mass media and acceptance of men's performance of some "traditionally" feminine housekeeping tasks could also play a crucial role in establishing an appropriate climate of opinion and social acceptance of the "normality" of such behavior. Movie and film presentation of men who have assumed some or all of the housekeeping responsibility—while they also enjoy and achieve in their jobs—portraying them as respected and admired men for their ability to cope with "both roles," could play a significant liberating role. Also if advertisements for housekeeping products (such as detergents, floor waxes, cooking ingredients, utensils, house deodorants, etc.) were addressed with equal frequency to husbands and wives, husbands would be more comfortable in making house-keeping decisions and performing certain tasks. And establishment of cook-ing, sewing, pressing, etc., competitions for men by church and other civic groups and organizations would also encourage men to feel proud of the high quality of their performance of housekeeping tasks.

Finally, the *word* "househusband" should be officially incorporated in the language, together with the *concept* of "househusband" in family law, so that men who opt to be househusbands can be paid a salary by their wives commensurate with the type, quality, and current cost of such services. Only by means of all these policies will men (as well as women) have the entire range of possible options in the continuum from total housekeeping responsibility to no housekeeping responsibility.

Social Policy for the Educational, Occupational, and Economic Liberation of Men

In these areas men do not suffer from the same problems and restrictions as women. Men have always had a large range of educa-tional and training options, particularly options leading to the better-paying jobs, with higher prestige and advancement possibilities. The kinds of options considered inappropriate for men fall into two categories: first, auxilliary, "nurturant," supportive occupations such as, nursing, nursery school teaching, secretarial training, medical or dental assistance, or primary school teaching (only in some societies); and, second, artistic, expressive occupations, such as acting, painting, ballet dancing, poetry, singing, which are supposed to require sensitive, temperamental, and emotional personalities, that is, characteristics stereotyped as "feminine." In most societies both sets of occupations are usually low-paying and low-prestige. Artistic occupations are characterized by employment instability and financial insecurity.

As a matter of fact, it is worthwhile to mention that in whatever societies any of the above occupations are, for some reason, well-paid or prestigious, men rather than women tend to occupy them. Thus, in the United States and England where rock groups are extremely profitable and popular, men have almost exclusively dominated the field. In several African nations such as Nigeria, most of the well-paid typists and secretaries are men. It is at a later stage of social and economic development that men at this level of education can find better paying jobs, with greater advancement possibilities, and can then leave the typist and secretarial jobs to women. Even an "utterly feminine" endeavor such as embroidery comes to be defined as "complicated" work that only men can perform in a country like Senegal, where the market for the product is quite good since embroidery is a necessary part of men's attire.

So why change things? What kind of "liberation" is this, if all it does for men is allow them to enter less "desirable" occupations? First, it must be remembered that the less "desirable" nature of these "feminine" occupations is not inherent, but has appeared, has become reinforced, consolidated, and perpetuated because only, or primarily, women, that is the cheap, "second-rate" labor force, have been performing them.

Second, it must not be forgotten that some men have showed inclination and preference for, as well as talent in, those occupations labeled "feminine," despite all the socialization experiences that were meant to discourage and disinterest them. Therefore, it is logical to believe that many other men have had similar inclinations and talents but could not let them surface or could not realize them because of a very "effective" socialization that never permitted them to consider these options. Liberation would permit these men to consider and to take these options, and would allow them to realize their inclinations and develop their talents. In the past in the rare circumstances in which a man performed "feminine" jobs (private secretary, butler, hairdresser for women, social worker, primary school teacher), he usually managed to be better paid and to have more prestige than women doing the same things. At present, the entrance of men in such occupations would play a very important role in upgrading them for women and men. Special attention must be paid so that sex-differentiated specialties and careers do not develop within the same type of occupation. That is, men primary school teachers must not always become principals, superintendants, and administrators; or men nurses must not become only "medics," a new health specialty with a higher authority line than women nurses. If proper attention is paid so that men in "feminine" occupations have equal footing with women, there will be a wider range of educational and employment opportunities for men.

A third reason for changing sex-occupation stereotypes is that men have always, as part of their "masculinity" package, taken courses to learn and/or to work in so-called serious, solid, practical, scientific subjects and concerns. "Fun" subjects have been considered appropriate only for women. Men have had to achieve in some concrete way. This achievement was measured in terms of earned income, at least within North American societies and some other Western European societies. In other societies, the more difficult it was for men to consistently earn satisfactory incomes through hard work, the more socially acceptable were alternative types and measures of achievement (Safilios-Rothschild, 1970b). But in all societies men have had to achieve, and their jobs have usually been keys to achievement. They have therefore been forced to become trained and educated for jobs that had a relatively high probability of good and stable remuneration and a reasonable chance for advancement. This obligation, accentuated by the fact that women and children have depended upon men for economic support and security, has most often excluded men from the pursuit of favorite subjects, talents, and inclinations that were not considered serious, because of the uncertainty of "making a living" from painting, writing, poetry, music, etc. In many nations (e.g., Greece) for many years sociologists and psychologists were primarily upper-middle- and upper-class women who had enough money to live well despite the fact that jobs for sociologists were scarce, badly paid, and seldom permanent (Safilios-Rothschild, 1968). Once, however, sociology and psychology became "established" professions men came in, and usually secured the most prestigious and powerful positions for themselves.

Another characteristic of occupations labeled "feminine" has traditionally been their subservient position in relation to a "masculine" occupation or to the few dominating men in the "feminine" occupations. Thus nurses are under the authority of male physicians; female medical and dental assistants under the authority of male physicians and dentists; female schoolteachers and social workers under the authority of male administrators. That is why "feminine" occupations have been "appropriately" defined as auxiliary to the important "masculine" occupations, and why men have been always obliged to be dominant in relation to women, even when they were "deviant" enough to enter "feminine" fields. Actually men entering "feminine" or artistic, expressive occupations were often suspected to be lacking in masculinity or to be homosexuals. Thus, the only way to shake off the potential stigma of inadequate masculinity or homosexuality was to prove their masculine superiority by outstanding achievement and by control of the field and their women colleagues.

It is, therefore, important to "liberate" men from the constantly constraining obligation to spend their time in serious and achievement-producing pursuits. It is important to expose men to subjects and activities that may be considered frivolous, nonproductive, esthetic, artistic, or nonintellectual but which they enjoy, or for which they have a definite inclination and talent. Thus men could take courses and training in child care, child development, sewing, embroidery, cooking, home economics, music and art appreciation, literature, ballet, interior decorating, typing and secretarial skills, etc.

In order to break established sex stereotyping of courses offered in primary and high schools, as well as in colleges, some definite strategies, corresponding to the ones discussed in the previous chapter, are much needed. During the transition period some courses, particularly those that help break the existing sex stereotypes, should become obligatory for *boys* and girls. Such obligatory courses in child care, home economics, sewing, and cooking could be obligatory, as in Sweden, at the primary school level. At the high school level *boys* as well as girls should have to take typing and secretarial skills, social graces, family and child development, and home economics, as well as scientific subjects. The development of an equal aptitude in typing and secretarial skills in men as well as women might help rescue women from the eternal "no-cost" secretarial role to boyfriends, husbands, or brothers. At the college level, the availability of scholarships and fellowships for men interested in studying nursing, child development, nursery school education, home economics, music, art, literature, theatre, or primary school education could serve as very potent motivation for male freshmen students.

In addition, advisors should encourage boys, especially during their freshman year, to explore their inclinations and to be exposed to a variety of fields and subjects, including those previously considered "women's fields." Particular emphasis should be placed upon subjects and fields considered "unprofitable," "fun," and frivolous—at least as masculine pursuits—such as art, history, poetry, painting, music, classical and modern dancing, literature, acting, etc. A possible strategy would be that a certain number of hours be required in some of these fields, especially for freshmen men who declare engineering, premedicine, chemistry, physics, business, or economics majors. While a few men might in this way discover their "true" talent and inclination for a totally different field than their original traditional "masculine" choice, other men will be exposed to important areas in life and knowledge other than the "appropriate" masculine world within which they have been restricted. Here, of course, the role of vocational counselors is extremely important. Counselors have to be liberated to allow and, even more, to encourage college men and make them feel quite comfortable in making a switch from a field traditionally labeled "masculine" to one labeled as less important and therefore "feminine."

However, as different types of child care facilities develop throughout the United States, there is a great opportunity to correct the conscious or subtle sex-stereotyped socialization styles of parents. Children at all types of child care centers and nursery schools should be exposed from a very early age to de-stereotyping educational experiences and training. There the choice of distribution of toys, games, and educational play activities could be carefully controlled so that no sex labeling occurs. On the contrary, boys could be encouraged and urged to play with toys that are not related to war or to space, and to take part in games and activities traditionally considered "feminine." In this way boys' emphatic socialization for violence, aggression, and adventure would be somewhat toned down, and they would have the opportunity to develop human relation or artistic skills.

In addition, a great effort must be made continuously by nursery school and child care center teachers and aides to place girls in leadership positions over boys in a variety of games and educational play activities. Only through the implementation of such a strategy from a very early age can boys, and later men, be helped to free themselves from the nerve-wrecking compulsion to always be the leaders, especially of women, and to feel comfortable under the leadership and direction of a woman. Of course, the same strategy, extended later into the primary and high schools, would also assure that girls and women would be willing to assume leadership and to gain experience in being good leaders.

Besides strategies to be used from children's earliest contact with educators, many of the educational techniques, materials, styles, and rationales must be examined very carefully in order to determine what aspects and features, explicit or subtle, are sexist and must be changed. There is evidence, for example, that a very popular letter kit, called Alpha One, widely used in schools throughout the United States to teach children their ABC's, is quite sexist in the way the images of the twenty-one male consonants and the five female vowels are used. The "girl-vowels are shown as weak, weeping creatures who must ask the chauvinist consonants for protection and support." Also the male consonants are shown discussing and choosing which girl-vowels belong to them without ever consulting the girl-vowels (Sherr, 1972). Thus the stage is set: girls belong to boys, boys make all the important decisions, and girls must cling to boys in order to amount to anything. How can boys ever get rid of their "need" to dominate, possess, and protect the "weak" women? Although some people may tend to shrug their shoulders at such "trivial," unimportant details, the influence of such "details" is very significant, especially since a great number of such small and unimportant details accumulate through life and reinforce each other.

In summary, then, the most important aspect of the educational and employment liberation of men is the resulting liberation from the compulsion to achieve and dominate, and the possibility of entering creative or auxiliary fields for which they may have talent and inclination. The masculinity syndrome cannot break down unless men can enter fields that, on the one hand, are not and will never be highly paid or highly prestigious, or fields in which economic security or continuous full-time employment are not guaranteed, and, on the other hand, that call for them to play a subservient, auxiliary role to other *women* and men.

Liberation will be achieved when a poet with limited financial means will be able to love and marry a wealthy businesswoman, or when a male dental assistant can attach to the woman dentist for whom he works without feeling "less of a man." In both of these cases the wife's salary and occupational status will determine the family's standard of living and social status, while the husband will be able to pursue his interests and vocation freely with only a minor economic responsibility for the family, or to become a househusband.

A recent research study conducted among Ivy League male college students shows dramatically men's persistent and deep-rooted ambivalence toward intelligent, competent women whom they perceive as their equals or their superiors. On the one hand, they tend to admire such women and to judge their intelligence and competence as desirable, but, on the other hand, their internalized masculine norms of dominance and superiority make them feel uncomfortable or downright theatened when dating such women. Thus, they would like to marry intelligent, well-educated, competent women—provided they would not have uninterrupted careers and would assume the traditional "feminine" responsibilities and familial roles (Komarovsky, 1973). These findings show that men have a long way to go before they are liberated enough to marry women who are their intellectual equals, and especially women who are superior in terms of intelligence, fame, financial achievement, or occupational rank or prestige. Strong societal supports are needed during the transitional period. Ridicule of unusually intelligent and famous men who marry very "inferior" women will have to be done before men's ambivalence and fear of highly intelligent and achieving women can be solved. As women develop their potential and their intellectual abilities to the fullest and are unwilling to make sacrifices in their careers in order to avoid inconvenience to their husbands, men will have to overcome their ambivalence, since the women within the field of desirable eligibles who will be willing to conform to their norms will be very few.

The entire discussion above by no means implies that men can be liberated only if they cease to achieve, to dominate, to be superior, to have authority over others (especially women), and to carry the financial responsibility for the family. The important point is that men *cannot* be liberated unless they actually have the *option* to underachieve, or to not achieve at all, to be inferior in terms of prestige or achievement, to enter auxiliary or creative "feminine" occupations, to relinquish the main economic responsibility to a woman "significant other," and, unless they can feel equally comfortable, from a psychological viewpoint, to take any one of these options.

The strategies discussed up to now are relevant to the coming generations, and so mostly touch men who are now in their teens. There is actually some research evidence indicating that male college students are increasingly liberated from the exaggerated preoccupation with career and high achievement. Thus, while Horner found that in 1965 the motive to avoid success in favor of familial concerns and preoccupations characterized University of Michigan women but not men, Hoffman in 1971 found that on the same campus men were as likely as women to report a motive to avoid success. While achievement and career were not central for only 8 percent of male college students in 1965, this was true for 78 percent of them in 1971—a finding that represents an important step toward men's liberation from compulsive high achievement (Wladis Hoffman, 1972).

But what can be done for those over thirty, or forty, or older? One solution would be the institutionalization of continuing education for men and the establishment of continuing education centers that would include a counseling section. Adult men would be able to come to these counseling sections to discuss the nature of their restlessness and dissatisfaction, to explore a variety of new educational and occupational opportunities and alternatives, and to be aided in discovering untapped talents, inclinations, and goals that they were not able to develop and pursue, partly because of prevailing sex stereotypes. Once these adult men have been able, with the help of vocational counselors, clinical psychologists, and/or psychiatrists, to find what they really want to do, the necessary structures should exist within colleges and universities to make their transition smoother and less painful. The availability of fellowships and training grants for men who would like training to pursue a nonsex-stereotyped career would render such changes more socially acceptable. The institutionalization of continuing education for men would provide them with another important option; to have at least two major phases in their lives, one during which they strove to achieve as high as possible and to dominate, and one during which they tried to satisfy their "expressive," creative, and fun-oriented needs. The possibility of alternating between these two phases represents a very important and satisfying option, since most people would have great difficulties in choosing between the two, and would prefer to find some way to combine them. In essence, the greatest profit that liberation holds for men is their freedom to work for as long as they wish in jobs they like, regardless of prestige and pay, rather than working in full-time high-paying jobs, whether they are fulfilled or not, or whether they like them or not. Men who have left jobs they loved because they did not pay enough money to maintain their families in a high enough standard of living can well appreciate this precious freedom and benefit.

There are actually already some indications that something like this is happening to some upper-middle-class men in their early or late forties— what has been called "the middle-age crisis." Some of these men, after having a significantly high level of achievement in their jobs, become dissatisfied and start asking very basic and disturbing questions about their roles, identities, and whether they want to continue their achievement-oriented life style for another twenty years. In most cases, however, and unless their wives have meanwhile managed to become economically independent and to assume a considerable part of the family's financial responsibility, these men have in fact only limited options for change. Unless their wives can and will carry the major financial burden, husbands can make only minor changes. Those changes may be a switch from a high-paying, prestigious, and very demanding job to one that pays relatively less, or to a prestigious job that is less demanding, but gives them a little more time and flexibility to enjoy life.

But most men cannot afford to take one to two years off to take courses in a subject they had always wanted to study but could never find time for, or to travel and think, or to write the novel they always dreamed of writing. It is not possible to make such a drastic break from their bread-winning responsibilities (Farrell, 1970). Actually, it seems that even the relatively small drops in income and prestige they are willing to take to have greater freedom from responsibility and stress and more time is not always approved by their dependent wives, as indicated by divorces initiated by the wives who still prefer a high-achiever for a husband.

An important liberation for men in the occupational sector, closely related to their sex-stereotyped obligations to work hard and achieve to support their families, is liberation from overtime work. Men within the American and some other Western societies are required to work overtime regardless of the type of work and their social class in order for them to be considered "real," "fulfilled," masculine men. In some blue-collar occupations, men have had to work overtime as a condition in their employment. In white-collar work, especially academic, executive, and managerial jobs, men have not been formally required to work overtime, but they have definitely been expected to. Failure to work overtime could result in being slowed down or refused promotions, raises, tenure, and eventually in being dismissed.

The obligatory nature of overtime work has served to accentuate the primacy of the occupational role for men, and therefore to clearly underscore the difference between women and men (especially since blue-collar women workers in many states were allowed to work little or no overtime). It has tended to alienate men from their familial roles, especially the father role, and made it almost impossible for men to ever take an active and responsible role in housekeeping and other family-centered activities. And the glorification of overtime work for men has left them with little time to pursue leisure interests, or soul-searching, or thinking and evaluating their lives (Polk, 1971).

Men cannot become liberated until overtime becomes legally and informally a voluntary activity shared equally by women and men. And men's liberation cannot be complete until part-time work becomes institutionalized and socially acceptable. Only then would men who opt not to work overtime or opt to work part-time not be unduly penalized, but would instead be judged on the merits of rather than hours spent on their work.

Finally, the economic liberation of men can be greatly facilitated by significant legal reforms that would hold both wives and husbands (or women and men) equally responsible for the economic support of their children, and would treat women and men as economically independent individuals. Wives and husbands would be taxed individually on the basis of their income, and those among them who rendered housekeeping and child care services would be taxed upon the amount of remuneration they receive from the other spouse for services rendered. In this way, very rarely would either of the spouses be considered legally and financially "dependent" upon the other.

Strategies for the Psychological and Sexual Liberation of Men

While psychological and sexual liberation is of crucial importance to men, it is the most difficult to achieve because the enactment of legislation can have no effect. Only indirectly can social policies and social pressure influence parents to change their style of child socialization. Images and messages presented by the different mass media would be helpful.

But what is the meaning of men's emotional liberation? According to the established and prevailing stereotypes of appropriate masculine behavior, men are not supposed to show their emotions, especially any weakness. That is, they are not supposed to show fear, affective weakness, or extreme sorrow, including crying. They are, however, permitted to express "positive" emotions such as, anger, pride, and a moderate degree of joy. It is a terrible emotional strain for well-socialized males to never "break down" and admit their fears and weakneses. But it would be a great relief for them to be able to cry when they are unhappy, to ask for help when they are faced with great obstacles, to admit that they are scared, to avoid an overwhelming situation, and to be able to admit how much they love, need, and are dependent upon the women they love (Polk and Stein, 1972).

Masculine stereotypes also require men to be "tough," uncommunicative, insensitive, and rough. The same stereotypes, if taken seriously by well-socialized males, make it difficult, if not impossible, to establish a good or real relationship, especially with a woman who is supposed to be gentle, expressive, sensitive, and tender. These stereotypes about masculinity (in combination with all the previously mentioned ones) actually constitute a kind of emotional slavery for the oppressor. The oppressor cannot be tender, sensitive, or understanding if he wants to be respected and effective. He cannot show weakness or fear, especially of the oppressed woman, or his reign might be challenged and overthrown. Liberated men do not have and do not like to be oppressors of women, but want to be equals who are able to share deeply rewarding relationships with them.

But how can men be liberated from all these psychological hangups? Part of it may come about as men find themselves in subordinate positions to women in the occupational setting, and have to take orders from them, are obliged to communicate with them, and have to be agreeable to them. As men discover the necessity and the desire to cooperate with female co-workers, some of their uncommunicative behavior toward women, based on rigid sex stereotypes will change; they will find that they can talk with women as well as with men. Similarly, having to accept subordinate positions to women in jobs, and their ability to choose among job options that do not require courage, physical strength, endurance, physical risks, or toughness might contribute to being able to be and feel weak, sensitive, or afraid without shame that they are not being the men they ought to be.

Child care centers and nursery school teachers, as well as primary and secondary school teachers, could play a very important role in men's emotional liberation. All these teachers should be taught to actively discourage (or even punish) the display of tough, "masculine" behavior on the part of boys, and to reward and admire sensitivity and the expression of the entire range of emotions and feelings for girls and boys. From the earliest stage, teachers should not discourage boys from crying, from being afraid or weak.

Mass media could also make a significant contribution by changing the image of the admired and beloved male from the tough, independent, courageous, and "cool" man who expresses his feelings and emotions very sparingly to the warm, sensitive man who openly expresses his feelings and emotions, who can be a good friend to women and men, who is by no means a superman. Actually, it would be very helpful if the stereotype of the "he-man" and tough guy who is not afraid and talks little were ridiculed in comedies on television. Heroines should be shown as falling in love with men with whom they can be good friends, who can be warm, sensitive, understanding, and who are able to admit and show their weaknesses, including their love and their need for the woman they love.

Of course, it must be clarified here that the image of the admired man as tough, independent, cool, and affectively restrained is very American and Anglo-Saxon, and is not shared by other countries, not even by all Western nations. For example, the image of the Swedish (and generally of the Scandinavian) man is by no means one of toughness, aggressiveness, and rough competition (Herman, 1972). The image of Mediterranean men (at least of the middle-class, educated ones) is one of easy expression of feelings (even when they do not really feel them, but expressing them serves a particular purpose), of considerable emotionality, warmth, but also of trickery, instability, and unreliability. Thus, changes in the stereotyped image of men would imply and require very different types of changes in different cultural contexts.

Men can quite effectively help themselves to liberation. Those few men who, either through "deviant" socialization experiences or through introspection and consciousness-raising, have been able to psychologically and emotionally liberate themselves can publicize their road to liberation and advantages of liberation in interviews, articles, T.V. appearances, books, and commentaries. Television program organizers could give thought to setting up programs for men in which they interview not only well-known men in politics, arts, science, and business but also the "common man," that is, bank tellers and policemen, construction workers and assembly line workers, bus drivers and mailmen. Some programs could present only "accomplished" liberated men and their experiences on a variety of occupational and social class levels. Other programs could present discussions by panels of men, each of them at different points on the liberation continuum, each with a different set of hangups and rationalizations, as well as liberating achievements and resources. Such programs would encourage many more men to become introspective and critical. They could then, without a sense of shame, examine behaviors, attitudes, and thoughts that they had always taken for granted. From such thought could come change of some things that they had unquestionably accepted, even though they may have disliked them, as part of the "masculinity package."

The experience of men's liberation consciousness-raising groups has been that men have had great difficulties in communicating with each other, especially in disclosing fears, failures, weaknesses, anxieties, dependency needs, feelings, and other concerns that make them vulnerable. The reluctance to freely, openly, and spontaneously talk about themselves, their thoughts, feelings, and emotions often prevents the establishment of deep friendships between men, friendships based upon the intimate knowledge of each other's thoughts, doubts, wishes, and fears. And it stands as a block in the way of men's psychological and emotional liberation. Expressing one's weaknesses and emotions represents the liberating ability to openly admit vulnerability and imperfection (Fasteau, 1972; Farrell, 1970).

It is important to note that the psychological liberation of men that would permit them to openly admit failure and weakness without any decrease in their self-esteem would have many far-reaching effects. Some of these effects would render all types of relationships among men and between women and men more honest, sound, deep, and humane. Furthermore, as we shall see in the next chapter many serious diplomatic, political, and international misunderstandings, conflicts, and wars could have been avoided (and may be avoided in the future) if the men in power could have accepted defeat, weakness, failure, and errors without undue self-depreciation and had not reacted aggressively (Farrell, 1970 and 1971; Amundsen, 1971). Thus the psychological liberation of men could have very important, extensive ramifications in the lives of both women and men in many nations.

Another of men's obligations has been taking the initiative and the risks involved in attempting to establish or to redefine all woman-man relationships. Men were always supposed to ask women out on dates, to ask women to make love to them, or to marry them, and to cope with the emotional strain of rejection that inevitably occurs in many instances (Polk and Stein, 1972). Many men have not been able to cope with the rejection pains, and have used quite drastic coping mechanisms, such as beating, raping, attempting to kill or actually killing, or less violent forms, such as defaming or otherwise punishing the rejecting woman[1] (Safilios-Rothschild, 1972c and d).

Throughout history some women have directly or indirectly sought or chased the man they wanted, and were quite persistent, but they have always represented the rare, outstanding exception to the rule. Quite often the obviously pursued male fled because he was threatened by the woman's "open" declaration of feelings, her straightforwardness, independence, "aggressiveness," and "unbecoming," "unladylike" behavior.

Liberated men would be able to share with liberated women the risks of the initiation or consolidation of a relationship. Both would be able to calmly and objectively evaluate the pros and cons of an offer and accept it, if desirable, as well as to pursue a woman or man they like. Thus liberated men would be freed of the obligation to do all the pursuing of women they like (this obligation transformed into an option), and would be able to accept the offers from desirable women to date, make love, or marry.

In this area, the liberation of men will be greatly and directly facilitated by the liberation of women. As women gain economic and psychological liberation, they will tend to "pick" their own men rather than to wait passively to be found by the "enchanted prince." Men will be faced with

---

[1] For example, a common punishment of a graduate student who has refused the sexual advances of her advisor is the requirement to endlessly rewrite her dissertation.

very attractive and appealing offers on the part of women for friendships, affairs, and marriages, and will find it less necessary to be always chasing women. This trend does not, however, signify, as some pessimistic and un-liberated men have predicted, that "pursued" men will become "coy" and hesitant, if not reluctant, due to satiation or boredom because of the avail-ability of sex partners (Rosenfeld, 1969). First, not all women will pursue all the time. Some of them will prefer to be pursued by men, and many would like to alternate between the two styles of courting. Second, men will not be pursued only for sex but for a variety of relationships combining friendship and affectivity in a variety of proportions.

What might be, however, the most important consequence of this type of liberation and its implications for men have seldom been discussed. The fact that men will be "picked" and pursued by women as much as they will pick and pursue implies that men will, for the first time, have to look at themselves also (but not primarily) as sex-objects. They will become increasingly aware that some physical and personality characteristics tend to be much more attractive to women, and they may start to make deliber-ate efforts to exhibit these characteristics. For how could some men's vanity (a very human kind of vanity) permit them to be rated as less desirable? Then they will start learning to some extent the anxieties that women have experienced for centuries about their attractiveness and appeal, although, of course, men's anxieties would be considerably lessened by their already established options for economic independence, high achievement, and the possibility to pursue a desirable woman, even at the risk of rejection (the probability of this instance increasing as women become liberated enough to feel freer to reject men).

There are actually some indications that men will have to radically change their present conceptions of the nature of their own sex appeal. A recent survey by the *Village Voice*, despite its lack of methodological validity and sophistication, suggests a very interesting discrepancy between women's and men's conceptions of what the most important aspects of men's "superficial sex appeal" are. Women thought that the most important assets of a physically appealing man were, in order of importance: a "small and sexy" behind, slimness, a flat stomach, eyes, and long legs. And the least important in descending order: tallness; penis (as seen through tight-fitting pants), a muscular chest and shoulders, muscular arms. Men's conceptions are almost the exact reversal of women's conceptions, since they think that a man's most important assets for superficial sex appeal, in order of impor-tance, are: a muscular chest and shoulders, muscular arms, penis (as seen through tight-fitting pants), and tallness ("Superficial Sex Appeal," 1972). Thus, men must become liberated from their own "masculine" images of sex appeal that envisage strong, muscular brutes. Slimness and trimness seem to appeal to women!

It is interesting to note that the cluster of attractive characteristics as reported by women mainly require slimness and trimness, that is, characteristics that one can achieve if strongly motivated and disciplined. Also, men's increasing preoccupation, not only with their physical appearance and their trimness but also with their clothes, fashions, and hair, and their increasing acceptance of and desire for vivid colors, longer hair, fancy clothes, perfumes, and overall beautification can be interpreted as good signs for men's liberation. Liberation from the austere, classical look of masculine attire that was practically immune to fashion and was perfectly compatible and in tune with the stereotyped masculine behavior can only be an advantage. The present attraction to, preoccupation with, and adoption of colorful and "vain" fashions tends to indicate a breakdown of the solid, serious masculine stereotype, devoid of frivolous tendencies, feelings, and weaknesses (Valabrègue, 1968; and McLuhan as quoted by Valabrègue).

These changes have significant implications for the psychological liberation of men. Men will have to learn how to make efforts to please women not only in terms of their slim appearance, and their attractive and fashionable clothes, but also in terms of their understanding, sympathetic attitude, supportive behavior (that is, playing an "expressive" role). Men will be free to behave with women they love as they have behaved up to now with male friends. In this way men will be freer to express all the tenderness, understanding, love, and warmth of which they are capable, and will be permitted (or obliged) to make definite efforts to please the woman they love in all ways. And then they will be able to enjoy the advantages and pleasures of being selected and pursued by women, advantages not without particular merit.

A Swedish writer captured the flavor of one of the possibilities ensuing from successful and independent women pursuing attractive men in a delightful short article called "Playgirl." It is quite possible that at least some women, once they reach a considerable psychological and sexual liberation, may look to men for sex, recreation, stimulation, and fun, and not for intellect or friendship that they can satisfy in a variety of relationships with other women and men colleagues and friends. Thus, a journal resembling "Playboy" but called "Playgirl" is now marketed with pictures of the Playmates of the Month—attractive, slim young men to be admired by female readers (Moberg, 1969). And it is possible that men who are so inclined may choose to be sex objects and to make this role the predominant one in their lives without any stigmatization or shame.

Here it is interesting to note that in January, 1973, a new club opened in Detroit with a floor show of attractive male strip-teasers who undressed to a tiny slip, while undulating to the appropriate "stripping" music. The audience was primarily composed of women between the ages of twenty-five and forty-five who smoked minicigars, drank, and commented upon the relative merits of the performance and anatomy of the male strip-teasers.

The increasingly liberated women will also be in a much better position to reject men's sexual advances without fear of open or subtle punishment. In addition, however, it is possible that at least in the early stage of the transition, women in powerful key positions may be tempted to use their power on desirable men in inferior positions. After all there has for too long been a bottled-up powerlessness in women, especially in the sexual area. The temptation may be great to reverse the role, whenever possible, and intimidate the man to accept their sexual advances and to satisfactorily respond to their affective relationship. Or they may tend to openly or subtly punish men who reject their sexual advances. But this potential trend, if it occurs, is expected to be a transitory symptom.

Generally, in the sexual area men must change many of their values and attitudes before they can be liberated. They must be free themselves of anxieties tied up with their sexual performance: duration and frequency of performance, variety and number of sexual conquests, and total domination of a woman through sex.

Many men have believed that it is a boost to their masculinity to have sexual relations with as many women as possible, even once, especially with sexually desirable women (Hawley, 1969). The assumption behind this belief (shared by nonliberated women) has been that a sexually conquered woman will forever belong to the man who conquered her. Actually, it is interesting to note that the law concerning rape makes exactly this assumption: a woman once sexually "conquered" by a man remains his property. Thus women who were once married or who have had sexual relations at some time with a man can never charge this man with rape at a later time, even if he actually raped them (Reynolds, 1971). The assumption here is that once a woman has voluntarily had sexual relations with a man, she can at no later time become totally indifferent to and sexually rejecting of him. This belief might have had some basis in the past in societies in which women were secluded and forbidden any contact with men, when sexual relations frequently resulted in pregnancy that rendered the woman dependent. But even then sexual conquest of a woman was not always foolproof emotional conquest. Today, of course, this belief is out-dated, meaningless, and silly since sexual intercourse need not lead to pregnancy and birth if the woman does not desire such an outcome, and even unliberated women indulge in sexual relations with different men without attaching any particular importance to the event.

Sexual liberation for men, therefore, would first entail acceptance of the fact that women with whom they have sexual relations react to this experience in much the same way as men. That is, they both have same probability of becoming emotionally attached to each other after their shared sexual experience and for reasons mostly external and unrelated to it.

Sexual liberation for men would also entail acceptance of sexual rejection by women as a nonthreatening experience to sex-identity. Liberated men can accept the fact that women have the same right as themselves to refuse the sexual advances of another person, without this meaning that they are frigid or that the man involved is not a "masculine" and attractive man. Rejection of sexual involvement does not necessarily imply *total* rejection. Very often the rejecting woman (or man) may like the other person tremendously as a human being, and may greatly cherish him (her) as a friend. An asexual friendship does not imply rejection. Men have to learn to appreciate such friendships with women as desirable and durable, not as "second-rate" relationships created by default (Safilios-Rothschild, 1972 b and d).

In the next step, deemed by some as the most important change, liberated men must be able to make a shift from the quantitative, consumer approach to sexual relations to a more qualitative approach. This new qualitative approach would consider as a criterion of "high" quality the orgasmic experience and the degree of sexual satisfaction felt by the woman as well as by the man. Thus men would be able to move away from the "ejaculative" potency, which is measured by number of conquests and numbers of ejaculations with each conquest, to an "orgasmic" potency, measured by the degree of sexual satisfaction experienced by both partners (Israel, 1969). Men could be freed from their "consumer" attitude toward attractive women, who are to be possessed and accumulated as prestige commodities (Israel and Eliasson, 1971).

The sexual liberation of men can come about only in conjunction with, not as an aftermath of, women's sexual and emotional liberation. In order for men to be able to become friends with women, women must develop distinct personalities with distinct attitudes, values, aspirations, and goals; that is, they must be liberated from the binding empty shell of Freudian-style femininity. In order for sexual encounters to be high quality experiences for both partners, both must be social equals. Only then can the dominance-submission syndrome that characterizes woman-man relationships be eliminated (Hawley, 1969). In order for sex to become only an ingredient in some but not all relationships, women must have other resources at their disposal for achieving their goals. Sex can then be redefined as an activity to be enjoyed for itself rather than used as an instrumental activity. Then women will stop feigning orgasms that they never experience, and they will stop pretending to be satisfied in sexual relations that they find frustrating, disappointing, or even disgusting. And it is only when women do not feign sexual satisfaction and feel free to honestly show their lack of satisfaction and frustration that men may become liberated enough to accept women's sexual autonomy and sexual role, not as a passive, receiving partner, but as an equally initiating, active, and stimulating person. Men could thus become liberated enough to accept women's expression of sexual dissatisfaction, the sources of this dissatisfaction (that may well be faults with their sexual performance), and suggestions or acts to bring about specific changes. In this way men can learn from and enjoy sexually experienced women, and the shift could be actually made from the quantity to quality sexual relations.

In addition, the mass media can again play a very important role in changing the image of the "masculine" man and protector or the sexy lover to one of a man who is very sensitive to and understanding of the woman's needs and wishes, and is successful in achieving a mutually satisfactory and stimulating sexual relationship with the same woman for ten or twenty years. For to have a high quality sexual relationship with a new partner is not a particular feat, but to accomplish it with a partner for ten, fifteen, or twenty years indeed requires special effort and talent.

Where mass media as well as liberated men can most help others is in the institutionalization of friendship between women and men as a socially desirable and admirable relationship. Movies, novels, and stories could glorify beautiful and important friendships between women and men that gave a deeper meaning to their lives, helped them in difficult moments, and rendered them better spouses, lovers, and parents because of the great understanding and respect they had developed for each other. Friendship between women and men in its pure form can be conceived as a relationship between two human beings who like each other, understand and admire each other, are very interested in each other, are bound to help and love each other as human beings rather than as members of different genders. Hence friendship enriches and supplements one's life and other relationships: colleague or co-worker relationship, marital relationship, and love and/or sexual relationships. This does not imply that one's love and/or sexual relationships are devoid of friendship. Between liberated women and men there will always be friendship too, but love and/or sexual relationships are more complicated and involved because of the variety of other feelings, emotions, and experiences that are intricately intertwined with it. But what is important is that love and/or sexual relationships are not mutually exclusive to friendships. Instead they tend to supplement and enrich each other and to provide individuals with a wide range of options and alternative sources of emotional, affective, and intellectual satisfaction.

One could still ask: How will these men who at present are dead-set against any introspection or consideration of sex role redefinition, are quite resistant to change, and find the concept of "men's liberation" simply ridiculous become motivated to change? Why will they start facilitating, encouraging, and emotionally supporting the liberation efforts of their wives, mothers, and daughters? And why will they be willing to redefine sex roles and familial roles if they see not advantages but new burdens and obligations?

Many men are, after all, terribly suspicious and fearful of the Women's Movement as the "women's conspiracy" against them, aimed at taking away the power and the privileges that they have enjoyed up to now, and at depriving them of their rights and pleasures. Much of the rhetoric of the Women's Movement is aimed at making women angry, since this anger plays an important role in politicizing and organizing women. Such rhetoric has deeply touched and scared men. In coping with this all-pervading fear, many men (and even quite perceptive and intelligent social scientists) convince themselves that the Women's Liberation Movement is a passing fad, invented by middle- and upper-middle-class women, that will be forgotten as fast as the latest fashion fad (Adelson, 1972). It seems then that a tactical strategy recommended for Women's Liberation Movement groups and all the supporting women's groups and individual women is that men be reassured concerning the advantages, gains, and benefits they can derive from Women's Liberation, their own liberation, and their motivation to strive and achieve emotional and psychological liberation.

Here again public opinion and social pressure can be quite effective. More and more women should openly and publicly criticize and ridicule men who blindly resist, oppose, and reject sexism-free articles, books, movies, programs, statements, and research as unimportant, unscientific, and unsound. On the other hand, public recognition should be given to men who actively engage in liberating themselves, as well as in encouraging and facilitating the liberation of women, their wives, daughters, students, and co-workers or colleagues. Those men should become ideals to be emulated by others, whether they share the same values and convictions, or go through the right motions for opportunistic reasons. During the transition period, it is important for men (and women) to make the appropriate steps toward liberation. Sometimes their values, attitudes, and beliefs will change first and will affect their behavior; sometimes their behavior will alter at the beginning (especially their public behavior), although their values and beliefs have not yet changed, because they conform to effective social pressure. Men's liberation can be achieved both ways, although in each type of evolution they will be liberated faster in some areas than in others, with their psychological and sexual liberation most probably coming last.

Chapter 4

SOCIAL POLICY TO LIBERATE MARRIAGE, THE INSTITUTION OF THE FAMILY, AND FAMILY LIFE

Social Policy to Liberate Women and Men from Compulsive Marriage and Parenthood

The ongoing process of women's and men's liberation is not compatible with traditional, compulsive marriage and parenthood. Women and men have increasingly more options, including those of remaining single or childless. From among them they can choose the one that seems to be most palatable and best suited to their personalities, needs, and life styles. The obligations to marry as soon as possible (and to quickly remarry after divorce) and to have children in order to be accorded a certificate of "normalcy" by society and peer groups drastically limit people's freedom to explore and adopt whatever marital or familial style they find most appropriate. Up to now the married status in the United States automatically included one in societal living as a full-fledged member, while single people, especially past a certain age, have been considered unstable, immature, and overall suspect. Many jobs were not formally or informally open to single adults; social circles tended to be closed to them; the American tax system up to 1971 discriminated against them; they could not adopt children; and they were reacted to as a class of people possessing a definite set of undesirable psychological characteristics. Due to the extremely potent social pressure placed upon single people, up to very recently most of them succumbed so that the few who did resist were often in fact "deviant," thus fulfilling the predictions.

There are, however, indications that since the middle 60s there has been a significant increase in the percentage of single people in the United States, especially among people between twenty-five to thirty-five years old; this is due mainly to marriage postponement. There is also some research evidence that in the late 60s and early 70s a considerable number of college students and young adults have been living together in a variety of arrangements and styles, without the legal sanction of marriage, and for varying lengths of time. Actually it seems that, among college students, living together is becoming widely practiced and almost "natural." A recent study showed that 34 percent of junior and senior women and 60 percent of graduate students had experienced cohabitation at least once. These living-together arrangements seem to substitute for early college-age marriages, to provide valuable training for marriage (Macklin, 1972), and to postpone marriage for some years. These trial relationships and living-together arrangements provide them with the opportunity to balance privacy, autonomy, independence, and freedom with social and affective closeness and exclusivity, discovering which combination in what context makes them happiest and most comfortable (Macklin, 1972).

But despite these ongoing changes in the American society, marital status and gender are still very important characteristics of individuals; they determine several aspects of their lives as well as the lives of their offspring. For example, in the United States a married professional woman pays more taxes than a single woman with the same income simply because she is married, especially if her earnings approach those of her husband or are above $10,000. The difference is around $500–1,000 as the wife's income moves from $14,000–16,000 to $18,000–20,000. The implication seems to be that working married women are particularly "deviant" and are penalized by the current tax system when they are successful professionals or businesswomen competing with men at the high levels! In these cases not only the wives but their husbands are also penalized. These husbands most often file separately (in order to avoid higher bracket taxation) and must pay more tax than single men at the same income level because they are married to "deviant" women. Furthermore, until 1971 married women could benefit from tax deductions for child care only when their income was close to subsistence level, and only divorced mothers could claim such deductions, regardless of income (Bader Ginsburg, 1971). The 1972 tax rules permit adequate deductions when the joint gross income of the couple is under $18,000 and some deductions over this level. While these new tax rules represent an improvement over past rules, they still leave much to be desired since married women going to school, working part-time and going to college, or just working part-time are not permitted any deductions for child care expenses. And finally, a child is still considered illegitimate if his parents were not married when he was born (rather than when he was conceived), and has, therefore, very different social and legal status than a child born in wedlock. Furthermore, a married woman cannot in most states legally establish residence in another city or state than her husband, and so may suffer serious occupational penalties.

There is, then, a definite need to end discrimination both on the basis of sex and on the basis of marital status. All persons should have equal chances and should be evaluated, taxed, judged, and considered equally, regardless of these two conditions. Here the required social policy is rather simple and the appropriate model exists in Sweden, where these issues have been dealt with for many years. In spring 1972 the final recommendations of the Committee on Family Law and Policy in Sweden formulated policies abolishing marital status as a basis for legal distinctions (*Abstract of Protocol on Justice Department,* 1969).

While a series of reforms are needed in the United States and other Western nations to abolish all distinctions in family and taxation laws that in any way discriminate on the basis of sex *and* marital status, the Report of the American Task Force on Family Law and Policy (1968) concentrated on the elimination of sex discrimination from different aspects of family law but did not touch in any way the existing discrimination on the basis of marital status. Thus the suggestions and recommendations offered do nothing to free women and men from the standard of marriage as the ideal, normal state.

In order to end all existing legal discrimination on the basis of marital status, a close examination of societal law is necessary. In all aspects the law should treat women and men as independent, legally equal individuals, regardless of their marital status. With such a legal basis, many of the present inequities that, depending upon the individual's sex, sometimes benefit married people and sometimes benefit single people could be rather easily corrected. Only through legal equality can people begin to choose freely the life style that is the most suitable and appropriate for them, rather than selecting the least penalizing option.

Only, for example, when some of the important attractions of marriage for many women cease to exist, such as financial security for the rest of their lives regardless of the outcome of the marriage, will they be able to evaluate their wish to marry more clearly. Only then, will women (and men) be able to refrain from marrying, unless they find some intrinsic value in marriage besides sexual attraction. If a woman knew that her husband's money was primarily his, and that in case of divorce it would still be his, many opportunistic, short-lived marriages would not take place. The individualization of the spouses' income and property throughout marriage and after the dissolution of marriage might be quite instrumental in improving the quality of marital relationships, especially in the elimination of marriages for money. In addition, many divorce complications would be eliminated. More people could divorce without bitterness, and could remain friends.

If women and men knew that children born outside wedlock would not be legally stigmatized and penalized, they might, in many cases, decide against marriage. Tying parenthood to marriage may have contributed more than any other factor to the compulsive marriage habits of Americans, who often marry because they want to have children or because of a premarital pregnancy. Some family studies have shown that women and men seem to be strongly attached to their children even when they are not affectively attached to their spouses, and are disillusioned in their marriage (Cuber and Harroff, 1966). Thus it could well be that the possibility of having one or more children without marriage would free women and men to enjoy parenthood without the entire marriage package, and would help render marriage a more voluntary decision.

At this point, it is interesting to note that in Sweden up to now unmarried (but not married) fathers were discriminated against in separation from the women they were living with, in that they could almost never be granted custody of their children. There a different legal standard was applied to unmarried and married fathers and mothers in the case of divorce. Custody of children was granted according to the best interests of the child rather than automatically to the mother, but only in the case of married couples (*Abstract of Protocol on Justice Department,* 1969). In the United States there is no such legal double standard. All fathers, whether married or unmarried when their children are born, and while they are growing up, cannot live with their children unless they are also living together with the children's mothers, either in marriage or in some living-together arrangement. The only exception is the proven moral or mental unfitness of the mother.

Of course, in the United States there is a considerable social stigma attached to "illegitimate" children, but the Swedish experience shows that once two conditions are present the social stigma disappears: (1) the equal legal recognition of children conceived and born under any marital status or form of cohabitation; (2) the birth of out-of-wedlock children to and public acceptance of such children on the part of powerful, influential, well-known personalities as well as many "respectable" upper-middle and upper-class women and men.

Complete equal legal status and the equalization of benefits for married and unmarried women and men (such as tax benefits, social security and health insurance benefits, salaries, bonuses, special work-related benefits, exemptions from active military duty, etc.) set the stage for people to make free choices as to life styles and cohabitation without being penalized for any choice. In addition, however, some new types of societal structures and arrangements could make the transition to the equal acceptance of all types of marital status and cohabitation smoother and less painful.

Near the center of many American cities small clusters of modern apartment houses have developed that often attract divorced and single men and women who live alone or with other members of the same or opposite sex in a variety of cohabitation styles. These apartment houses are usually located near services, facilities, and a small shopping area; they have swimming pools, tennis courts, child care facilities, and large rooms to rent for parties and receptions. This type of apartment house should multiply, not only in large cities but also in smaller cities and towns. They should be appropriately modified after joint teams of architects, sociologists, and psychologists, who have studied housing arrangements, recreational facilities, common spaces, and other facilitating mechanisms, recommend what conditions encourage and stimulate meaningful interaction between the residents, and what situations encourage the breakdown of social and psychological isolation and loneliness.

Communities, townships, and neighborhoods (for example, the cluster of six to seven apartment houses in the same area) could devise and organize different activities and structures to facilitate the social integration of residents, regardless of sex, marital status, or age. After all, it must not be forgotten that one of the very potent justifications for marriage and parenthood has been to avoid loneliness in old age. The creation, therefore, of a social integration option for older unmarried, widowed, or divorced women and men takes on additional crucial importance. Apartment houses could have a policy of admitting a minimum quota of older persons, especially the unmarried (possibly 20 percent of all residents), and using them in the child care facilities as well as, whenever possible, in other community projects. Older people should always be invited to and encouraged to actively participate in all common recreational gatherings, parties, and other get-togethers. Effective mixing of the generations at the social and affective levels would have a significant impact on people's fears of loneliness and isolation in old age, a presently dreadful reality (not always alleviated by marriage or parenthood). And it would provide older people with some attractive alternatives. The option for true affective, social, and residential integration (regardless of marital status) would tend to be greatly facilitated by changes in occupancy rules that would permit a group of people of different ages and sexes to live together as friends and companions with various affective and sexual commitments. This would mean that leases or ownership of apartments would have to be written to a group of unrelated persons (rather than to a family head) who make a commitment to co-lease or co-own the apartment.

Here it must be mentioned that old people in Southern European and

Middle Eastern cities like Rome, Athens, or Beirut, in which different generations intermingle socially at dinners, parties, excursions, and other gatherings, enjoy tremendously and are stimulated from these interactions with younger people. Because up to now old people in the United States have been socially isolated and cut off from normal interactions with younger people, they *appear* to prefer interacting with their peers. This preference is actually the result of awkward, uncomfortable interactions with younger people, even their own children, and their inability to go beyond "fictional acceptance." Everyone is "nice" and polite to old people but very few can accept them on an equal basis with everybody else and relate to them individually rather than categorically as "old." Opening the avenues for social interaction and friendships between the old and the young could provide the old, single or married, with enjoyable alternatives to interaction only with their peers or loneliness. New images of the old projected by mass media which portray middle-aged and older women and men as vital, fun-loving people with a sense of humor, relativity, experience, and sound judgment who can be great friends to younger people might also be helpful in breaking through "fictional acceptance."

SOCIETAL ACCEPTANCE OF CHILDLESSNESS

Liberation for both women and men from compulsive parenthood is another area where new societal attitudes must be encouraged. Some demographers have supported the thesis that when women do in fact have alternative sources of identity that gratify them or give them status, they will cease to opt (not only once but repeatedly) for motherhood as a source of "instant identity" (Blake Davis, 1970). Others have pointed out that it is very true that childbearing and childrearing are the *only* sources of creativity and achievement for women within the confines of the traditional "feminine" role (Wladis Hoffman and Wyatt, 1960). Thus the liberation of women in terms of employment and occupational careers might help women opt for motherhood as a privilege rather than as a duty or as the only possible choice. Liberation from compulsive motherhood will only take place if women become psychologically liberated from "femininity" hangups, and if their occupational options can provide them with considerable rewards and satisfaction.

When women hold demanding, important, responsible, or "masculine"-stereotyped jobs, they will not feel that they have to prove their "femininity" by having several children, as it has been true up to now (Poloma, 1972; Fortney, 1972). The implications of satisfying, rewarding occupations for women's fertility will become clear-cut and very significant. Free of "femininity" constraints, women's fertility will be influenced by the degree of their commitment to work, that is, by the meaning work has for them; the importance they attach to it in comparison to other activities and commitments; the degree to which they invest time, energy, and emotional involvement in it; and the satisfactions and sense of identity they derive from work. Only in the case of psychologically liberated women, living in a liberated society that provides them with satisfying work options, will the working role become a significantly competitive alternative to motherhood.

Furthermore, liberation from compulsive parenthood cannot be achieved for all women and men in the absence of implementation of a broader range of pertinent social policy. First, of course, until a variety of 100 percent safe contraceptives that can be used by all women and men have been developed, different types of "corrective" mechanisms and techniques must be easily available at low cost to all women and men. At present the only type of almost 100 percent safe contraceptive available, the oral pill, cannot be used by all women because of health complications, side effects, as well as fears about potential long-range related problems. Thus a considerable number of women of childbearing age cannot use the oral pill; but even among those who use it some conceptions do occur because of a variety of mistakes in using the pill.

Similarly, women using some kind of an intrauterine device are seldom perfectly protected. Anatomical peculiarities and local inflammations and infections often dictate temporary or permanent removal and other complications. A potentially considerable number of "unwanted" pregnancies must therefore be controlled if women are to be able to choose to become parents. And there is no safe contraceptive that can be used by men. It seems, then, that until a range of safe contraceptives for women and men are developed (so that everyone can find one type that she [he] can use), abortion, on the one hand, and vasectomy, on the other, must be available on demand. Expenses must be covered by all available health schemes, or be free to low-income women who are not covered by health insurance. The repeal of all antiabortion laws by the Supreme Court of the United States on January 22, 1973, represents a landmark in significant social change. The model is now there for other nations to follow.

Much, however, remains to be done in the United States before abortions become accessible to women at all income levels. As things now stand, the cost of an abortion ($250–350) and not covered by health insurance schemes is forbidding to low-income women. Thus the change is not spectacular since upper-middle- and upper-class women have always been able to secure abortions, regardless of the type of prevailing abortion law, by traveling to another country (or more recently to another state within the U.S.) with "liberal" abortion laws, or by paying the exorbitant fees of the few physicians who were willing to perform the operation.[1] The present

---

[1] Actually higher income women even in "liberal" nations like Sweden can afford to travel to Poland to have an abortion when their demand for a legal abortion is rejected.

changes in the American law make abortion widely accessible (but not cheap) to middle-class women but not to low-income women for whom it is still problematic.

It is interesting to note that Russian and most Eastern European women definitely have the right to determine the fate of their own bodies and their reproductive lives. Abortion is granted on demand—in Russia without any explanations or council approval, in the Eastern European countries after relatively easily obtainable bureaucratic approval (Barker, 1972; David, 1970). They are therefore able to effectively opt for childlessness, or for one child, and to accurately control the timing of their childbearing so that it interferes minimally with their other life plans. Liberation in this area is not, however, related to liberation in family life and husband-wife interaction. Russian women, however, can divorce very easily and painlessly when their marriage does not involve children (Barker, 1972).

Men, on the other hand, must also be able to control the outcome of their reproductive behavior—independently of the women involved. There can be a variety of situations and circumstances in which the man does not want a child as the outcome of sexual relations but the woman does. Both are motivated by different sets of wishes, values, and needs. Up to now the man could never implement his preference with a great degree of certainty, and in such disagreements he most often fathered a child. In the current absence, then, of safe contraceptives for men, vasectomy should be readily available to men, and be covered by all health insurance schemes (or free of cost for low-income men,) so that they can father only as many children as they want. An important condition, however, for safeguarding the individual rights of women and men (and the privacy of relationships between them) would be granting an abortion or a vasectomy on demand, regardless of marital status and without the consent of anyone else.

Social policy is also needed to change the image of childless and one-child families, and to free these options from the stigma of "deviance" presently attached to them. The scientific committees that will have to review all existing family sociology, family life education, child development (and related fields), textbooks and make recommendations for needed revisions and changes will have to consider the way in which parenthood, childlessness, and one-child families are treated. Current research has shown that spouses in childless marriages are much happier with their marriages than are those who became parents, even when couples married for the same length of time are compared. There is evidence too that the birth of children decreases spouses' satisfaction and happiness with their marriage and their ability to be close and affectionate companions and lovers, especially when their relationship before children had been very close and companionate (Feldman, 1964 and 1969; Rollins and Feldman, 1970). Such findings, however, are not usually integrated in family textbooks because they "go against the grain" and are not compatible with the flowery rhetoric of the guaranteed-instant-motherhood-happiness.

Research proposals and projects should be preferentially funded or commissioned which deal with single women and men living in a variety of familial arrangements, including different types of relationships with one or more persons of the same or the other sex, and with different degrees of permanence and affective and sexual commitment. Findings from such research would provide us with valuable information in an area where we have only started to scratch the surface. Also, research focusing upon voluntarily childless couples (preferrably on a longitudinal basis) and on developmental issues in one-child families would help to test out many of the negative stereotypes that exist about these "deviant" options. The present lack of adequate and valid information from cross-sectional and longitudinal studies facilitates the perpetuation of stereotypes and prejudices against them.

Dissemination of findings by a variety of mass media and "experts" would help to break down negative images and beliefs. Television programs in which childless and one-child couples discuss the advantages ensuing from having taken these options could be shown. Childless couples could be presented in movies and soap operas as happy "normal" couples living full, satisfactory lives, who have developed close, warm, vital companionate relationships, and who have no remorse about their decision. The portrayal of the childless couple's old age is of particular importance. Older childless people must escape the label of loneliness and despair, the probability of which they share equally with those who have children. They must be portrayed as happy people who still enjoy the company of each other very much and who are surrounded by friends of all ages. One-child families should be similarly presented. The child should be shown to have a "normal," happy childhood, with the same "normal" experiences as children in larger families.

Another very important step in liberation is that the parental history of people introduced in television or referred to in journals and newspapers be omitted. Parenthood should in fact cease to be an identity label. The information Mrs. X, "mother of three children and grandmother of four," must come to be a meaningless phrase devoid of identity information. Or the presentation of a woman or man political candidate, an influential businessman, university professor, labor union representative, or very well-known artist or entertainer can no longer be made on the basis of their reproductive history or prolificacy.

All these policies aimed at liberating women and men from compulsive parenthood will also serve to control and stabilize population growth, a desirable and necessary goal if the quality of life is not to deteriorate seriously for everyone now living and for those to be born in future decades.

The Meaning of the Liberation
of the Institution of the
Family and Family Life

Since it may be less self-evident than in other areas, the meaning of liberation in the context of the family and family life must be carefully elucidated. The institution of the family in its traditional form has come under heavy attack and drastic criticism for restricting and distorting the lives and potential of adults and children, especially of women of all ages (Cooper, 1971; Laing and Esterton, 1971). Hence one goal of liberation is to allow all family members to develop their potential and individual personalities and to find the most satisfactory arrangements and combinations for their needs, rather than to achieve an "ideal," standardized family life model.

Another pervasive characteristic of family life up to now has been that the dynamics of the wife-husband and child-parent relationships; the type and distribution of power structure; the influence techniques used; the type of division of labor; communication, leisure, and companionship patterns; and the very tone of family life have been largely determined by sex stereotypes concerning "appropriate" roles and behavior for women and men. Liberation of family life would therefore mean the freedom of wives and husbands and mothers and fathers, as well as girls and boys, to behave according to their inclinations, preferences, and abilities rather than stereotypically as women and men.

Actually, of course, both structural and personal liberation in the family are highly interrelated, but they merit separate treatment because they refer to different aspects of family life.

LIBERATION OF FAMILIAL STRUCTURE
AND ORGANIZATION

A basic, common, and influential assumption made up to now has been that there is *only one* ideal family life model. This model, referred to as the nuclear family, is composed of the father, the mother (married before or during their early twenties), and their three children. The father is a successful breadwinner, and the wife is a devoted mother, housekeeper, and wife. Their happy and love-filled marriage will last throughout life (that is, on the average, about fifty years). This has been the ideal image against which people have had to measure their marriage and its success. Very few deviations were allowed for differences in values, beliefs, and needs. Every woman and man had to fit into the narrow definition of family or face social ostracism, if not more serious occupational sanctions, regardless of her (his) idiosyncratic needs, inclinations, wishes, values, and beliefs. Familial behavior in the past represents a most striking example of boundless conformity. Childless marriages were not even considered families. Extended, one-parent, and dual-career families represented "deviant" types of family constellations. And several women and men and children living together without any legal ties and under a variety of social, affective, and sexual ties and combinations represented Sodom and Gomorrah.

Conformity to one model of "good" family life has been restricting and suffocating. One restriction has been the lack of many marital and familial options, such as remaining single, marrying late, not having children, having children in late twenties, limiting family size to one child, living with compatible and beloved close relatives or friends attached to the nuclear family, maintaining dual-career families, or living in a variety of arrangements with other couples or individuals of both sexes or with one or more members of the same sex. Such options did not exist—even theoretically. Women and men could not even imagine the potential advantages of alternatives, let alone choose them. Women and men were only free to do what they wanted as long as what they wanted fell within the ideal model of "good" family life.

In addition, the economic and social vulnerability of women has discouraged (and is still discouraging) most women from considering family life styles which do not provide them with financial security and legal safeguards. As long as women are not economically and socially liberated, they will not be able to opt for flexible, often short-lived family life styles, perhaps without security, even when such family life styles become more socially acceptable. And unless women become psychologically liberated from "femininity" stereotypes, they will not be able to consider or to opt for singlehood, childlessness, or homosexual relations without feelings of total failure and self-depreciation. Liberation, then, of family structure and organization in this sense entails creation of a society where women and men may opt for different types of family life styles (some of them marital and others nonmarital), and often for several different family life styles at different stages of their lives.

A second serious structural restriction results from some of the so-called ground rules of marriage. According to them, spouses must be the exclusive sources of sexual and affective satisfaction for each other throughout the fifty years of marriage. Even close friendships with members of the opposite sex have been taboo, they might involve potentially threatening intellectual and emotional involvements. One could actually question the extent to which binding and meaningful friendships even with members of the same sex have been tolerated in the past, if these ties involved sets of specific reciprocal commitments beyond ordinary social, recreational exchanges. The range of permitted relationships with other persons than the spouse has been narrow and constricted, and the relationships shallow and superficial.

Furthermore, even the nature of the husband-wife relationship has been by definition restricted, and has not allowed for a real exchange of feelings and the mutual interinfluence that leads to the self-discovery and growth of two individual personalities. Instead, husbands and wives were supposed to blend their personalities—or more accurately the wife was. She was not supposed to have a distinct personality when she married, and was to be shaped and molded according to her husband's values, attitudes, and beliefs to become a mirror image of him (Safilios-Rothschild, 1972a). Also, husbands and wives were not supposed to have serious disagreements and quarrels, but were instead to want to please each other; to spend most of their free time in each other's company; and to love, cherish, and never try to manipulate each other.

Thus spouses could not have a variety of deep and meaningful relationships with any other person but each other, and even the relationship between them was restricted and made artificial by the proscriptions for expressing feelings (especially negative feelings). The prevailing prescriptions dictated behavior according to sex-stereotyped norms.

Of course, the existence of all the taboos, prescriptions, and proscriptions included in the ground rules of marriage does not mean that spouses have followed them consistently. On the contrary, proscriptions have been honored mostly in being violated. Such breaches have often been functional in making many marriages tolerable and livable for a considerably longer time. They very often have provided the necessary breathing spells for restricted lives and relationships which have bound spouses in marriage. Furthermore, the existence of frequent violations rather clearly indicates that the traditional ground rules regulating the marital relationship tend to be oppressive to and incompatible with the needs of most people. But the fact still remains that people commit infractions of the marital ground rules, even when they do so to be able to have a better relationship with their spouses or to stay in the marriage. Unfaithful spouses, for example, know all the time that, at least according to the rules, they have deviated, and many feel quite guilty over their deviance (Cuber and Harroff, 1965). It seems that this rule-breaking is an area in which behavior has altered before the corresponding attitudes have changed to the same extent. But there is considerable evidence that attitudes are also changing quite drastically and at quite a rapid pace (Cuber and Harroff, 1965; Johnson, 1970; Mulligan, 1969; Bartell, 1971). It then remains to change the rules and structures so that behavioral options considered "deviant" up to now can become institutionalized, and thus become socially acceptable and stigma-free.

What would these changes entail and what are the facilitating strategies? Legal changes that would treat all men and women equally, regardless of their marital status, nature and mode of cohabitation, and private life style, could considerably diminish a certain degree of social stigma that is still attached to some life styles and living arrangements, such as swinging couples, group marriages, or homosexual couples. Two conditions must change: First, people must be able to create the model of "family life" that suits them the best, as long as all the involved adults consent and are willing to live in such a "family." Second, the particular model of "family life" that one chooses and the involved sexual patterns and arrangements must not in any way reflect on this person's character, or competence.

Legal safeguards should be established so that people living any type of life style are not discriminated against in terms of taxation, housing, occupational opportunities and promotions, active political participation, or legal treatment in case of any type of violation or offense. Also, in order for the lack of discrimination on the basis of marital status and living arrangements to become institutionalized, a new constitutional amendment might be necessary to guarantee the equality of people under the law, regardless of their marital or familial status. Of course, much more resistance is expected to be shown here on the part of many different conservative groups, but it may be important that recommendations be already moving in this direction, if the change is to take place sometime in the not-too-distant future.

Another restrictive structural characteristic of marriage in the United States and most Western nations has been the domiciliary rules for married women. Up to now the legal domicile of a married woman was for all purposes automatically considered to be that of her husband, except in five states (Alaska, Arkansas, Delaware, Hawaii, and Wisconsin), where women have the same right as their husbands to their own domicile (*Report of the Task Force on Family, Law and Policy,* 1968). This type of legal restriction becomes increasingly important as people recognize that cohabitation is not necessarily obligatory or desired by the wife and husband throughout their married lives, throughout the year, or every day. In the last years, for example, partly because of the scarcity of jobs, academic women have sometimes had to accept good offers in universities in other cities or states than the ones in which their husbands lived and worked. Thus they spent some of the days in the city where they were working and usually came home for extended weekends to see their husbands and children, or they may have taken the children with them. In these cases it is obviously sensible to consider the city and state where the woman works and resides most of the time as her legal residence for purposes of taxation, voting, or even holding public office. It also represents a tax injustice for the woman not to be able to claim her traveling expenses as business expenses.

As dual-career families increase, even with compensatory adjustments and mechanisms to facilitate their simultaneous and equal chances for advancement through geographic mobility, it will often happen that for one to two years spouses might have to live separately in different states until they can secure advantageous and satisfactory positions in the same location (Poloma, 1972; Rapoport and Rapoport, 1972; Lytle Holmstrom, 1972). Or exceptional job opportunities may take a woman away for a year to a foreign country or necessitate traveling around the world. Or a married woman may have the opportunity to be nominated and elected to a public office if she establishes legal residence in another city or state. The law has to adjust to already present and developing trends in the occupational and political careers of women that will require temporary, long, permanent, or semipermanent separate legal domiciles from their husbands or/and their children, so that these women are in no way discriminated against or penalized.

Only through a series of modifications in existing laws and policies, can family structure and organization become more flexible and adaptable to the needs and requirements of two adults (instead of just the husband). Then marriage will become compatible with many women's needs for independence, achievement, and commitment to a career. Up to now the relatively few women who had such needs and felt strongly about realizing them, as evidenced by their occupational success and high earnings, generally remained single or opted for divorce (Havens, 1973). As more women aspire to high achievement, it is important to decrease and eventually eliminate the incompatibility between marriage and success for those women who would like to marry.

Liberation of Familial Roles and Family Dynamics

This restrictive element of family life is much more closely and directly related to traditional sex stereotypes concerning appropriate roles and behavior for women and men. Women and men, under the influence of prevailing sex stereotypes, have been prevented from playing certain roles and engaging in some behavioral repertories which would earn them the label of "deviance." Of course, in many instances socialization had been so effective that many of these "deviant" behaviors and roles held little appeal, and their unavailability created little discontent in the minds of wives and husbands. But even in cases of most effective socialization, there were at least some sex inappropriate behaviors and role elements that were attractive, or that were actually engaged in, with various ensuing guilt, discomfort, or stigmatization.

It seems, for example, that even in the past only working- and lower-class black and white American (and other Western) fathers restricted their role strictly to the breadwinning function, while many college-educated fathers played, with different degrees of intensity, a variety of affective-expressive roles. Working- and lower-class men in the United States and other Western societies bound by rigid concepts of masculinity cannot openly express love and affection for their children, since such behavior would represent a "flaw" in their tough, inscrutable, and unconquerable facade. College-educated men, however, seem to be more liberated in this area, since they consider expression of love and affection as a very important component of the parental role (Safilios-Rothschild and Georgiopoulos, 1970). In India, however, even middle-class fathers have been reported to be inhibited in establishing a warm and affectionate relationship with their children, but can do so with their grandchildren later on when they are viewed as "asexual" and the sex-related norms no longer apply to them (Gore, 1961; Ross, 1962; Narain, 1969).

But even when American men have been liberated enough to want to be good friends with their children, to interact with them, and to show them love and affection, the mothers have often successfully kept them in a marginal position in their attempt to safeguard the primary importance of the mother-child relationship, a relationship crucial to justifying their existence, indispensability, and identity (Lopata, 1971; Safilios-Rothschild, 1972a). And the mothers' behavior was motivated by their wish to avoid further restriction of the meaningful life options that were available through prevailing sex stereotypes. Of course, it must be noted here that the few studies in which mothers and fathers were separately interviewed report that fathers perceive that they play a much more active and affectively supportive role than their wives are willing to attribute to them (Safilios-Rothschild, 1969). But even so their reported involvement (affectively and time-wise) is most probably greatly influenced by their stereotyped version of the male role in society and the family (Miller, 1972).

The prevailing sex differentiation in marital roles based on sex stereotypes further restricts married women's and men's behavior in that some options cannot be even theoretically considered. Since, for example, the main role of husbands has been the "instrumental" breadwinning role, the option not to work could not be considered as a possibility, even for a short period of time. In addition, the options to work part-time or to work at a less prestigious or less well-paying job in order to have more time to spend with and enjoy their families have also not existed for men. Because the family's social status and standard of living depend upon men, some occupational options that would give them more time and flexibility to enjoy life have not been possible.

And since the main sex-stereotyped roles of women have been those of "housekeeper" and "mother," with the mother role further specified as a twenty-four-hour-a-day job (especially when children are very young), the option to have a continuous career has been unavailable to married women. Consequently, women could not hold important, responsible, prestigious jobs. They could generally only engage in unimportant, low-prestige, low-paid, meaningless, routine work. Thus, women were for the greater part of their lives forced to derive all satisfaction from their marital and familial roles and interactions, a condition that rendered them much more dissatisfied with their marriages and their lives than men (Bernard, 1972), and seemingly contributed to their depressed feelings in middle-age (Bart 1970a and b and 1973). In fact all available research evidence reviewed by Bernard indicates that the married status (versus singlehood) is much more favorable to men's happiness and mental health than to women's (1972). Women can be further frustrated and disappointed by marriage since they have been socialized to have very low aspirations for personal achievement and to achieve vicariously through the successes of their husbands, sons, and, to a lesser extent, their brothers (Tangri, 1969; Birnbaum, 1971; Veroff and Feld, 1970; Wladis Hoffman, 1972).

As for men, the option to be "househusband" and father has never existed. And the desire for these options could not be voiced, since it would represent an extreme "deviance" and would tend to be treated as an indication of serious mental disturbance. There is, however, some evidence that, despite those potent, forbidding norms against such an option, some skilled and semiskilled forty to fifty-year-old men with back injuries preferred to stay home and take care of the house and the adolescent children while their wives worked, rather than continue to be the breadwinners. Despite the strong disapproval of social workers and other rehabilitation agents, they often carried out their wish, and the "deviant" restructuring of the family seemed to be both stable and satisfactory to all family members (Safilios-Rothschild, 1970b).

Furthermore, in Sweden, where the option not only to work part-time but also to become "househusbands" is open to men and is socially approved, a small but slowly increasing number of men is taking them. Some options, such as the "househusband," have been such an almost total impossibility for married men that even the desire has been repressed and rationalized on the basis of the low prestige of the option. As the option becomes available, however, it tends to become attractive to some men who find many of its features appealing on a permanent or temporary basis.

In addition to exclusion from the above-discussed options for one of the spouses on the basis of sex stereotypes, wives' and husbands' behavior has, on the basis of the same stereotypes, been restricted in many important areas of family dynamics. One very basic type of behavioral restriction running through all aspects of family dynamics is that men must always take initiative, play the most active role, and dominate interaction, while women must follow in a passive, submissive, and supportive role (Polk and

Stein, 1972). Any deviation from this pattern has up to now been considered (by sociologists and the spouses themselves) unsatisfactory for both spouses, or even pathological. For example, a Detroit study showed that whenever decision-making was reported to be dominated by women, the same women reported low marital satisfaction. This finding was duly interpreted by the researchers to mean that women who are dominant in familial decision-making have become dominant not by choice but by default, because their husbands were passive and incapable of making decisions and undertaking responsibilities. Therefore, since these women had to "step into the shoes" of their husbands, who did not behave according to the "masculine" norms, they were unhappy with their marriage (Blood and Wolfe, 1960).

Another recent study showed that whenever the wife tends to initiate communication more often than the husband, both spouses find their conversations and their marriage less rewarding (Feldman, 1964), because this behavior is defined as "deviant" on the basis of prevailing stereotypes about the roles of women and men. Furthermore, in psychological studies of "normal" and "disturbed" clinic families, the main isolated "pathological" characteristic of "disturbed" families was the fact that mothers spoke more often, for a greater length of time, and hence tended to dominate the communication patterns in the family. An active role played by mothers in communication and their dominating behavior was considered to represent a "deviant" role-reversal in the socially acceptable familial model, and practically a cause of the existing psychopathology (Leighton, Stollak, and Ferguson, 1971).

Finally, the existing sex stereotypes influence the behavior of spouses, and particularly that of husbands, in two important areas of family dynamics: communication and empathy. Thus husbands who feel bound by masculinity norms (as seems to be the case for most working-, lower- and even lower-middle-class American and other Western men) do not feel that they can talk to their wives about anything beyond simple information (Komarovsky, 1967). They cannot express their feelings, their worries, their anxieties, their insecurities, their weaknesses, and fears to their wives because they would lose their "cool" and their rational, brave, tough facade. It would also be more difficult to dominate wives who knew their secrets, their failings, and their anxieties. Communication with wives is kept at a minimal, informative, superficial level, while true communication, whenever (very rarely) it occurs, is only with other men who can "better understand" them and not use the communicated content to manipulate them or undermine their dominant role.

Of course, it must be noted that there are important cross-cultural differences in the extent to which stereotyped masculinity allows depth of communication in feelings, doubts, fears, and emotions with other men.

Mediterranean, Middle Eastern, and Latin men tend, much more than American or Western European men, to communicate inner feelings, anxieties, and emotions to close male friends than to their wives.

However, sometimes these "masculine" husbands from different cultures have "poured out their souls" to their mistresses or prostitute girlfriends, possibly because they were in a different category from the "good" women they married. This differential treatment could be also explained by the fact that they were not afraid to lose their dominant position in this relationship, since by its nature they had the "upper hand"; that is, they could always sever it. But it may also indicate that men felt the need to have intimate communication with a woman, and they felt freer to do so in a secret, prohibited relationship.

Because of these attitudes, two different worlds were created: the women's world and the men's world. The men's world included the husband and his male friends and confidantes (and eventually his growing sons), and the women's world included the wife, her female relatives, a few female friends and confidantes, and eventually her growing daughters (Komarovsky, 1967). The overlap between the two worlds was minimal and superficial— or solely sexual. The model of separate communication and companionship outlets represents an extreme, but with certain "face-saving" modifications, it holds true even for a considerable number of higher-status and better-educated families.

Another important area of family dynamics in which behavior has been effectively regimented by the prevailing sex stereotypes has been in empathy between spouses. Husbands, due to their "masculine" nature, are not expected to understand the feelings and desires of their wives. Wives, on the contrary, are endowed with "feminine" intuition and are supposed to understand their husbands, even guessing their feelings and desires in order to satisfy them. Husbands do not feel that they have to make any particular effort to understand their wives' feelings, needs, and desires, or to accurately assess how well they satisfy these needs and desires, simply because they are men and can unilaterally expect this type of understanding and empathy without significant reciprocity (Komarovsky, 1967). In many circles, in which the prevailing sex-stereotypes have been quite influential, husbands who were understanding of and sensitive and empathic to their wives' feelings, needs, and desires were often ridiculed as weak, henpecked, and not too "masculine." They were viewed in such negative terms because the implication was that they did not occupy the superior position provided by their maleness, but behaved instead "like women," trying to understand and please their wives instead of dominating them. Thus, men often did not in fact have the option to play socioemotional, expressive roles; they had to restrict themselves to stereotyped "masculine" behavior.

Husbands have had to be powerful and to dominate their wives and children in order to be respected. Even when they were actually unable to dominate or make all decisions, their wives and children had to take all kinds of precautions and use a variety of strategies in order to "save their face." There could never be open admission that somebody else had, in fact, decided or imposed his (her) opinion. Husbands were always to have at least the illusion of power whenever they were unable to have the family power in their hands. This pretense was necessary and functional as long as sex stereotypes influenced familial behavior. Women and men had to pretend in order to maintain the appearance of "normalcy" within the family, the level of marital satisfaction, and the mental health of all family members.

Obligatory dominance and constant power display within the family made it necessary for husbands to select as their domain all major pace-setting decisions, and to continuously struggle to orchestrate the important movements and acts of all family members. Husbands could therefore not tolerate a family in which an extremely competent and dominant woman openly pulled the power strings, thus challenging their power and authority. Having such a dominant wife was an extremely deviant act for men, and labeled them as weak, inadequate, passive, and seriously disturbed psychologically.

Men also had to manage the family's budget and make all important financial decisions because they are "masculine," even when they performed badly and their wives could have functioned in a much more competent manner. Women, on the other hand, were forbidden to openly assume and exert power. They could only play the power game "underground" by means of "sneaky," "feminine" influence techniques that were hardly satisfactory to their egos since they could never receive and enjoy credit for any victory (Safilios-Rothschild, 1973). In this way both husbands and wives could not use their skills, talents, and inclinations in making the decisions for which they were best suited. The best person did not win in the family power game. Instead, both husbands and wives' behavior had to be restricted by sex-stereotyped notions of appropriate behavior.

Strategies to Liberate
Family Structure and Dynamics

The previous discussion of the meaning of liberation in family structure and dynamics indicates that much of it is closely related to the psychological and social liberation of wives and husbands. During the transitional period, however, and until women and men become quite liberated, some additional, specific strategies would be quite helpful.

A very crucial strategy focuses upon all experts that are in some way related to the family (marriage and family counselors, family life educators, family sociologists, clinical psychologists, psychiatrists, as well as social workers). All such experts who are often called in to help family members in critical moments, or who intervene in family situations without invitation, or who study families and establish norms and models have to be resocialized and helped to become liberated from their own sex-stereotypic notions of familial behavior and modes of interaction. Liberated family counselors, consulting psychologists, and psychiatrists would learn not to try to mend family crises by helping spouses "accept" their sex-stereotyped niche, behavior, and roles. Instead they would help them to express themselves freely within the familial setting, according to their particular needs, talents, wishes, and inclinations, in order to be able to accept each other as independent, valid, and integral personalities. They would try, for example, to help husbands overcome their masculinity "hangups" and feel comfortable, relaxed, and pleased in a wife-dominated relationship, instead of trying to suppress the wife's domination inclinations, needs, and talents as "deviant," undesirable, disturbed behavior. And they would aid wives who wished to assume power to do so without guilt or threat to their femininity. They would try to find ways to help spouses discover what behavioral options would be best suited to each of them, and would try to aid them in increasing the degree of satisfaction they derive from their marriage, as well as from their lives. They would not exclude any option as deviant or inappropriate for a woman or a man, and would not compare the different types of marital relationships to a monolithic "ideal" family model.

But how can such liberation of the family counselors and advisors be achieved? Again, eventually very few strategies will be needed; their training should liberate them. But until all basic textbooks are rewritten, enough liberated research has accumulated, and basic theories have been reconceptualized from a sex-stereotype-free viewpoint, transitional strategies are necessary. The National Institute of Mental Health and other governmental as well as private funding agencies and foundations should establish funding for programs aimed at exactly this type of liberation. Special intensive workshops could be funded throughout the nation for different types of family counselors, psychologists, psychiatrists, and social workers. These workshops, designed and conducted by liberated social scientists and clinicians, would concentrate on different techniques of consciousness-raising and would present problematic cases to be discussed and handled by the participants under the critical evaluation of the instructors. Mental hospitals, state and city psychiatric clinics, welfare units, as well as departments of psychiatry, psychology, and sociology, schools of social work, and family counseling training institutes and centers, could be required to send their staff and students to these workshops as an integral part of their training and specialization.

Furthermore, substantial pressure can be placed upon family counselors and therapists (psychiatrists and psychologists) to become liberated (or at least to behave in a liberated manner regardless of the degree of their psychological liberation) by widely publicizing those who are "liberated," thus enhancing their prestige and profits. Women's groups such as the National Organization for Women and Professional Women's Caucuses could (and some of them have already started to) compile lists of liberated family counselors and family therapists, as well as child psychiatrists and psychologists, and distribute them not only to their local members but to the wider public (academic women and men, students, members of different women's associations and organizations). Whenever women's programs on television or radio, or conferences on sex roles require the presence of a family counselor or therapist, this roster would provide the organizers with the appropriate people. In this way these gradually increasing lists could become very prestigious. Here the clientele can exert great pressure and can be quite instrumental in changing the values and attitudes of counselors and therapists by refusing to see a family counselor or therapist who is not on the "liberated" lists.

In addition, family textbooks at all levels, particularly those at the high school and undergraduate college level, desperately need "liberation." Those widely used at present are thoroughly permeated by sex stereotypes and are clearly insulting to women. Here the large number of women teaching assistants, part-time teachers, instructors, and assistant professors who teach large undergraduate family courses have considerable consumer power in their hands. By complaining and putting pressure on the publishers of these sexist textbooks, they can "convince" them to contract with liberated women and men family sociologists to write family textbooks. Similarly, students can exert considerable pressure on nonliberated instructors to use liberated textbooks by refusing to read sexist family texts or to register for courses given by professors who assign such materials.

In addition to a new constitutional amendment guaranteeing equality regardless of marital status and family style, in order to provide marital relationships with flexibility and to assure the actualization and social acceptance of all types of "familial" arrangements, two specific social policies are necessary. First, individual marital contracts mutually agreed-upon by those entering a marital relationship must be legalized. This mutually agreed-upon individual marital contract would have to be discussed and deposited with a lawyer, as is presently done with wills, and would be legally binding upon the countersigning individuals, unless changed by mutual consent. It could include much more than agreements concerning responsibilities toward children, wages to be paid to the spouse(s) undertaking housekeeping activities, type of division of labor, ownership and use of money, property ownership, or contractual duration of marriage. It could contain the ground rules regulating the relationship, as well as the built-in mechanisms for changes, adjustments, and renegotiations. In this way marrying individuals would feel reassured that their relationship was "legally protected," a desirable feeling for some women and men, without any loss of flexibility and power of self-determination. Individuals entering a marital relationship could in fact largely determine their familial lives and the type of relationship they would have with all due legal approval.

The existence of such contracts might render renegotiation of ground rules easier, since potential change would be built-in, and there would be no need to reconcile the new proposed ground rules with established legal, cultural, and religious rules concerning marriage. The people who make them will be able to change them freely within the limits of general laws regulating human relations. Family laws could, in addition, establish some requirements concerning the economic and psychological welfare of children, psychological welfare being defined beyond moralistic pseudo-scientific limits.

Passage of the Equal Rights Amendment would, of course, require some significant changes in the present family law that would eliminate inequalities in the marriage relationship based upon gender. Thus, women would be able to keep their maiden name, to establish another domicile, if they wished, to manage community property and to establish credit. Furthermore, men would no longer be held legally responsible for financial support; women would be equally responsible. And women would no longer be held legally responsible for providing housekeeping and sexual services to their husbands; men would be just as accountable legally for provision of the same services. The amendment would make many features of liberated persons' marriage contracts more legally binding, although in many cases litigation would be necessary to establish new legal rulings and precedents. Several lawyers have voiced the opinion that the financial contractual arrangements between spouses have a better chance of standing up in court than contractual arrangements affecting personal aspects of the marriage. Probably the most difficult financial agreement to receive legal validation would be the contractual arrangement for providing payment for household services, but even this may have a chance after the Equal Rights Amendment is passed and implemented in the courts (Edmiston, 1972).[2]

In the area, however, of contractual agreements affecting personal aspects of the marriage, legal approval will be much more difficult. Contractual agreements, for example, granting both spouses sexual rights and freedoms beyond monogamy and marital fidelity (such as swinging, or experimenting with group marriage, or occasionally indulging in extramarital affairs) would have a very difficult time in court because they run counter

---

[2] It must be noted, however, that the cost of the services rendered by wives is quite high. In 1972 a British management consultant firm evaluated that a mother of two working overtime for 85 hours per week should be paid by her husband a salary of $192.40 a week ("British Wives Found Worth $192.40 a Week").

to public policy. Passage, however, of a legal reform, according to which all types of cohabitation, with or without "marriage," would become legally equal would tend to diminish the legal stronghold of monogamy. Similarly, contractual agreements to remain childless might be equally invalid from a legal point of view. Anyway, passage and implementation of the Equal Rights Amendment in the courts will require considerable time, and establishment of more laws will most probably be necessary before individual marriage contracts become legally binding.

Meanwhile, however, the drafting of such marriage contracts by couples intending to marry could have an extremely important liberating function in their family relationships. The fact that people who have decided to marry will think out carefully and in detail all the important aspects of their marital and familial relations would oblige them to face and anticipate many situations and problems, as well as to better understand each other's needs, preferences, wishes, hangups, weaknesses, inhibitions, values, and attitudes (Edmiston, 1972). In some cases the process of drafting this marriage contract would show that the two people who had decided to marry are, in fact, quite incompatible and cannot agree on the basic aspects of family dynamics and organization. They will be able to see their future family life in a short preview, and can decide whether they want to—or are able to—make a go of it. In other cases, by clarifying their views of and wishes in important areas of family life, couples will have settled some important issues early. They can then enter marriage and family life on a solid basis.

Here is a suggested model for an individual marriage contract specifying some important financial agreements, agreements concerning a number of personal aspects of the wife-husband relationship, as well as the reproductive and contraceptive behavior of the couple:

THE UTOPIAN MARRIAGE CONTRACT[3]

1. The wife's right to use her maiden name or any other name she chooses.
2. What surname the children will have: husband's, wife's, a hyphenated combination, a neutral name, or the name the children choose when they reach a certain age.
3. Birth control: Whether or not, what kind, and who uses it. (One couple—the wife can't use the Pill—splits the responsibility 50–50. Half the time she uses a diaphragm, the other half he uses a condom.)
4. Whether or not to have children, or to adopt them, and if so how many.
5. How the children will be brought up.
6. Where the couple will live: Will the husband be willing to move if the wife gets a job offer she wants to take? Separate bedrooms? Separate apartments?

[3] Reprinted from Susan Edmiston, "How to Write Your Own Marriage Contract," *Ms.*, Spring 1972, p. 71.

7. How child care and housework will be divided: The spouse who earns less should not be penalized for the inequities of the economic world by having to do a larger share.

8. What financial arrangement will the couple embrace? If husband and wife are both wage-earners, there are three basic possibilities:
   a. Husband and wife pool their income, pay expenses, and divide any surplus.
   b. Husband and wife pay shares of expenses proportional to their incomes. Each keeps whatever he or she has left.
   c. Husband and wife each pay 50 percent of expenses. Each keeps what he or she has left.

9. Sexual rights and freedoms. Although any arrangement other than monogamy would clearly be against public policy, in practice some people make arrangements such as having Tuesdays off from one another.

10. The husband might give his consent to abortion in advance.

Item 9 have can be of crucial importance since through it prospective spouses can provide for each's necessary degree of privacy, independence, and autonomy as well as for proper safeguards to insure that these needs can be expressed and mutually respected.

Passage of laws establishing the legal equivalence of all types of cohabitation of two or more persons would also help to establish the legal validity of "marriage contracts" between two or more persons of the same sex, or between groups of men and women in a variety of family life styles (Firestone, 1970). Only then will the present type of constricting marriage and family life become truly one option among many other options, all of which are equally socially acceptable and legally sanctioned.

The second social policy needed to assure acceptance of alternate familial arrangements concerns different types of zoning ordinances. Occupancy and use of private property ordinances in the United States, as well as in other Western societies, restrict the occupancy and use of privately owned houses or apartments, or the lease of houses and apartments, to nuclear families with few deviations (such as the mother of a spouse, or two or three college students of the same sex). Such regulations should be carefully examined and changed to allow occupants the right to determine how they will use owned or leased housing units. Laws and ordinances regulating the sale and lease of houses or apartments should not be allowed to discriminate on the basis of sex, marital status, or family style. Zoning restrictions can still apply (if deemed appropriate and necessary) to the external appearance and maintenance of the housing unit but not to its functional use. Without this type of reform most people who choose some type of communal-like life style will not be able to be housed outside rural or slum areas.

In addition, mass media can, of course, play a very significant role in liberating family dynamics and in permitting spouses to behave according to a much wider range of behavioral alternatives. The presentation of familial behaviors and models that are free of sex stereotypes and that satisfy the particular inclinations and needs of each individual as "normal" in different types of T.V. movies, soap operas, and programs, and magazine articles, and the ridiculing of sex-stereotyped familial behaviors could be crucial for the socialization of the young, as well as in the redefinition of familial roles and contracts that many married people may want to undertake or are in the process of realizing. Here again the same types of strategies discussed in the chapters on the liberation of men and women could be tried in attempting to change the messages presented by the different mass media, especially by television.

Chapter 5

SOCIAL POLICY
TO LIBERATE THE SOCIETY
FROM SEXISM

The liberation of men and women and the familial institution and family life has to go hand-in-hand with the liberation of the entire society and other social institutions. Of course, if the liberation of all women and men could be rapidly and efficiently achieved, there would be no need to make special efforts to liberate the society. Liberated people would bring about all the necessary changes in all aspects of social life and in all social institutions. But since the liberation of women and men is a slow and painful process that may never be totally successful, simultaneous efforts to liberate social structure, and norms, and social institutions are absolutely necessary. Such social policy is necessary both to facilitate the liberation process of individuals and to minimize the suffering and frustration of increasingly liberated persons in a nonliberated, sexist society.

For how can liberated socialization be successfully given new societal members when, despite all the sincere and appropriate behavior on the part of their parents and teachers, language, religion, the law, history, literature, the arts, and mass media remain sexist in content and orientation? And how can liberated people be treated for their psychological problems and disturbances, identity crises, life-meaning uneasiness, etc., when they have to consult sexist therapists who often tend to treat many aspects of their psychological and social liberation as pathological symptoms?

Social Policy to
"Liberate" Language

Linguistic studies have shown that women tend to use different language than men in their everyday interactions, speech, and writing patterns. It seems, then, that some parts of speech have become more identified as "feminine"—such as adjectives. Furthermore, it has been found that in referring to events men tend to use verbs more often than women; women tend to use nouns. The same research study concluded that men tend to "...involve themselves more in their references to the events, to locate the event in their personal sphere of activity, and to refer less to others...," while women instead of a personal achievement orientation are more concerned with "being" and with satisfactory primary relations (Warshay, 1972). There is also evidence that the grammatical structure drastically differs. The one employed by women demonstrates their relatively greater concern with internal psychological states, while that employed by men shows their greater involvement with implementation of action (Barron, 1971). But the use of language both influences the type of thought process and ensuing behavior, and tends to reflect one's value system and behavior. Thus, women's and men's reality is constructed according to a model that closely resembles language patterns and models of language utilization. The differences in language are actually so significant that some raise the issue about the extent to which communication is effective and feasible when respective cognitive realities and modes of linguistic expression are so far apart (Barron, 1971).

Furthermore, recent analyses of the American language have quite clearly shown a high degree of sexism in a wide variety of words and expressions referring to women and men and to "feminine" and "masculine" behaviors (Miller and Swift, 1972).[1] The consistent sexist pattern is that whenever a behavior is sensible, rational, brave, "cool," intelligent, or innovative, it is semantically identified as "masculine." Whenever a woman behaves in one of these ways, she is said to have behaved "just like a man." Whenever a behavior is inconsistent, irrational, illogical, temperamental, emotional, or dumb, it is semantically identified as "feminine." A man displaying such behavior is said to behave "just like a woman." One of the definitions for "womanish" is: "unsuitable to a man or to a strong character of either sex." And the word "sissy" (derivative of "sister") connotes timidity and cowardice, while the word "buddy" (derivative of "brother") connotes a close and strong friendship. In addition, supposedly generic terms such as

---

[1] Here it is interesting to note that while the traditional usage of language requires authors to write "men and women," throughout this book the opposite sequence of "women and men" has been used. Many readers, even the liberated ones, must have found it a little strange after socialization in the contrary usage.

"man," "mankind," "the average man," "American men of science" are in fact words referring only to men as the masculine pronouns clearly indicate (Miller and Swift, 1972). In the same vein, unless one specifies that the doctor, professor, chemist, scientist, or president referred to is a woman, everyone assumes that he is a man since such important occupations are identified with men and not with women.

A recent research study of the images elicited by such generic terms as "political man," "urban man," "economic man," "industrial man," or "social man" commonly used in sociology and other social sciences textbooks showed that they are not "generic" at all. The majority of images (64 percent) elicited by students corresponded to males only. Whenever, however, the "generic" label "man" was omitted, only 50 percent of the students illustrated the concepts with pictures of males only. While the representation of male images was much higher for political, urban, economic, and industrial man, even in the case of social man, males were represented as surrounded by women, but women were seldom an elicited image under the generic term "man" (Schneider and Hacker, 1972).

This semantic sexism is extremely important because its subtlety and pervasiveness can be most effective in socializing young people to grow and develop according to stereotyped conceptions and models of "masculinity" and "femininity." From the time the child is first spoken to, it hears different words, speech patterns, and expressions from females and males who come in contact with it. Further differentiation is made according to its own sex, since girls and boys tend to receive different frequencies and types of verbal and nonverbal stimuli (Lewis, 1972). Mothers have been observed to look at and talk to their girl infants much more often than their boy infants during the first two years of life. This fact may well explain the usual trend that girls develop language functions earlier than boys and generally have throughout life a greater verbal fluency and facility (Lewis, 1972a; Kagan, 1972).

Furthermore, often from the first efforts to teach the alphabet to children, sex stereotyping continues, often through personification of the different letters. It has been found, for example, that the multimedia teaching kits widely used in the United States are quite sexist in that they personify the vowels as girls, who are weak and entirely dependent upon the consonants (the boys) for protection, support, and their very identity (Sherr, 1972). Many teachers in many lands have been doing the same thing by attributing all "feminine" characteristics to the vowels.

Because the language is permeated with sexism, so is the expression and formulation of ideas. Thus teachers, parents, and others associated with the young think and express their thoughts, and create and express their creativity in a sexist fashion, partly because of the sexist patterns already built into the language. Novels are written, paintings painted, poems inspired, history re-created, research designed and interpreted, all done according to sexist patterns, because ideas and expressions are "naturally" channeled in this direction.

Thus children's socialization is influenced in many ways by sexism. They have to think and express themselves in a sexist language, and they have to read classic and modern literature in which women play appropriate "feminine" roles or are duly punished for their "unnatural" behavior. They have to learn a sexism-permeated history in which the role and contributions of women, other than sex-stereotyped ones, are underplayed or entirely omitted. They have to study and build on scientific findings and theories often more or less seriously distorted by sexist beliefs and stereotypes (this is more true for the behavioral and biological sciences). What is presented to them as proven scientific truth is in fact shaky because it is biased by sex stereotypes. For example, a definite bias seems to exist as to what animals are exhaustively studied by biologists (those in which the male plays a dominant and stereotypically "masculine" role), and those which are not (those in which there is a "role-reversal"); or what types of artifacts archeologists are searching for in their excavations and in what sites.

But the main concern is to liberate language, and thus aid the liberation of thought processes and expression. Here the linguists have an important role to play in "cleansing" the language of all sexist words, expressions, and connotations. Before, however, a new liberated dictionary is written and becomes the official one to be used by all people in all circumstances, different types of action can be taken to speed up liberation of the language.

Novelists and writers should start writing high quality short stories and novels which are free of sex stereotypes. And historians should rewrite the history of the world in a more balanced and liberated manner. They should carefully consider and evaluate the role played by women and their contributions in different nations' critical moments and during peace. Actually, there is considerable evidence that during crises such as wars the roles of women in the occupational and political sphere become de-differentiated (Lipman-Blumen, 1973). Also sex stereotypes cease to limit women's interpersonal and sexual behavior. This process of de-differentiation has been conducive to women's ability to make significant contributions during crises. Thus, while throughout history women have often and in many societies played a very active and meaningful role even in active combat, their contributions have usually been belittled or entirely ignored by most historians. More attention should be paid to social history in addition to political and military history. Finally, scientists, especially behavioral and biological scientists, should carefully assess "established truths" to determine to what extent sexist biases have entered into the design of research, the selection of populations, the formulation of theories, and the interpretation of data. Everyone must take special care to consider how the use of sexist language has betrayed them, even when no other particular bias was operating.[2]

In addition, all the different types of explicit and implicit forms of sexism in the language must be detected, uncovered, and widely publicized and ridiculed. Following extensive publicity of the sexist elements and forms of language, different groups of women, as well as all liberated women and men, should take it upon themselves to uncover, underline, and ridicule sexist expressions, words, and connotations in classic works of literature and science, as well as in contemporary and current documents and speeches of scientists, politicians, lawyers, friends, colleagues, spouses, children, teachers, newspaper and journal editors and writers, T.V. commentators, and other mass media people. Constant ridicule and verbal and written attack on sexist statements and expressions can place a significant pressure on most people who need the approval of others, and who would, therefore, be made to feel, depending on their reference groups, either "old-fashioned" and "out of it" or simply sufficiently "deviant" to change.

Furthermore, passage of a legislative act would make it legal to sue mass media[3] or leading figures or scientific authorities for using a sexist rhetoric; politicians for making sexist speeches and decisions; journals and newspapers not only for carrying sexist features, but also for using sexist expressions (such as "a charming woman sociologist" or "a woman chemist in a very unlady-like fashion attacked her critics") and connotations; and advertisers for attributing stereotyped "feminine" characteristics and qualities to vanity products and "masculine" characteristics to useful, practical, rational products. In this way, expressed thoughts, opinions, and ideas will gradually tend to become sexism-free, regardless of whether or not (initially at least) the person is actually liberated. With time even those who are not liberated will be at least to some extent influenced by the sexism-free language and expression. They may start thinking in a relatively more liberated manner.

The gradual disappearance of sexist references, expressions, and con-

---

2 Because the behavior of boys and men is always taken as the norm according to to which girls' and women's behavior is judged, behavioral and biological scientists often use sexist expressions to describe differences in processes. Kagan, for example, writes of the "precocious" development of the left-hemisphere of the brain in girls and not of the "retarded" development of the left-hemisphere of the brain in boys (Kagan, 1972).

3 It is interesting to note that the National Organization for Women has petitioned the Federal Communications Commission to refuse license renewal to WABC-TV in New York on charges of "blatant sexism." The charges are based on the findings of an in-depth study of WABC-TV programming over eighteen months that showed that women were portrayed as "unintelligent, irresponsible, dominated by men, defined by their anatomy, and incapable of independent thought or action." In addition, the study showed that only 3.6 percent of the air time was given to "significant women issues" ("N.O.W. Charges WABC-TV with Blatant Sexism," 1972).

notations from our everyday language would have a very important effect upon women's self-concepts and degree of self-esteem, as well as upon the degree of esteem for and the type of image men have of women. For much of the currently used language is clearly offensive to women and serves to continually accentuate their inferior "nature" and subservient position.

Social Policy to Liberate Therapy, Counseling, and Clinical Psychology

Even before the onset of the Women's Liberation Movement, several sociologists and psychologists (women and men) conducted research and wrote articles indicating that the scales measuring femininity and masculinity were not valid and were based on old-fashioned, sex-stereotyped attributes and behaviors that did not characterize "normal" girls and boys (Vincent, 1966). And findings from different types of studies on the family and mental illness in the 60s showed definite symptoms of maladjustment, unhappiness, and mental illness in those who were trying to adhere to the prevailing sex-stereotyped roles and behaviors. Thus Bart found that depression was a very common syndrome among middle-aged women who, according to prevailing sex stereotypes, devoted their entire lives to motherhood and housekeeping, but it was not as common among those women who had deviated by taking on the working role (Bart, 1970 a, b and 1973). Housewives, in general, were found to show more frequent symptoms of psychological distress than expected, while married working woman showed them less frequently than expected (Bernard, 1971b; 1972). Finally, Dizard, on the basis of longitudinal data collected in the late 50s, concluded that the more the spouses tended to adhere to sex-stereotyped role-differentiation, the more they tended to grow apart, to quarrel, and to feel unhappy and dissatisfied with their marriage (Dizard, 1968). A study of blue-collar marriages showed that when the husbands adhered very closely to masculinity stereotypes and associated appropriate behaviors, the wives often felt frustrated and unhappy, and felt they had been denied fulfillment, companionship, and warmth (Komarovsky, 1967; Shostak, 1969). In addition, a variety of data about blue-collar marriages showed spouses tended to follow the stereotyped sex roles faithfully and to report marital unhappiness much more often than those in higher strata (Shostak, 1969; 1972).

All this accumulated evidence shows a close relationship between unhappiness and mental disturbance and conformity to the stereotyped sex roles and the sex-appropriate behaviors, especially in the case of women. The more pronounced effect on women can be easily understood when one sees the more constrained and limited range of options, as well as the intrinsically less rewarding content of the options permitted to women by traditional sex roles.

But if the effects of adhering to the traditional sex roles are so negative, why have women and men, and especially women, continued to conform to them? Why did they not protest, revolt, and reverse the roles or undifferentiate them so that they reflected their needs, inclinations, potential, and desires? The answer lies in the operation of a very potent social control that assured conformity, particularly the conformity of women, and the perpetuation of the status quo. This social control was mental health as defined by male psychologists, psychiatrists, and psychoanalysts.

According to prevailing definitions of mental health, adult women must behave very differently and have very dissimilar personality characteristics than men. Healthy women, according to the mental health criteria of psychiatrists, clinical psychologists, and social workers, differ from healthy men in that they are more submissive, less independent, less adventurous, more easily influenced, less aggressive, less competitive, more excitable in minor crises, more sensitive, more emotional, more conceited about their appearance, less objective, and not as competent in math and science. Furthermore, the clinicians' and therapists' criteria for mental health are similar for healthy adults and healthy males but not for healthy adults and healthy females, the implication being that healthy women are perceived by them as significantly less healthy than men by adult standards, or that women are not perceived as adults (Broverman, Broverman, Clarkson, Rosenkrantz, and Vogel, 1970)!

Not only are clinicians' and therapists' mental health criteria and definitions differentiated along traditional stereotyped sex roles and sex-appropriate behavioral lines, but the criteria and definitions of women's mental health are also less socially desirable than those for men. The implications of these facts are extremely grave and can explain a great number of curious findings and observations. First, a woman "must adjust to and accept the behavioral norms for her sex, . . ." and find fulfillment and happiness in the stereotyped "feminine" role if she is to be judged "well-adjusted" and mentally healthy. Second, since the definitions of mental health and maturity for adults and males involve self-actualization, mastery of the environment, fulfillment of one's potential, and high need-achievement, women must accept second-class adult status. They must exhibit less socially desirable and less healthy behaviors (for a competent adult) in order to be considered "feminine," and, therefore, mentally healthy women (Broverman, Broverman, Clarkson, Rosenkrantz, and Vogel, 1970).

The second of the two implications mentioned above explains why a considerable number of women have rejected the stereotyped "feminine" role and the associated second-class adult status in order to fulfill themselves and develop their potential as much as possible. But what price have these women paid? They were constantly aware that they were breaking the rules and were made to feel by everyone around "unnatural," deviant, and immature. Depending on how much they themselves felt the conflict between their desire for personal growth, self-fulfillment, independence, dominance, and achievement on the one hand, and the requirements of traditionally defined "femininity" on the other (and the degree to which they perceived it as a serious conflict), the penalty for their deviance varied. For some, the lucky ones, a series of happy coincidences, the presence of supporting and approving significant others (including husbands), and a certain economic ease made the two sets of behaviors compatible enough so that they could "make it."

It must be pointed out, however, that even in the cases of successful, "deviant" women, there is considerable evidence that certain aspects of the stereotyped "feminine" role had to be faithfully adhered to if they were to be able to manage the conflicts emerging from their deviance. Thus, for example, successful women physicians, lawyers, and university professors carefully depreciated their professional achievements and commitment, and stressed their maternal role (also emphasized by having many children) and their housekeeping skills. These women constantly feared that they might become more famous, gain more money, or achieve a higher rank than their husbands, thus seriously threatening a precarious marital harmony that depended upon maintaining a lower salary and prestige position than that of their husbands (Poloma, 1972; Garland 1972). Only this doubly subservient and secondary position in the familial and the professional setting, along the lines of the stereotyped "feminine" role, secured for them the "normalcy" label and their husbands' as well as society's tolerance.

But most women, either because they lack supporting and approving significant others, or because they reject many more behavioral norms of the stereotyped "feminine" sex role than society is willing to tolerate, find themselves in a stigmatized deviant position, and suffer serious and often unmanageable psychological conflicts. Women who reject the marital role as defined by the prevailing sex stereotypes, and who either remain single, divorce after some years of marriage, or manage to reverse the roles and be the dominant partner often become clients of family counselors, psychiatrists, and other therapists in their search for a resolution of the conflict.

Phyllis Chesler, a psychologist, has written that "both psychotherapy and marriage, the two major socially approved institutions for white, middle-class women," function effectively in keeping women "in their place" and behaving according to the traditional sex stereotypes. Being unmarried or being unhappily married is considered an illness that must be cured by a (preferably male) therapist. The essential element in the therapy becomes the elimination or modification of the "nonfeminine" personality characteristics, attitudes, and expectations blocking her "fulfillment" as a woman (Chesler, 1971).

Family counselors, psychiatrists, and other therapists try to help "maladjusted" women (those who reject or "fight" their femininity and the sex-stereotyped behavioral requirements) to become "happy" and "normal" by accepting their womanhood, a subservient role to their husbands, and a self-sacrificing role to their children. Up until to very recently, in many instances the therapeutic treatment entailed helping women adjust to and accept their stereotyped sex role and feel happy in doing so (Bernard, 1971a).

Those women who have been unwilling or unable to change and accept the traditional feminine role and associated behaviors, persisting instead in playing a dominant, active, or aggressive role, especially in their interactions with their husbands or significant male others in authority positions (such as fathers, therapists) seem to have been punished by being diagnosed as mentally ill (Cekala, 1972; Dworking Levering, 1972). Several studies show that the most significant recognized behavioral difference between female schizophrenics and their "normal" controls was their overactive, dominating behavior in interacting with others, especially with significant male others in authority positions (Cheek, 1964; Leighton, Stollak, and Rau Ferguson, 1971). Psychiatrists and other therapists act as very potent agents of social control in assuring the conformity of women to the stereotypic range of "feminine" behaviors. Since, however, the "feminine" sex roles are constraining and frustrating to many women, a large number try to escape the stereotyped role of womanhood. In trying to do so they are met with many obstacles, stresses, and conflicts, and have a high probability of becoming mentally ill. Thus, the significantly greater number of women than men who, during their sixties, diagnose themselves or are treated as mentally ill at all types of psychiatric facilities (including private practitioners) (Gove and Tudor, 1973) can be partly explained by the extreme stress that "deviant" women usually experience. But it can also be explained in part by societal and "expert" diagnosis of such deviance as mental illness when acted out by women.

Recent research on the current status of psychosurgery in the United States, Canada, and several European and Asian nations undertaken by Dr. Lindstrom, a prominent California neurosurgeon, showed that the majority of lobotomies are performed on women who are often labeled neurotics, that is, who are relatively well functioning. He reports that 72 percent of the psychotics and 80 percent of the neurotics who are lobotomized are women (Roberts, 1972). Also even when lobotomies for men are frowned upon, as is true at many psychiatric hospitals, they are performed on women. It seems that lobotomies, which decrease or destroy the person's unique emotional responsiveness, creativity, abstract thinking, and overall intellectual functioning, are with much greater impunity performed on women than on men, because lobotomized women are believed by many leading neurosurgeons to make "good housewives" (Roberts, 1972). One prominent psychiatrist (Dr.

Peter Breggin) claims lobotomies can be better performed on women because of their passive conditioning, and because they are more socially acceptable for women since the destruction of women's creativity is less serious,
creativity being an "expendable quality in women" (Roberts, 1972).

Lobotomies are performed mainly on "restless," "neurotic" wives who
rebel against their traditional "feminine" roles as housewives, against the sexual double standard, against sexist barriers to their growth and self-actualization. Depressed, middle-aged women who often became depressed because they
have lived according to traditional sex-role specifications receive lobotomies
too. After the lobotomy they become quiet, calm, "satisfied" housewives; all
the seeds of rebellion have been destroyed forever. Thus, "unlike burning at
the stake, psychosurgery can silence rebellion while preserving the useful
work women can do with their hands, their backs, and their uteruses"
(Roberts, 1972).

The punishment for nonconformity is heavy; it reminds one of the
severe punishments (often death) meted out to deviant women by their
male relatives in many traditional cultures, especially those where women's
subserviance and obedience were inforced through a powerful honor code
(Safilios-Rothschild, 1972c).

It is important to note that rejection of the stereotyped "masculine
role" by men, especially in interaction with significant female others is
handled just as harshly by psychiatrists and other therapists. Again the consistent difference between male schizophrenics and their "normal" controls
is the fact that the former tend to be more passive, less active, to take the
initiative less often, and to be dominated by their interacting females (Cheek,
1964; Leighton, Stollak, and Rau Ferguson, 1971). Men who reject their
superior position in the family and in their relationship with other men,
and who permit women by default to control are threatening to the maintenance of the social order. They must be helped to assume their "masculine" role, or if they are unwilling or unable to do so, they must be labeled
"mentally ill" and, thus, irresponsible for their deviance. In this way, other
men will be more motivated to assume the appropriate masculine sex role in
order to avoid the unhappiness and serious psychological disturbance resulting from rejection.

Actually, however, some evidence exists that points to serious maladjustment and mental disturbance among men, particularly among adolescent
and young adult males, who try very hard to conform to all the behavioral
and psychological requirements of masculinity. Serious automobile accidents
due to speeding are many times more frequent among young adult men than
women. Suicide and homicide rates tend to be higher among men than
among women. And mental illness seems to be more frequent among boys
than girls up to the end of adolescence. These behaviors are indications of
the stress experienced by men in coping with society's standards of mas-

culinity. Despite this type of evidence, however, psychiatrists and other therapists have not been willing until very recently to permit men to choose the behavioral and psychological sets that were best suited to their needs, personalities, abilities, and inclinations.

The meaning, then, of the liberation of all kinds of therapy implies a radical change in the orientation of clinicians and therapists. They will have to make a full turn from trying to help women and men conform, adjust to, and accept the stereotyped sex roles and associated behavioral sets to helping them to choose freely from among a wide range of behavioral sets, regardless of their patients' gender. Clinicians, counselors, and therapists can actually play a significant role both during the transitional period and after liberation has been achieved. It is very important that therapists become liberated (regardless of whether or not they are themselves liberated in their private lives) in order to be able to help others find an emotional and psychological balance in searching for new and more satisfying ways of life.

During the transitional period, a great number of women and men will need to be helped to feel comfortable in choosing behavioral sets previously considered "deviant" for members of their sex. Women will have to be helped to feel adjusted and socially accepted when they want to openly and actively compete with their husbands for family power. They will have to be counseled, guided, and shown how to effectively compete and engage in power battles, as well as to feel comfortable and be able to enjoy some degree of equality (or power and dominance) with their husbands. Men, on the contrary, will have to learn how to be passive, sometimes dominated by women (their wives and/or their colleagues), to have less control and power, and not to always take the initiative, when these behavioral sets are most congenial and best suited to their personalities, needs, inclinations, and wishes (Safilios-Rothschild, 1973). In both cases the women and men will often have to be reassured by therapists that, when opting for choices stereotypically defined as "deviant," their sexuality is by no means affected, they can still function sexually as females and males, and they will be equally well liked, loved, and respected by members of the opposite sex, particularly by their significant others.

It seems that in some Eastern European countries some of these radical changes in psychotherapy have already been occuring. There is evidence that therapists try to help men adjust and accept the professional achievements of their wives and their emancipation without feelings of inadequacy or threatened sexuality (Knoblochova and Knobloch, 1965).

Therapists and counselors will also have to help women and men (not only during the transition but also afterwards) discover their own needs, potential, inclinations, wishes, abilities, and desires, and to find the appropriate behavioral and psychological set to represent the best fit for each different and dynamically changing stage of their lives. In fact, therapists and counselors will have to help women and men to utilize and benefit from the ongoing liberation movement and its processes without the possible harmful and undesirable side effects and consequences. Some psychiatrists have recently reported that a new growing type of impotence has been observed among young men interacting with partners who, freed from traditional "feminine" sexual hangups, demand high standards of sexual performance from them (Ginsberg, Frosch, and Shapiro, 1972). Therapists have to learn how to cope with such short-range side effects of liberation, which are expected to multiply in the future in both frequency and variety. These side effects affect men more frequently, because they have to undergo many psychological changes and adjustments in reaction to women's sexual and psychological liberation.

What *is* the recommended action that could lead to the liberation of all types of therapy? Some of the needed models of action have been already put to work. Liberated women and men (or those trying to find their road toward liberation) have become sensitized to the importance of having a liberated therapist when finding ways to cope with their problems. As a result, they tend to be intolerant of a therapist who is subtly guiding them toward "acceptance" of stereotyped sex roles and behaviors, and often terminate therapy under these conditions.

A journal that recently appeared, *The Radical Therapist*[4] (with the subtitle: "Therapy is Change...not Adjustment), carries articles by liberated social scientists, clinical psychologists, and other therapists who are trying to delineate a new type of liberated therapy, to set new standards and definitions of mental health, and to find ways of helping women and men liberate themselves and make the most appropriate decisions for their needs and personalities. Furthermore, different articles and sections critical of the basic premises of psychoanalysis have been written, but they are just beginning to scratch the surface and have not yet suggested viable alternatives.

One increasingly popular therapeutic model that could be compatible with the liberation orientation is lay-therapy by and with a number of people suffering from similar problems, who have been successful in overcoming them to varying degrees. This basic model, encountered under different names and varied in application, often encourages women and men to express and experience feelings and emotions that are not sex-role-appropriate. Furthermore it also helps free people from the economic and intellectual restrictions of most traditional methods that render therapy inaccessible to low-income, low-education, or low-intelligence individuals (Scheff, 1972).

Here it is interesting to note that there is some evidence to suggest that

[4] The title of the journal has now changed to *Rough Times* (address: The Radical Therapist, Inc., P.O. Box 89, West Somerville, Ma. 02144).

feminism and in general a higher level of consciousness, freedom of choice, and confidence have themselves had a psychotherapeutic effect on many women, who could have been diagnosed as "neurotics," "character disorders," etc. In some cases women were able to avoid hospitalization in a mental hospital and to function as private patients of more or less liberated therapists (Chesler, 1972). In other cases they were able to bypass therapists of any kind and to successfully cope with problems. This evidence indicates indirectly that the basic root of much of what was labeled and treated as mental illness in women was connected with the restrictions that stereotyped femininity imposed upon all women, regardless of their potentials, talents, aspirations, and desires. Once women are able to rid themselves of the psychological restrictions and taboos of femininity, they can better fight the social-structural restrictions on their path to self-actualization and can maintain their mental balance while doing so.

PRESSURES TO HELP LIBERATE THERAPY

The liberation of therapy might come about under three different types of pressure: (1) *economic pressure* exerted through the refusal of clients to have unliberated therapists; (2) *prestige pressure* exerted through publicity and recognition rewards and special prizes for outstanding liberated therapists for either a reconceptualization of the existing principles of psychoanalysis or for outstanding service rendered toward the liberation of women and men; and (3) *professional pressure* exerted through the institutionalization of changes that alter the training of young therapists and that require special training sessions for established therapists to enable them to practice in a liberated manner.

Different women's groups and organizations can exert economic pressure, without which the other two types of pressure cannot and will not come about. NOW and other women's groups could (and are beginning to) establish lists of liberated, trustworthy therapists that would be widely publicized not only among their members but also in the wider community. Women could then be encouraged to boycott therapists not on these lists. An effective "economic pressure" would eventually also have serious implications for the therapists' prestige. Furthermore, the mass media could play an extremely important role in establishing the second type of "prestige pressure" by projecting images of liberated therapists who guide women and men to find the behaviors that best represent their personalities and relationships, regardless of sex stereotypes. The mass media, especially different TV shows and the popular journals, could feature liberated psychiatrists and other therapists on talk shows, and other programs, or have them written up in special columns or articles. For example, the Feminist Psychology Coalition has set up a therapy referral service (located at the City University of

New York, Graduate Center) that refers about fifteen women per week to the fifty or so screened therapists, some with, some without professional credentials, some "straight" and others gay, but almost all women ("Feminist Psychology Coalition Therapy Referral Service," 1972).

Professional pressure is the most difficult to bring to bear since the most powerful and influential men are most probably opposed to changes and would tend to boycott the efforts of the younger liberated women or men therapists. Here the key to change—that is going to be slow and uneven—may be first, through the ascent of liberated women therapists to powerful and influential positions, and second, through the policies of fund-granting federal institutions and foundations. Research grants and institutional support could be given preferrentially to basic research and service projects seeking answers to basic questions raised by liberation—both for women and men and for social institutions. Such basic research and service projects would help liberate the theory as well as practice of clinical behavioral sciences from sex stereotypes that constrain the behavioral options of women and men. Here again the role that funding from federal and private foundation sources can play in bringing about changes can be quite significant. Some stirrings in this direction are already evident, but they must grow into well organized, strong, and consistent efforts before fruitful changes can be made concrete.

WOMEN AND HEALTH CARE IN GENERAL

Finally, it should be observed that sexism in medicine is not confined just to the evaluation of women's mental health and the type of received treatment. It extends into *all* aspects of health and rehabilitation. Thus physicians and surgeons seem to hesitate very little in a decision to remove women's ovaries, even when the reasons are not urgent and clear-cut, but they would think twice before removing a testicle. As one surgeon cynically stated, "No ovary is good enough to leave in, and no testicle is bad enough to take out" ("Women M.D.'s Join the Fight," 1970).

Furthermore, because physicians believe and are taught that women are hysterics who exaggerate pain and symptoms, who develop psychosomatic symptoms out of boredom or in order to attract attention, they tend to de-emphasize or totally overlook reported pain and symptoms, and so to frequently underdiagnose women's illnesses and conditions (Bondurant, 1972). In general, physicians and surgeons seem to pay much greater attention and to take better care of men than women patients in alleviation of pain and valuation of the integrity of the body and physical functioning. A recent analysis shows that although women constitute the large majority of physicians's clients and are the exclusive clientele of gynecologists, they are nevertheless treated as "lesser" persons with little concern for the impor-

tance of the roles they play, as well as for their needs, anxieties, and potentials. Furthermore, the available rehabilitation research and statistics show
that women are considered to be "bad risks" for rehabilitation and are often
refused such services (Safilios-Rothschild, 1970b). In order to establish the
role that sexism plays in the delivery of medical care, much more research is
needed in the form of a series of clinical observations in different hospital
settings such as that of *Sickness and Society* (Duff and Hollingshead, 1969).

Social Policy to Liberate
the Legal System

Existing evidence from all societies and times indicates that
women have always tended to break the law less often than men, because
stereotyped sex roles demanded a greater degree of conformity, docility,
gentleness, and passivity from them than from men. The same trends seem
to persist in modern developed societies such as the U.S.A., Canada, and
England, although the rate of difference between women and men seems to
be decreasing in the U.S. and in Canada (*The Status of Women in Canada,*
1970; Pollak, 1950; Heidensohn, 1968). In general, however, the deviance
and crime rates for women have not increased at the same pace as their
rate of participation in higher education and gainful employment, or in
accordance with the overall improvement of their status in society, as might
be expected (Wooton mentioned in Heidensohn, 1968).

But there are some indications in the early 70s that women's involvement in serious crimes (assault and battery as well as murder) and acts of
violence have been increasing both in the United States and in Western
Europe ("Crime Rate of Women Up Sharply Over Men's," 1971; "The
Hooker's Boswell," 1972). Statistics available from the Federal Bureau of
Investigation show that the national percentage of arrests for women rose
from 2.9 percent in 1968 to 15.0 percent in 1971, while the national percentage of women committing violent crimes rose from 14.2 percent in 1968 to
17.2 percent in 1971. Furthermore, detailed data from the Detroit Police
Department show prosecution charges for larceny in the case of women rose
from 15.1 percent in 1968 to 18.0 percent in 1972, and charges for narcotics
went from 2.1 percent to 12.3 percent (Bannon, 1973). This increase may be
at least partly due to policemen's, judges', and social workers' decreased
tolerance of and paternalism toward women criminal defendants (Nagel and
Weitzman, 1971), and partly because their crimes tend to deviate from
those considered compatible with the "feminine" personality.

In some developing societies such as Greece it has been noted that the
rate of women involved in assault and homicide increased already in the 60s
as women achieved a significant level of occupational and economic emancipation. Urban Greek women, for example, began for the first time to defend

their own honor by assaulting (mainly by throwing vitriol in the faces of men) or killing the men who "dishonored" them usually by jilting them after having promised marriage or after having had sexual relations with them. (Safilios-Rothschild, 1972c).

This persisting crime differential between women and men has been explained by different theories by leading criminologists. Pollak, for example, believes that women are, on the average, as deviant as men and break the law as often but are less frequently apprehended or convicted because they can better hide the evidence of their deviance. This greater ingenuity in concealing evidence is, of course, attributed to the "feminine" personality and its associated talents (Pollak, 1950). Others have tried to explain the difference by pointing out that women's lives focus mainly on marital/sexual preoccupations, while men's lives center on economic/occupational concerns, and these preoccupations determine the nature of their respective deviance (as well as the rates?) (Grosser, 1951; Cohen, 1955; Gibbs, 1966).

In fact, however, it seems that in general women's criminal deviance has been little studied, and the existing data are not always systematic, complete, or valid (Heidensohn, 1968). Probably the only exception to this is the considerable number of studies of prostitutes and prostitution, a deviance that is more of an occupational nature and not intrinsically a deviance. The common criminal acts, such as theft, assault, extortion, blackmail, sex exploitation, drug addiction, may be deviance punishable by law, but prostitution in itself (unless it is connected with soliciting) does not constitute a punishable offense in most nations. Actually, until very recently in most states in the U.S., prostitution was considered a violation or a noncriminal offense usually carrying a sentence of fifteen days in jail if the prostitute were arrested. In 1969, however, a bill was passed in New York which made prostitution a crime punishable by a maximum sentence of ninety days (Roby and Kerr, 1972). Despite these severe sentences for prostitutes, their patrons are rarely arrested, although there has been legal provision for such arrests since 1967. In fact, only 6 percent of all arrests involved with prostitution between 1967 and 1971 and less than one percent of all convictions were for patronizing (Roby and Kerr, 1972).

The fact that in many states there are no laws penalizing the clients of prostitutes, and that where there are they are not treated seriously shows gross legal discrimination on the basis of the offender's sex. Only one party to the crime or violation is subject to arrest and especially to conviction: the woman. Despite the fact that prostitution cannot in fact exist without actively participating males, men who have sexual relations with a prostitute are rarely arrested and practically never convicted. In fact it has been decided in court that resorting to a brothel or a prostitute for "an isolated act of intercourse does not warrant conviction," and that soliciting a prostitute for "personal gratification" cannot be penalized as "soliciting" (Kanowitz,

1969). This legal *de jure* or *de facto* exemption of male participants from blame in prostitution demonstrates a clear-cut case of sexism in the law and implementation of law.

Because of the lack of accurate, systematic, and complete data on women's criminality, it is difficult to ascertain to what extent the existing differentials in rate and occurrence are due to the women's lesser involvement in crime, to a less frequent apprehension of women involved in crimes, or to a smaller rate of detention and conviction of women criminals. The possibility exists, and is consistent both with stereotypic beliefs about the feminine "nature" and with chivalrous notions as to how women must be treated (especially since it is believed that women are seldom, if ever, callous, professional criminals), that women are less often sued, arrested, brought to trial, or convicted than men, even for the same types of committed crime (*The Status of Women in Canada,* 1970). Data available from the Wayne County and Detroit Recorder's Court show that in 1971, despite the fact that 16 percent of all arrests for prosecution were women, only 7.3 percent of the cases were disposed of by the court in such a fashion as to become a responsibility of the department of corrections. Also of all those committed to correctional institutions in 1971 only 2.8 percent were women (Bannon, 1973). Thus, at least in the case of Detroit the case can be made that women tend to be jailed less often than arrested men.

There are, however, no systematic data to permit us to tell for what kinds of crimes women are sometimes not arrested and for what kinds they are always arrested. There is some evidence that among juveniles girls tend to be arrested for offenses incompatible with their stereotyped "feminine" role, that is, for running away, pregnancy, or sexual misconduct (Olson, 1971). But we do not know whether or not there are some types of crimes and some circumstances that maximize the probability of being forgiven because such offenses tend to be more in character with the stereotyped feminine sex role. There is some evidence, however, indicating that women tend to be jailed more often in assault cases, stereotyped as "masculine"-type crimes, than in larceny cases (Nagel and Weitzman, 1971).

In the case of rape and seduction, women cannot be legally prosecuted for having seduced or sexually assaulted a man, or for having had sexual intercourse with a boy who is considered a minor (Kanowitz, 1969; *The Status of Women in Canada,* 1970). The implication here is that women do not initiate, much less force, sexual relations on a man, because it is not compatible with their passive, "feminine" nature. Furthermore, men cannot be raped by women because being physically stronger they cannot be forced, even if they are under age. In addition, the consent to sexual intercourse, even on the part of minor males, is upheld as valid (but not so in the case of female minors), probably due to the stereotyped masculine unsatiable sexual urges and interests. And men are free from the biological and social complications of pregnancy, complications that have at present lost most of their gravity since they can be eliminated. In summary, all rationales for laws that convict men (but not women) of statutory rape (sexual intercourse with a consenting female under eighteen—or in some states under twenty-one) are based on sex-role stereotypes and may often, and increasingly, not reflect the actual behavior of women and men (Kanowitz, 1969).

Actually, the implementation of rape laws again shows considerable sexism, since the raped adult woman's testimony is usually doubted and not considered sufficient evidence for conviction in the absence of witnesses. (But what rapist would choose to have witnesses?) Furthermore, any degree of previous acquaintance between the woman and the rapist practically always acquits the man. Her lack of consent to sexual intercourse is not considered valid, the implication being that she "provoked" the man or that "she was asking for it." And the raped woman's sexual life prior to the rape plays a very important role in the rapist's conviction—a fact indicating the judges', juries', and lawyers' sexual double standard with regard to women (Reynolds, 1971; Weinman Lear, 1972).

There is also evidence that, once women are arrested for larceny or assault, they tend to be treated paternalistically, in the same way as juvenile delinquents, in that they are either much more frequently released on bail during the pretrial period than men, or have their cases dismissed or are acquitted during the trial. Arrested women, in general, tend to avoid jail during the pretrial and the postconviction periods because, according to the prevailing sex stereotypes, women are "weak" and can be seriously harmed by imprisonment (Nagel and Weitzman, 1972). Because of the same type of judicial paternalism shown toward women litigants, they tend to be informally tried more often by a judge without the benefit of a jury, a fact that can often be a detriment, since juries tend to favor women in their criminal verdicts more than judges (Nagel and Weitzman, 1972).

With regard to the seriousness or length of sentence given to women and men litigants, the evidence is mixed, but it shows that sex differentials are definitely operating. There have been recent court cases in which the Supreme Courts of New Jersey and Maine failed to find differential sentencing, on the basis of the offender's sex, for the same type of offense unconstitutional. On the contrary, such sex differentials were legally justified because "female criminals were basically different from male criminals..." (Nagel and Weitzman, 1971), and because there are "significant biological, natural, and practical differences between men and women" (Kanowitz, 1969).

And there is evidence that the few statutes that specifically differentiate sentences for men and women generally provide more indeterminate sentences for women. Such treatment is based on the belief that women can be rehabilitated easier and faster than men, and thus can be released from jail earlier. In practice, however, indeterminate sentences usually result in a much longer stay in prison than fixed terms. Thus, for the same type of crime, women are in fact punished with longer jail sentences than men (Kanowitz, 1969). In the absence of such statutes, convicted male defendants tend to receive indeterminate sentences much more often than women (Nagel and Weitzman, 1972).

Finally, the available evidence from Canada shows rather clearly that women litigants in general receive lighter sentences than men, when the type of offense is not controlled. Thus, 6.7 percent of men and 1.3 percent of women are sentenced to imprisonment for twenty-four months or more; 37.8 percent of men and 14.4 percent of women go to prison for up to twenty-four months; 24.9 percent of men and 46.7 percent of women are fined; and 30.6 percent of men and 37.6 percent of women are given a suspended sentence (*The Status of Women in Canada,* 1970). It seems that, unless there are statutes such as the Muncy Act that specify higher or differential sentencing for convicted female offenders, women tend to be more leniently sentenced by judges and juries.

Once women are jailed, their treatment is again significantly influenced by sex stereotypes, especially with regard to the type of vocational training they receive. While men are "rehabilitated" by preparation for financial independence through the acquisition of occupational skills, women are "rehabilitated" by moralizing attitudes and are prepared for little else than the dependent role of mother and housekeeper. Whenever any vocational training is available, it is limited to low-paying and low-prestige "feminine" skills, and is followed up after release with placement in low-status and low-paying jobs ("Women in Prisons," 1972). And in some states, such as Michigan, there is no correctional facility for women. Instead, women serving long-term sentences (that is, over 90 days) are housed in the Detroit House of Correction, a facility designed for short-term sentences and lacking the various rehabilitation programs available to male prisoners (Bannon, 1973).

Another type of very important sex differentials in judicial decision-making has been well documented in all types of personal injury cases. In general, adult women are less likely than men to file suits, to establish liability, and to receive considerable awards, especially for some types of personal injury. Basically, women are discriminated against on the basis of sexist beliefs about the inferior importance and "value" of women. Men therefore receive much higher awards than women for the same type of personal injuries. And the same is true in cases where they sue for loss of consortium (affection and love) caused by their wife's injuries than when wives sue for loss of consortium caused by their husband's injuries. While higher awards for personal injuries interfering with men's breadwinning functions could be to some extent more justified than those of economically dependent women, the fact that men collect more for loss caused by their wife's injuries than women collect for loss caused by their husband's injuries very clearly indicates a sexist bias (Nagel and Weitzman, 1971).

Discrimination on the basis of sex in the legal system is also demonstrated by the fact that in many states the law does not permit wives to sue for loss of their husbands' love, affection, and sexual relations since the wife is considered to be her husband's property and cannot therefore sue the owner of the property (Nagel and Weitzman, 1972). And in the case of one type of bodily injury, namely urinogenital injuries, men's awards are three times those given to women. Despite the fact that part of the difference could be explained by the more severe and often more permanent damage to the male urinogenital system, the differences of awards are too large and tend to reflect the sexist value system in American courts (Nagel and Weitzman, 1972).

The sex composition of juries seems in addition to play an important role in the judicial treatment of female and male litigants. Thus, while the sex composition of the jury does not make any difference in the establishment of liability, it does make a great difference in the average amount awarded to women and men. Men-dominated juries tend to give men higher than average awards for personal injuries and give lower than average awards to women, while women-dominated juries tend to in the same manner favor women more often than men (Nagel and Weitzman, 1972). Mainly because of the rarity of women judges there are no data indicating how their sentences for women and men offenders compare to those pronounced by men judges.

The evidence of discrimination in the judicial process and findings on the effect of the sex composition of the jury upon the type of decision require extremely important social policies to liberate justice. First, the easiest policy concerns reformulation of legal statutes that still discriminate against the one or the other sex, so that at least such statutory discrimination can totally disappear. Second, men and women should have the same right and responsibility to serve on jury duty without any sex-linked sets of exemptions. Presently in many states women are allowed more legitimate excuses for abstaining from such duty. These first two types of legal reforms are, of course, expected to occur soon after the ratification of the Equal Rights Amendment, since the involved discrimination on the basis of sex will become clearly unconstitutional.

But what is even more important than just making sure that women serve on juries to the same extent as men is finding a mechanism that would guarantee the equal sex composition of each individual jury. By law it can be decreed that a jury must be composed of an exactly equal number of women and men (50–50), but safeguards should be built in so that the final sex composition of the jury does not depend entirely in the end upon the relative sharpness of the defense and prosecution attorneys.

Another very important step is the opening up of law schools to women, probably by establishing a minimum quota of women to be admitted (provided, of course, that they meet the admission criteria). In addition, the establishment of fellowships for women (of all ages) to study law would be an extremely useful policy. Finally, the appointment of women in high positions in the legal structure in cities and states and at the federal level would help establish the image of women as lawyers, judges, and attorneys, all equal in respect, prestige, and weight with men in the professions. Significant representation of women among judges and lawyers will consequently help end sexism and discrimination in the courts.

Furthermore, women lawyers in collaboration with family sociologists, law sociologists, criminologists, and other social scientists should continue the excellent work that Nagel and Weitzman have started in exposing the different areas and ways in which court decisions have been permeated by sexist values and beliefs. In many instances much work must be done in analyzing and systematizing the trends followed by court decisions in different areas and in showing the explicit and implicit rationale on which these decisions are based. Once all the necessary evidence is collected, the action to be taken will become clearer, and it will not be necessary to appeal the case to the Supreme Court every time sexist values influence a court decision. Of course, once a few cases have been reversed by the Supreme Court as unconstitutional due to sex discrimination, similar types of decisions will tend to become rare. However, some statutory safeguards may be also needed regarding some basic principles, such as those concerning the relative economic value attached to personal injuries incurred by a woman and by a man. All types of personal injuries incurred by women and men should become legally equivalent. The plaintiff's sex should not play any role in the determination of awards for personal injuries or for loss caused by the spouse's injuries.

Social Policy to Liberate Politics, Power, and Political Decision-Making

The crux of sexism is undeniably the desire for the exclusive right to power. Since men want to have power over women at all levels and in all areas, they soon realized that the only way to perpetuate their exclusive right was to brainwash women into thinking that they neither desired nor were able to control power. Only through such an effective socialization would men be spared from continuously having to control women by exercising physical power, violence, and physical or intellectual superiority.

Women became convinced that they did not want to and were unable to handle power because men consistently portrayed power as cruel, inhuman and undesirable—but necessary for social order. Men in a sense played the self-sacrificing role of being willing to control power and do all that was necessary (cheating, lying, killing, etc.) to obtain and keep power in their hands, so that women could live a "good" life, free of such base and soul-eroding preoccupations. Thus, men appeared to be heroes who became worn out from the hard competitive struggle to gain and exert power, while their wives, who outlived them, could enjoy the entire range of benefits from their efforts and achievements (Amundsen, 1971).

Of course history can show many power-thirsty queens, empresses, and women heads of states who distinguished themselves by scheming, lying, plotting, and killing on a par with political men of all times. But then these women were always brought up in powerful families and have had the model of a politically strong father, brother, husband, or son that permitted them to acquire the necessary political socialization. This has been a very important and almost necessary requirement for women to desire and/or to acquire power in many contemporary societies, including that of the United States. In many cases women who ran for or were elected to significant political posts were the widows, wives, or less frequently the daughters of political men (Gruberg, 1968; Gehlen, 1969). The great shortcoming for the majority of women has always been their socialization to the traditional sex roles and sex-appropriate behavioral sets that made the desire for or the holding of power basically incompatible with "femininity" and the "nature" of women. The control of power in most cases requires at least a certain degree of rationality, objectivity, stability, strength, and a high sense of responsibility, properties lacking in women who, according to sex stereotypes, are (and must be) sweet, passive, and helpless (Amundsen, 1971).

The most tangible and clear-cut evidence of traditional sex role typing upon women's political behavior comes from research findings concerning women's voting behavior. Among the 21 million women nonvoters in 1968, the majority of them were women in the lower educational levels (grade school) and women living in the South, that is, women adhering to much more rigid sex-role stereotypes than more well-educated, northern women. It seems, then, that adherence to traditional sex stereotypes has inhibited women even from the most elementary political right and exercise of political power—voting (Amundsen, 1971; Gruberg, 1968).

At the elective level, despite the fact that women senators and congresswomen have often not been feminists, they have been described as "femininely militant," ambitious, and somewhat ruthless (Lamson, 1969). There is also some research evidence that women in politics are better accepted in informal political networks, considered more competent and more often rewarded the more they deviate from traditional "feminine" rules and norms. The more they can think, speak, and act "like men," that is, along the traditional masculine norms of rationality, coolness, intelligence, courage, ruthlessness, purposeful compromise, and straightness and squareness with issues and problems, the more they are considered to be "good" politicians and the more they can exert political power (Gehlen, 1969). Thus, the traditional notion of "femininity" seems to deter American (and all) women from effectively exerting political power at all levels, from voting to competing for political posts to making political decisions and influencing others.

On the contrary, women have been rather adequately socialized to influence those who had power (men) through a range of subtle, devious, and indirect techniques that were compatible with and based on their "femininity." Like all oppressed people, women were taught these techniques, and many of them became quite skilled in operating backstage, in the underground, diplomatically, tactfully so that the powerful men would never discern that they were being influenced. Throughout history women have been the very influential wives, mistresses, daughters, and sisters of powerful presidents, dictators, ministers, generals, or governors. They have probably often been responsible for significant decisions made by these men. But history gives them a very cursory mention, if any at all, and their political influence and power is underplayed. In more recent times, and still at present in the United States and Canada, the political campaigning and the continuous and never-tiring aid and support women give in terms of time, money, and organizational skills have been responsible for the victories of political parties and the election of men to all the important political positions (Gruberg, 1968; *The Status of Women in Canada*, 1970).

Furthermore, the fact that, as we already saw, history and government textbooks at all levels do not mention women in any particular power context tends to reinforce girls' sex-role stereotypic concept that "politics are not for women." In addition, it seems that women with a grade school education (who adhere more faithfully to rigid sex-typing) have been found to have "the most impoverished level of political concept formation," and, therefore, to emphasize moral issues consonant with their feminine "nurturant" role (Amundsen, 1971). The fact that girls from an early age are given few opportunities and little encouragement to develop leadership abilities and to practice their talents in increasing the importance of leadership positions further contributes to women's alienation from leadership, politics, and power.

Research undertaken in Finland has shown quite clearly how women's socialization caused young girls sixteen to nineteen years old to possess significantly less national and international political information and to be politically less articulate than boys the same age. While these differences held true within each social class, the differentials were much more acute in the lower- and working-class, thus showing that this trend may be universal (Stolte Heiskanen, 1971).

In the last twenty years behavioral scientists (almost entirely male) have further reinforced ideas of the "nature of femininity" and all its implications by providing scientific research evidence indicating that women who sought and/or obtained power were "deviant," "unnatural," pathological, disturbed, and utterly unhappy. Thus, research put its seal of authority and truth on the sex-stereotyped nonsense that for years has distorted the relationships between women and men and has frustrated countless individuals.

This type of perpetuated socialization has handicapped women in political participation, in active trade union participation, and in involvement in any other aspect of the power-seeking social system. Yet it is remarkable to see that at the close of 1973, and after six years of an active and significant Women's Liberation Movement, women still believe many of the centuries-old myths about their "feminine" nature and their inability to seek and control power. Thus 63 percent of women (and 63 percent of men) still think that, "Most men are better suited emotionally for politics than are most women." Also 55 percent of women (and 62 percent of men) feel that, "To be really active in politics, women have to neglect their husbands and children." Furthermore, 52 percent of women (and 62 percent of men) believe that, "Men have more physical stamina than women." Similar percentages of women and men believe that, "Men are more aggressive than women" (and hence need and desire to have power and control over others). (All figures from *The 1972 Virginia Slims American Women's Opinion Poll,* 1972.) Canadian women downgraded their own political potential too by stating that, "Women do not have the necessary background to become candidates" (34 percent of them), or that, "A woman's chief role is to care for her family" (23.5 percent) (*The Status of Women in Canada,* 1970).

The only change in such opinions held in America can be discerned among the majority of young, single (and to a lesser extent divorced and separated), college-educated women (and more among black than among white women) who seem to have managed to overcome the above-mentioned traditional, sex-stereotypic beliefs that downgrade the potential of women and exclude them from active political life (*The 1972 Virginia Slims American Women's Opinion Poll,* 1972).

Another sex-linked stereotype about the "nature" of women that is still somewhat persistent, even among relatively liberated women, is the belief that women are more idealistic, peace-loving, humanitarian, gentle, and antimilitaristic. It is this belief that leads a considerable number of women and men (51 and 56 percent of them, respectively) to believe that, "This country would be better off if women had more to say about politics" (*The 1972 Virginia Slims American Women's Opinion Poll,* 1972). In Canada about one-third of women and men polled believed that Canada would be ruled better if women had more to say in politics, one-third thought that it would make no difference, and 24 percent thought Canada would be worse ruled by women (*The Status of Women in Canada,* 1970). In the same vein, a large percentage of American women and men believe that women would be more sensitive than men to the problems of the underprivileged, more interested in the arts and cultural concerns, but less able to successfully handle unrest and riots, and would be less skilled in international relations and in dealing with issues concerning big business (*The 1972 Virginia Slims American Women's Opinion Poll*, 1972).

This belief syndrome about women is, of course, based upon prevailing sex-stereotypes about women. The fact is totally ignored that women have up to now not had any real significant power, and thus have not been corrupted by it. While it seems true that women legislators and politicians have tended to be somewhat more humanitarian and idealistic, this may well have been due to the fact this was the only option open to them. Since they could not determine whether wars would or would not take place, they resigned themselves to protesting for peace, this being the only avenue of influence considered compatible with their "feminine" character. Idealism came rather easy because they themselves controlled little if any power, did not belong to the powerful political committees where decisions were made, were not part of the inner socially elite circle of male politicians, and were not courted by lobbyists (mainly because they controlled so little power). Under these circumstances, their best bet was being honest and sticking to issues, ideals, and righteousness, and they probably had few temptations to do otherwise (Joseph, 1972; Shanahan, 1972). Furthermore, their inclination has been always socially approved and rewarded as appropriately "feminine," since the men in power could comfortably continue to play their power games and intrigues with worthwhile pay-offs.

Similarly, women's artistic and cultural skills have often been permitted to develop, but only to the extent that they could enjoy and perform music, write poetry, or paint, not so that they could create masterpieces requiring the dedication of a large part of one's life. In this way, women (at least upper-class women) could be kept happily and pleasurably busy outside the masculine world of politics, wars, and power. But even so special care has always been taken so that these women would not take these artistic and cultural interests too seriously, produce something original and inspired, and thus replace their "real" purpose in life (that is, taking care of men and children) by such "secondary" pursuits. In the same way women have been permitted (or even asked) to function in auxilliary political roles (such as doing the busy work in political campaigns for the election of male politicians), but they have been openly or subtly discouraged from becoming political candidates themselves, especially for powerful posts of national importance. Women have been allowed to be "dilettante" politicians but never "real" ones.

The behavior of women up to now vis-à-vis power cannot, however, be taken as a good indication of how women react to power. Once women are given some real power, or even just a taste of it through watching those close to them enjoy it, they seem to change altogether and to behave as most men would in similar circumstances. They very often become authoritarian, rigid, unwilling to delegate control and responsibility, continuously hungry for more and more power, and they seem to lose much of their previous humani-tarianism and idealism. Even at present, when women are not socialized to hold and enjoy power, they seem to do quite well when they "make it." It is a very dangerous illusion to believe that when women obtain power and a greater say in politics, the world will necessarily be "better"; that there will be no wars; that the level of civilization will be higher; that there will be more compassion for the poor and the suffering, less harsh competition, and a more pleasant life. This type of a "social workish" dream world will not happen simply by establishing equality between the sexes and by making it possible for women to become powerful. It is true that at the present time such a vision and a presentation of the potentials of equality between women and men is quite attractive to many people who, discouraged and disgusted by a materialistic, competitive society devoid of ideals and humanitarianism, are looking forward to profound social changes. So they would welcome women in power, if they would automatically bring about important changes toward a more humane, civilized, and just society. But the promise does not seem to be based on solid ground.

It is possible, however, that during the transition, and before the socialization of women is freed of "feminine" sex-stereotypes, at least some women in power may behave in a more humane, cooperative, and status-con-sciousness-free way, at least in middle-range power. Whether or not these "transitional" women will show the same type of behavior when they reach the top and control "real" power remains an interesting empirical question. And whether the redefinition of sex roles and liberation itself will have any profound and long-term effect upon our conception of power so as to break down the rigidity of status hierarchies is even more questionable. But it is possible that we cannot at present very clearly conceptualize and visualize society and relationships once liberation has been achieved.

But let us now examine how sex-stereotypes have influenced, if not determined, the power-directed behavior of women. Leaving history aside, contemporary evidence from a variety of developed nations shows political apathy, ignorance, and lack of active participation on the part of women, even after they obtain the legal right to compete for power. Women in most developed societies (in which voting is not compulsory) tend to abstain from voting to a greater extent than men, but the gap between the two seems to be closing, according to data available for the United States, Canada (*The Status of Women in Canada*, 1970), and the Scandianavian countries (Haavio Mannila, 1972), but not in France (Dogan and Narbonne, 1955; Charzat, 1972). In developing nations, partly because of a number of restrictions that affect women to a greater extent than men (such as literacy), the percentage of women voting has consistently lagged behind that of men (Menon, 1968).

Of course, exercising the right to vote represents an elementary and to some extent misleading indicator of women's political participation and desire to influence or eventually control power. It does show, however, the first step toward breaking down the traditional woman's apathy toward politics and affairs of state. But the available data remind us that the overall trends in women's voting patterns are the same as men's. One quite important difference between the voting behavior of women and men, a difference that is more clear, accentuated, and important in the Western European nations than in the United States and Canada, is that women tend to vote more conservatively than men. Women particularly tend to vote much less for communist and leftist parties and more for "central," conservative, or to the right (but not extreme right) parties. Thus, women seem to be responsible for de Gaulle's election in 1965 and, most probably, for Pompidou's election in 1969, according to preelection Gallup polls in France (Charzat, 1972).

An examination of women's and men's voting patterns after the end of the Second World War showed that, at least in France, Germany, and Italy, it was the women's votes that prevented the establishment of communist regimes in those countries (Stanislas Devaud, 1968). The relative conservatism of women can be attributed partly to their underprivileged status in society and partly to the influence of the stereotypic sex-linked beliefs that render them less adventuresome and daring and less inclined toward radical social changes, protest, and revolutionary social movements.

Furthermore, there is considerable evidence that the majority of women vote as their husbands do. About 85 percent of French wives reported in the mid-50s that they voted as their husbands did, and about one-third of them did so, not because of same ideals and points of view, but because "they were not especially interested in politics and had confidence in their husband's opinion." So, at least in one-third of the cases the wives admitted using their vote to reassure their husbands of their "femininity" and their submission to their superior knowledge and judgment in such profound and "masculine" areas as politics (Dogan and Narbonne, 1955). A similar percentage of American women and men (33 and 37 percent, respectively) believe that, "When it comes to politics, women don't have a mind of their own and tend to vote the way their husbands tell them to" (*The 1972 Virginia Slims American Women's Opinion Poll,* 1972). Recent voting studies show that anywhere from 75 to 95 percent of American women vote as their husbands ("Toward Female Power at the Polls," 1972).

Furthermore, women have not, up to now, supported women candidates to any considerable extent, even in the Scandinavian countries where the prevailing sex ideologies strongly support equality. Obviously, women's voting patterns have been greatly influenced by the sex stereotypes about women's inappropriateness for and inability to obtain and control political power. The available Finnish data from the 1966 parliamentary election show that 5 percent of men and 42 percent of women in Helsinki voted for women, but only 15 percent of women living in small towns and 22 percent of rural women voted the same way (Haavio-Mannila, 1972). Although Finnish women tend to support women candidates more than French or Canadian women, the trend is strong only among urban women.

Here a parenthetical comment must be made on the effect of the existing electoral system and the degree to which women candidates succeed in being elected. It seems that the proportional representation system with single person lists is the least discriminatory system for women (Haavio-Mannila, 1972). The reason for this is the fact that women candidates have the same chance as men to be elected since each candidate's name is listed on a separate ballot rather than tagging the women's names at the end of multiple lists. The recent experience in the 1971 Norway elections clearly demonstrated that a slight change in the electoral proportionate system, such as placing women candidates at the top of the multiple person lists, swung the elections to women. Interestingly enough it was a Norwegian man, Per Hovengen, a journalist, who mobilized women to change the order of women candidates from the bottom of the electoral lists (where they were usually placed due to their "poor" chances to be elected) to the top of these lists. Result: women won forty-eight out of the eighty-five posts on the Municipal Council of Oslo. Similar results were obtained in two other Norwegian cities and in forty other communities (Heymann, 1972).

As in the distribution of women in any given occupation, there is a pyramidal pattern in politics whereby the higher the political position and the greater the power it controls, the smaller the percentage of women occupying such positions. In all countries the percentage of women holding some kind of position at the local level of politics and in low-level political offices is never outstanding or impressive, but is consistently many times higher than the number held at higher levels or at the national level (Duverger, 1955; Gruberg, 1968; Amundsen, 1971). This situation indicates the mode of ongoing change and has important social policy implications. As women start gaining in self-esteem and self-confidence, they start voting for women in positions of low or moderate power, but they still tend to mistrust ambitious and competent women who run for high political posts. Similarly, men find it a much easier and effective "cooling off" process to permit women to enter and win low-level political offices, and then to "freeze" them there rather than to keep them out of politics altogether. In this way aspiring women can be consoled and kept busy with unimportant and extremely time-consuming tasks and activities.

Furthermore, heavy social pressure against women, their own socialization and values, and a number of social-structural conditions make the realization of aspirations for high political office very difficult, if not impossible.

Because most women who enter politics have also been mothers and have had to do most (if not all) of the mothering in their families (due to the high cost and the social stigma of reliant, all-day long "mother substitutes"), they have not usually been able to start their political careers before their children were grown up. This significant delay in entering the political world, resulting in the average older age of women politicians, has tended to handicap women in terms of political experience, exposure, acquaintances, and seniority, all very important factors in a person's political career. Seniority is particularly crucial since it seems to be the basic criterion in the selection of congresswomen or congressmen to chair different committees and subcommittees (Gehlen, 1969).

Due to the prevailing sex stereotypes and the wide-spread discrimination against women in all areas and activities, women have seldom had the personal financial resources or the financial backing of wealthy businessmen and industrialists that would permit them to campaign for a high political office (*The Status of Women in Canada,* 1970; Dogan and Narbonne, 1955). And the doors to the all-important informal, powerful political networks— that determine many crucial decisions and help a candidate create and augment a significant following—have been pretty much closed to women, since they were not "one of the boys."

The influence of sex stereotypes can be further evidenced by the way in which they seem to determine women's behavior and the type of possible political contribution, even when women have "made it to the top," that is, to the congress, the parliament, or the corresponding political body. Women, having received the appropriate socialization and developed the appropriate "feminine" mentality and personality, tend to conform to sex stereotyping that makes them take the floor less often than men and use a different style in presenting their opinions than men.[5] The available French data show that the number of times women take the floor to speak was not different from that of men, but the style of their presentations was quite different. Their presentations and speeches were restricted to "feminine" subjects, such as family, health, housing, pensions, children, and education. Women deputies

---

[5] It is rather interesting that a Chilean congresswoman who in the early 60s tried to break the walls of stereotypic behavior found it very difficult to get a chance to talk and even more difficult to finish what she had to say or to be heard at all in a male-dominated and violence-permeated congress. So she started coming dressed in a cowboy suit, carrying a gun in one hand and a whip in the other. The first time she wanted to talk and they didn't let her, she fired a shot, and whenever they tried to interrupt her through ridicule or by any other means, she would raise her whip and threaten. After a few days, she was accepted and permitted to talk in the same way as her male colleagues.

practically never talked on economic issues, national and foreign policy, national defense, agriculture, or general administrative issues, all subjects considered to be areas of "masculine" competence.

This "feminine" behavior on the part of the women deputies cannot be attributed solely to their socialization, since a more determining factor is probably that women are seldom, if ever, appointed to serve on such male-dominated committees as finance, foreign affairs, national defense, and national public administration, appointments that would give them the necessary authority and knowledge to speak on the subjects (Dogan and Narbonne, 1955).

Recent American data concerning the political careers and behavior of the eleven congresswomen of the Eighty-eighth Congress showed, however, that the committee and subcommittee appointments of women members were spread over all types of committees, including the three most exclusive ones (Rules, Ways and Means, and Appropriations). While no particular "feminine bias" could be detected in the distribution of committee assignments, congresswomen tended more often (but by no means exclusively) to sponsor bills related to "soft" issues (such as consumer affairs, housing, health, special education, national parks, Indian affairs) more compatible with traditional "feminine" concerns (Gehlen, 1969).

Finally, in the 93rd U.S. Congress convened on January 3, 1973, the fourteen women members of the House of Representatives were assigned to some of the important committees. Thus, one (Griffiths of Michigan) is assigned to the Ways and Means Committee, two women to the Appropriations Committee, two women to the Banking and Currency Committee, and two to the Judiciary Committee. It is also important to note that twenty bills of specific concern to women have been introduced to date but many of these proposals involve taxing power. Therefore, the Ways and Means Committee is crucial for the fate of these proposals, a Committee to which only one woman is assigned (*WEAL Washington Report,* 1973).

Similar trends have been documented for most European countries (Stanislas Devaud, 1968), with the exception of Eastern European countries where women holding power are slightly better distributed among different areas of political concerns. For example, in Czechoslovakia in the early 60s the minister of light industry and the deputy chairman of the Parliament were women. In Poland two of the judges on the Supreme Court were women in 1966 (Chylinska, 1968). But even in the Eastern European countries, where the range of occupations in which women engage has been considerably enlarged to include most "masculine" fields, and despite sporadic impressive gains, the degree of sex desegration in political appointments is slow and lagging. In general even when women manage to overcome all the social-structural and internalized barriers to active political participation and manage to get elected, their problems are by no means over. They may still be delegated to committees and functions that are labeled "feminine" because they are women, regardless of their particular backgrounds, abilities, talents, and potential. They may thus be blocked in controlling significant political power, again, regardless of their competence.

Our discussion of the trends in women's political participation has indicated a number of crucial and often unsurpassable obstacles that have important implications for social policy. As we have seen, part of the problem is the internalized barriers to power that women acquire through their socialization. Here, the social policy and action measures already discussed concerning the liberation of the socialization of both girls and boys from sex stereotypes would also help women explore, develop, and satisfy their needs, potentials, skills, and desires for leadership and power, without experiencing conflicts, ridicule, or embarrassment.

But in addition to the overall changes in the socialization process that would free girls' mentality and behavior and would eliminate sex stereotypes and sex-linked behavioral restrictions, a concerted effort must be made to provide girls (at least during the transitional period) with concrete political socialization. Models of women as political leaders and the required skills for influencing large numbers of people, as well as for obtaining and effectively handling power, must be made clear to them. Such an effective political socialization extend the possibility for women to participate actively in politics and to obtain power beyond the small group of elitist women who happen to be born or marry into a "political" family. Since, however, the changes in the socialization process are bound to be slow, because all the scializing agents (parents, teachers, etc.) must thoroughly change their values and behavior, in the transitional stage the accent must be heavily placed upon the creation of appropriate facilitating social-structural conditions for women.

Available evidence from a number of societies indicates the factors that at present constitute the most seriously inhibiting conditions for women to assume and control power. First, discrimination in the nomination process is well documented. Parties have not given priority or serious thought to the recruitment of competent women. Even when such women came forth, they have often been discouraged or discarded on the basis that they would tend to lose votes for the party (Amundsen, 1971; *The Status of Women in Canada,* 1970). Second, the social, economic, social-structural position of women, with the incumbent consequences of financial dependency or limited financial means (due to low-level and low-pay jobs), the exclusive housekeeping and childrearing-child care duties placed upon them, and their limited independent geographic mobility have been significant barriers to important political offices (Amundsen, 1971; *The Status of Women in Canada,* 1970; Dogan and Narbonne, 1955; Charzat, 1972).

The first type of discrimination suggests a series of social policies and actions for the transitional period, continuing until the point can be reached at which it will be sufficient to establish and maintain political recruitment, promotion, nomination, election, and appointment systems that provide women and men with the same options and opportunities. At present, however, it is necessary to establish preferential political systems for recruiting, nominating, promoting, and electing competent, well-qualified women in important political positions. A preferential and well- organized campaign would help women to enter politics and reach high posts. It is crucial and necessary to break society's generalized resistance and reluctance to allow women to control power, a resistance that is often at least to some extent shared by the women themselves—even by those who are interested and actively involved in politics (Gruberg, 1968; Amundsen, 1971).

To some extent such a preferential recruitment and promotion system actually operated in the 1972 American electoral preparations and campaign, especially on the part of the Democratic party. The results were not spectacular, but women are now better represented in the Congress, and, probably more important, many of them are concerned with sexism. They may further aid political reforms that will encourage greater political participation of women.[6] As we noted earlier, fourteen women are in the 93rd Congress of the U.S., and twenty bills concerning women have already been proposed and are being actively supported by women representatives. Furthermore, the existence of the newly formed Women Lobby, Inc., a political lobby for women's issues, might further help stimulate and enhance the congresswomen's action-orientation and effectiveness ("Women's Lobby to Pressure for Women's Issues," 1972).

But nomination and election of women as candidates is not sufficient. They cannot wage an effective and successful campaign unless the obstacles mentioned above associated with their "feminine" role are removed or at least alleviated. Thus, unless the women candidates are single, or have no small children and considerably liberated husbands, they will meet unsurmountable problems, even if their party provides them with necessary financial and public relations resources to continue an active campaign. Of course, the eventual liberation of women and men would make these sex-linked obstacles disappear, but until this is achieved special measures must be taken by the political parties to help women overcome these difficulties.

Nobody, however, can change a candidate's husband so that he supports, facilitates, and encourages his wife to become active in politics. In addition to and in support of the socialization process that women must receive and give their husbands, mass media could do a lot to promote and reward the image of the supporting, liberated husband, and to ridicule

---

[6] It is important to note that in Finland, the sex role debate in the 60s (corresponding to the American Women's Liberation Movement) led to the election of women in 21.5 percent of parliament posts, a considerable increase over the past (Haavio-Mannila, 1972).

the intolerant husband who continuously torpedos his wife's plans and efforts.

Women must be preferentially recruited and nominated until their representation is proportionate to the population. Such a preferential system is necessary during the transitional stage (1) to establish the image of the woman candidate for the public; and (2) to facilitate the breakdown of sex stereotypes and women's and men's resistance to voting for women, especially in high and powerful positions. For after all, it must not be forgotten that only a small minority of women (one out of six, the majority of which are single or black) would be *more* likely to vote for a woman than for an equally well-qualified man for president of the United States. Two out of five women would be *less* likely to vote for the woman. In the case of men, only 7 percent would vote for a women president, and 49 percent would prefer the male candidate (and for 39 percent there would be no difference between the two). Acceptance of a woman as vice president is only slightly better to American women and men. Both envisage a woman president of the United States might become a reality only in the very distant future (in about fifty years)—later than a black or a Jew might have become president (*The 1972 Virginia Slims American Women's Opinion Poll*, 1972). A great deal of change in the image of women in power will have to take place in the United States before the majority of women and men are willing to support and vote women into powerful political positions.

One specific policy that might be most helpful is temporary establishment of a federal directive according to which one of the two senators from each state must be a woman. The same type of policy should be also applied at the state level whenever the same principle of representation is in operation. This type of transitional policy would not only help make the image of women appropriately political, but would also provide competent and qualified women with valuable political experience for higher offices. Actually, such a recommendation was recently made in Canada by the Royal Commission on the Status of Women (*The Status of Women in Canada*, 1970).

It is striking that recent opinion polls taken in France and Canada show that the majority of French women (72 percent) would accept a woman as president of the Republic and consider this quite possible (57 percent) (Charzat, 1972). The majority (75 percent) of Canadian respondents (women and men) said they would vote for a well-qualified woman chosen by the party as the candidate for the presidency (*The Status of Women in Canada*, 1970). Why this difference in attitudes between American and the Canadian and French public opinion? One cynical interpretation may be that for the Canadians and the French the probability of actually having to vote for a woman candidate for presidency very soon is rather small, while the same probability in the United States may in fact be greater (or may be perceived as being greater), and hence is much more real and threatening.

Another necessary social action is the drastic reorganization and refocusing of all types of women's organizations, particularly women's political organizations, so that recruiting, promoting, nominating, and campaigning for women candidates becomes their main goal and activity. Women's organizations should become especially active in raising money in support of well-qualified women candidates and in organizing a dynamic and effective campaign among all segments of the population.[7] Such action is essential during the transitional period, and might not be needed once there is in fact no difference in the recruitment and treatment of female and male candidates.

Another source of power, that provided by trade unions, has up to now been largely underutilized by women. Women in most countries have joined unions at a much lower rate than men, and as union members have tended to strike and fight for their rights less frequently and less poignantly (Charzat, 1972). In the United States out of 28 million working women, only 3.7 million are organized into trade unions. Most of the nonunionized women are office workers, and the others are domestic workers, farm workers, and retail sales workers. Most office workers have not been willing to unionize because they have been "brainwashed" by their employers to think that this is something only for lowly menial, blue-collar workers (Edelman, 1970).

The reality of the very small, or nonexistent, power that American women enjoy when unionized (and even within unions with a large female membership) becomes blatant when the percentage of women office-holders is examined. In 1968 (as in 1958) only 4.6 percent of all union officials listed in the Bureau of Labor Statistic's biennial directory were women. This percentage is, however much higher in a few unions, such as the International Union of Electrical, Radio, and Machine Workers or the Associated Actors and Artists of America. Furthermore, the percentage of women office-holders in local unions generally fares much better than in national unions where it seldom passes tokenism (Dewey, 1971; Cook, 1968).

A significantly greater participation of women as union members and office-holders is of great importance not only in that it would provide invaluable political attitudes, training, and skills, but also in that it would promote equality between working women and men. As things stand now many union and nonunion shops have different categories for women's and men's jobs that provide men with the more prestigious, responsible, and better-paid jobs (Cook, 1968). Unions often write separate agreements covering women's and men's jobs and are not sensitive or interested in

---

[7] It seems that increasingly these policies are being put into effect. In Detroit, for example, active academic women organized, raised money, and actively supported a women attorney for member of the board of trustees of Wayne State University.

women's issues, such as provisions for child care, paid maternity leaves with no loss of seniority, adequate maternity medical coverage, etc. A great number of issues have to be negotiated, bargained, and fought over before equality is achieved between working women and men and before women can learn how to obtain and utilize power in unions.

In the last few years there are indications that women's active participation in existing unions, initiative in unionizing, and their willingness to fight for their rights is growing and intensifying. Different types of women workers, such as saleswomen, gas station attendants, meat cutters, and butchers, are increasingly organizing, striking, and fighting for their rights (Jordan, 1972, 1972a; Maupin, 1972). The Harvard Square Waitresses Union, a grass-roots organization, made headlines in many newspapers across the United States for the tenacity and courage of the women involved as well as for the degree of sympathy received from the entire Cambridge community (Bingham, Golden, and Newman, 1972). In the case of the Farah Company, which fired or arrested striking and picketing women workers, women have been urged by the vice president of the International Union, United Automobile, Aerospace, and Agricultural Implement Workers of America–United Auto Workers to boycott Farah slacks for men and boys ("Don't Buy Slacks for Men and Boys, Says Olga M. Madar," 1972).

In order to achieve a stronger representation of women among important union leaders, a helpful transitional policy may be the organization both of women's unions for workers in specific occupations or trades and of women union members across many different skills and trades. Such organizations could serve a very important function in familiarizing women with organizational, structural, and political problems and in permitting them to gain valuable political experience. Such an effort is the Women's Alliance to Gain Equality (W.A.G.E.), comprised of women from forty different unions. Such union alliances are also important because they can make it possible for women to participate actively through providing child care facilities at reasonable rates.

It must be stressed, however, that the policy of women's unions, or women's departments within a union, or alliances of women unionists across occupations is only transitional and must not be institutionalized as the "Women's Department" as has happened in many European countries. Probably union alliances such as W.A.G.E. are preferable to other temporary solutions because they have less of a chance of becoming institutionalized and leading to compartmentalization within each union on the basis of gender.

Social Policy to Liberate Religion

While the different religions of early societies included several female goddesses of varying importance, most religions in the last twenty centuries have been patriarchal and male-dominated. The image of the Supreme Being or Beings is consistently masculine in Buddhism, Christianity, Islamism, or Judaism, and women in their contexts are considered to be "impure," sinful, and inferior. There is, however, an important theological controversy about the extent to which the original formulation of the religious philosophies were sexist and the extent to which only the superstructures of institutionalized religions and the inflexible interpretations of the original religion are sexist.

Thus, a professor of Islamic civilization has recently argued that the content of the Koran, instead of being permeated by sexism, contains safeguards for women's equality with men. The Koran affirms that both the woman and the man descend from the same soul (a good beginning for a spiritual equality) and recommends that the husband treat his wives (since he could have four) with absolute justice. Furthermore, the Koran gave the woman the right to own and manage her dowry, as well as the right to go to the Cadi for the correction of financial and familial injustices. The same professor claims that this treatment of women in the Koran can be considered "feminist" for the epoch and the social conditions under which it was written (Arnaldez, 1966). But the evolution of the interpretations of the Koran by the organized Islamic religion through time has become increasingly sexist, following closely and greatly influenced by the overall sexist trends in the Arab society and the male-dominated structure of the organized religious body.

Similarly, many Christian theologians argue that despite the fact that the Redeemer, Jesus, was the son and not the daughter of God, he talked freely with women and treated them as equal to men; and the first witnesses to his resurrection were three women. Furthermore, some theologians argue that the fact that Jesus and the Twelve Apostles were men can be understood in terms of the social conditions of the time that would have made the choice of women "unreasonable" and "farfetched." Some go even further and in a cavalier manner point out that the fact that Eve came from Adam's rib and not his foot indicates equality between the two. They even try to explain St. Paul's misogynic admonitions to the Corinthians in terms of Corinth's ethnic composition ("Father God, Mother Eve," 1972). Also in early Christian fellowship women were included equally and actively participated in the "banquets of Christian love." Women in early Christianity defended Christianity, proselytized others, and died for it under tortures with the same fervor as men.

However, despite the originally almost equal treatment of women by Jesus and the early Christian fellowship, the writings of the church fathers and the entire organized religion became sexist, partly because it reflected the tendencies and social conditions of the time. Thus, the "natural" inferiority of women, their impurity, and evil "nature" were established and took on a particular force and aura because of the stamp of divine approval that made sex stereotypes a part of an immutable "divine plan" (Daly, 1970). The vested interests of the hierarchical clergy, who controlled large fortunes and an extraordinary degree of power throughout most of European history, did keep the organized religion strictly male and contributed to the development of further "sacred" rationalizations for sexism in the church.

While all Christian religions share the same attitudes toward women and the same sex stereotyping, the Catholic Church has been most criticized from inside and outside for having most clearly accentuated these sex stereotypes and for still adamantly resisting any change in this area. Pope John the XXIII's *Pacem in Terris* conveyed an authentic recognition of women's equality with men, but since then the official Catholic position seems to have retrogressed. Women having authority or becoming "intellectual" are deemed "unnatural" and "defeminized" (Daly, 1970). The Catholic Church has not admitted women in its clergy while most other churches have already ordained women (Algrin, 1960; "Father God, Mother Eve," 1972; Bock, 1967). Of course, in the United States (but not in Sweden) many of these women clergy still occupy a rather marginal position, are not fully accepted, and are not granted all the rights, privileges, and functions of male clergy (Bock, 1967). But the beginning has been made, and as the status of American women improves, pressures will mount to fully integrate and empower female clergy.

Since up to now and in all religions ministry has been exclusively masculine and the image of God has been male, many theologians are in agreement that these facts have caused God to be personified and thought of in personal, male terms rather than in impersonal, abstract, spiritual terms (Cox as quoted in Miller and Swift, 1972). Recently feminist documents (directed at all Christian churches) of the Women's Task Force of the United Church of Christ declared references to God exclusively in the male gender as "heresy" and the exaltation of males as superiors as "idolatry" (Blau, 1972). In order to finally be able to abstract God and religion, all the sexist superstructures and rationalizations have to be removed from the current religious formulations. The ordination of women and their full integration at all levels (including top positions) seems to be the consistent expression of nonmale-dominated and "nonidolatrous" religions, despite the present reluctance of some women to become ordained in religions permeated by sexism.

Most theologians and women active in the struggle to liberate religion from sexism are not interested in developing a theology of women or institutionalized religious structures dominated by and only for the sake of women, as Claire Randall, head of Church Women United, a nationwide organization of active Protestant, Catholic, and Orthodox women recently declared. The ultimate goal is to infuse the new concepts of Women's Liberation into the mainstream of the religion, and to, therefore, increase the relevance and validity of religion for women's lives at present and in the future (Blau, 1972).

In order, however, for women to take a truly equal place with men in most religions, there is a need for a rather drastic theological reconceptualization of women. Thomas Aquinas' reduction of women's "theological significance to a biologically determined and divinely intended natural function: the reproduction of human creatures that still significantly influences Christian religions" (Maxey, 1972) must be replaced. Since research evidence from many fields has clearly shown that human sexuality does not primarily or essentially exist for reproductive purposes, theologian Margaret Maxey argues that the exploration of appropriate conditions and criteria for self-disclosures could provide a new set of data and bases for the new conceptualization of Woman and Man. This new conceptualization, Maxey believes, would not only free theology from sexism but would also be compatible with needed reforms and action regarding contraception, abortion, means of genetic control, as well as the issue of celibacy among priests. For, as she points out, the main rationale for celibacy was the desire that priests remain "pure" by not intimately associating with woman, and avoid distracting themselves from their holy service by having sexual intercourse with women (Maxey, 1972). The availability of a reconceptualized and reformulated theology is necessary if theology and religion are to be liberated.

While women and men theologians are groping with the reformulation of religions that would free them of patriarchal hangups and sexist biological models, and that would reflect the current equalitarian sex-role ideology, the best social policy for hastening theological reforms and changing the image of churches and religions seems to be greater active participation by women in all facets and levels of organized religion. The Union Theological Seminary passed a rule, according to which women must comprise one-half of all students, faculty, staff, and directors, the goal to be reached gradually within a few years, and to be implemented in all institutions of religious training (Fiske, 1972). Interested women who are barred from religious training on the basis of their gender might be able to sue the administrative boards for unconstitutional educational policy. Once admitted they can exert significant pressure for educational reforms, not only in the admission policies but also in the content of the courses taught. The recent case where a single female rabbinical student exerted some pressure, and made public statements about changes needed in Judaism to reflect equal status for women and men illustrates the importance of the presence of women students in previously all-male religious schools (Dugan, 1972).

There is also a great need for women who belong to and are active in a religion, and who are involved in studying the religious documents to clearly delineate how present religious conceptualizations discriminate against women and downgrade them to second-class status. It also is important to show clearly and publicize widely how current religious practices, beliefs, and concepts are incompatible with the present status of women, as well as with the laws and policies followed by the entire society, and a growing equalitarian ideology. Such actions as the ones recently taken by young Conservative and Orthodox Jewish women which aimed at "modernizing" and "liberating" Judaism (Nemy, 1972) must be multiplied for each religion and within each religion by different groups of women—and hopefully men too.

Multi-denominational special services, such as the one recently held on Reformation Sunday as "sister celebration" by feminist women of different religions in various parts of the Unites States (Blau, 1972), may also serve a very useful function in showing that liberated women feel alienated by the sexism in religious doctrines and practices, by the contents of the Bible and other religious documents. Through the actions of women within all religions and the discussions of liberated women theologians, it is becoming increasingly clear that all religions have to gain wider acceptance and influence among women (but also among men) by implementing modernizing and liberating reforms that would make them compatible with the social reality and ideology of the 70s.

Chapter 6

SOME REFLECTIONS
AND CONCLUSIONS

One of our basic assumptions not dealt with in Chapter 1 is that the Women's Liberation Movements in the United States and other Western nations will become increasingly more vocal, active, and powerful. At the same time, a growing number of women (and men), whether they formally join an active organization or not, will become more conscious of sexism in themselves and in society and will try to liberate themselves, as well as whatever aspect of the society they are particularly interested in and concerned with, or over which they can exert some kind of pressure and influence. Contrary to the wishful thinking of those women and men who are threatened by the existence, blossoming, and spread of the Women's Liberation Movement, there is no indication at all that the Movement and its goals are a merely passing fad that will be soon shelved with "midis" and pointed high-heeled shoes. On the contrary, all present indications point toward a mushrooming, not necessarily in numbers of formal members, but rather in terms of the influence the Movement has on people and in the nonsexist social policies and actions being implemented every day.

Even in countries where women had already made significant progress in educational and occupational liberation or advanced social policies combatting sexism, women are starting to organize into women's protest groups to advance liberation further and in more life sectors, and enforce existing laws and policies. Such active polemical groups have formed in Finland, Sweden (the "Group Eight"), and in East Germany.

Of course, gains toward liberation are by no means expected to follow a linear model consistently. On the contrary, because of the existing degree of divisiveness among women along different lines and most men's strong emotional resistance in guarding their vested interests, the road to liberation is expected to have many ups and downs (and several plateaus) before set goals can be achieved. Men in power will use the already reported blocking tactic of "playing up divisiveness within the women's ranks" and accusing active white middle-class women of not representing all women, even when they try to organize women clerical, technical, or service workers (Holden, 1972), or attempt to change welfare laws discriminatory to low-income women. And men may give power to women who choose to side with them against those who wish to put an end to sexism, only to use them as powerful proofs that there is no sexism and that the antisexist demands of other women and men are meaningless and nonsensical. Several middle-aged women known to be indifferent, if not hostile, to the Women's Liberation Movement and their proposals for change have already been appointed by powerful men to important decision-making positions; they can be trusted not to side with activist women and overturn the "applecart."

The existence of women who are indifferent or hostile to the Women's Liberation Movement itself and its goals is to some extent a generational occurrence. It is more prevalent among women over thirty than under thirty (*The 1972 Virginia Slims American Women's Opinion Poll*, 1972). Their numbers would therefore tend to diminish with new generations.[1] But it can be expected that as long as a considerable number of sexist men have power, at least some women will side with them. They will have considerable benefits and power to gain from this alliance. And as long as such dissenting women exist, sexist men in power will use them to legitimize their own sexist behavior (Dofny, 1970).

Under increasing political and social pressures, men will have to go beyond tokenism not only to relinquish marginal power positions, but also to give up some essential power posts. They will fight rearguard battles as long as they can. Women and the men who join in fighting sexism will have to persist in their efforts without becoming overjoyed, relaxing when significant victories are won, or becoming discouraged when ground is lost, or when little or nothing is happening as a result of pressures and actions they are engaged in. They must persist despite and against all odds, for it is going to be a long-range and difficult road to liberation.

---

[1] There are, however, some indications that as the Women's Liberation Movement becomes more institutionalized, successful, and better understood by women, some established women over thirty are joining it. They lend it more "respectability," credibility, and prestige. Men in power cannot dismiss them as "young activist" women who will forget all this nonsense as soon as they get married and have children (or simply as soon as they "have a man"). Also, these often-successful women have considerable experience, contacts, and some influence (and maybe a little power) that can be valuable to the Movement (Salpukas, 1972).

A recent study of the treatment of the American liberation movement by newspapers in Los Angeles showed that several distinct stages can be discerned. At first the Movement was totally ignored (in the hope that like a "bad dream" it might vanish away) while it was experiencing tremendous growth. Second, beginning in 1969, the Movement began to be mentioned, mainly in order to be satirized, ridiculed, or criticized. Third, only toward the end of 1970, did it become clear to editors and journalists that the Movement was there to stay after all the mass media's ridicule and mistreatment. As it gained momentum, the newspapers started presenting it in a more objective, unbiased, and somewhat favorable light (Morris, 1972).

These same stages that were followed by the Los Angeles newspapers in their treatment of the Women's Movement seem to have been followed by most media in most cities. The only difference may be that some newspapers or TV programs started ridiculing and criticizing the Movement a little earlier than the Los Angeles newspapers. And some prominent newspapers, such as the New York Times, did not start seriously and frequently dealing with issues and subjects connected with the Women's Movement until the beginning of 1971.

Analysis of the content of the more recent objective and informative articles and "news" about the Women's Movement published in the Los Angeles newspapers showed that certain goals and aims were usually presented. The prediction is that it is exactly this set of goals and aims that will gain public support, even from people who are basically against the whole idea of a Women's Liberation Movement. All these goals and aims have one common characteristic: they are in agreement with the central ideological tenets of the society, and their achievement can be managed without radical, social, or psychological change. The opening up and equalization of educational, occupational, and employment options for women and men fit in with this characteristic (Morris, 1972). Even people like Adelson (1972) and Etzioni (1972), two male social scientists who find the whole ideal of the Women's Movement frivolous and amusing, are willing to compromise and accept educational, occupational, and pay equity between the sexes.

It is exactly this trend that represents serious danger for the success of the American and some beginning Western European Women's Liberation Movements. The fact that very few people can seriously oppose women's educational, occupational, and employment liberation anymore, that they may be willing to grant them this kind of liberation to appease all the women, represents a temptation and a danger not to advance the Movement beyond this point. For it is when demands are made for liberation in other areas, that men throw up their hands and ask in amazement, "But what *do* these women want?" And the resistance really mounts when women demand a sizable piece of political or economic power; or when they demand the actual redefinition of the sex roles that will permit the psychological, sexual, and familial liberation of women and men; or if women demand that the language, history, therapy, the law, and religion undergo drastic changes to become free of sexism. The resistance to all these types of liberation is high because their realization would require several significant and drastic changes that would alter the basis of all women-to-men relationships and, to a considerable extent, the societal structure and dynamics.

The Finnish, Russian, and Eastern European model has existed for many years and can serve as a reminder of the existing danger that the educational, occupational, and employment liberation of women can be achieved to a remarkable degree without making any progress in any other type of liberation. Women in the Movement must be on guard not to become satisfied with relatively easy victories that may not be too far off and abandon their efforts. They must insist and persist from generation to generation until liberation in all areas has been achieved.

Another possible problem which the Women's Movements must be aware of is the possibility of a fairly quick, favorable change in public opinion that can take place when a sufficiently large portion of the population begins to support them. This is exactly what has happened in Sweden and was recently reported to be happening in Finland (Haavio-Mannila, 1972). The dangers of a quick, premature reversal in public opinion, before significant changes have taken place in the social structure, the different types of social policies, and in the behavior of men (and women), is that it finally becomes only lip service to the righteousness of the Movement. The Swedish experience indicates that the politicians', administrators', and other influential men's lip service to the Movement does not aid or speed in any special way the liberation process. It is pleasant when it occurs, but it may be dangerously misleading, if it gives Movement leaders and all the active, liberated individuals the impression that they have won the battle, and that from there on things will move without any special effort.

There are some indications that the process of giving widespread "accreditation" to the Movement is well on its way. Political candidates of all parties are trying to do "something" about women and to include some mention of their issues in their campaign speeches. It is good that this official "accreditation" has started but it does not mean much. All the battles are still to be won, one by one.

Women must keep another very important prediction (or fact?) in mind: Very little legislative and social policy change will come from above unless they continuously protest and demand these changes. Politicians will not yield power to women and will not bring about significant changes unless they are pressured. Actually, liberation can be won only if each individual woman does all she can to pressure, protest, and bring about changes—and there is a lot that each individual can do. All women have some valuable talent resources, some have money, others have legal skills, others can teach women and men at different educational levels, others are counselors or therapists, others have significant political experience and connections, and others have time—to mention only a few.

American women (as well as women in other nations) who have inherited large sums of money and have established foundations could assign a sizable part of their foundation funds to activities advancing and facilitating the aims and goals of the liberation of women (and men). Funds would become available not only for research through government funding agencies and the major foundations, but also for prizes for the best-liberated children's book, the best-liberated television program and movie, the best-liberated theater play, the best-liberated novel, or for the most liberated man in the United States. These funds could also be accessible for financing significant lawsuits, the outcome of which could be critical for the entire future of women's and men's liberation, or for sponsoring entire television programs that would project new images of women and men and advance their psychological and familial liberation.

Similarly, wives of businessmen could play an important role by pressuring their husbands not to sponsor television and radio programs that project sexist images or that show advertisements with sexist content. Women teachers and professors at all levels can not only have considerable influence through what they teach their students and what textbooks they use, but they can also exert considerable pressure on administrators, publishers, and colleagues, especially if they organize and have good channels of communication with city, state, and national women's organizations. Actually both teachers and students have considerable power. An increasingly large number of women teach large undergraduate courses as teaching assistants, instructors, and assistant professors, and a large body of women take undergraduate courses in universities and community colleges. All these women have not yet realized their consumer power and the significant changes they can help bring about by refusing to take courses offered by sexist professors or by refusing to adopt sexist textbooks. Such kinds of pressure are urgently needed to convince publishers that they can no longer make money on sexist textbooks and that a sexist reputation can have serious profit and prestige repercussions. Also such pressures would help stigmatize sexism as an immoral and punishable behavior.

This, of course, does not mean that all women must exert pressure on all kinds of issues that relate to the liberation of women and societal institutions. Some of them may prefer to channel their energy and contributions to writing sexism-free textbooks in their fields, to doing research in a relevant subject, or to giving speeches or conducting consciousness-raising sessions for different groups of women or women and men within or outside their work setting. Others may prefer to concentrate their efforts on counseling and guiding students. Still others may prefer to act within the framework of an organized women's group. But whatever their preference and choice, all women can play an extremely important role in the liberation process.

Women lawyers are already playing a key role in several women's organizations and in the formulations of official protests, lawsuits, proposals, resolutions, and demands. But a woman does not have to have any particular skill or resource in order to make valuable contributions. Any woman (or man) who wants and is willing to dedicate some of her time to some kind of activity or effort that can advance liberation can find a valuable contribution she can make to advance liberation a step forward.

While all women's individual contributions mentioned up to now refer mostly to middle- and upper-middle-class women, the implication is by no means that only these women can make significant contributions or that the Movement is relevant and meaningful only to them. Actually, recent survey data show quite clearly that twice as many black women (67 percent) are sympathetic to the efforts of "Women's Liberation Groups." Slightly more women with an income under $5,000 (45 percent) than with an income of more than $15,000 (41 percent) are sympathetic to the efforts of Women's Liberation. Also 71 percent of all women find that "if women don't speak up for themselves and confront men on their real problems, nothing will be done about these problems" (*The 1972 Virginia Slims American Women's Opinion Poll,* 1972). It seems, then, that the goals and ideals of the Women's Liberation Movement have reached the consciousness of many women—across classes and races—and have become relevant and meaningful to them (Etheridge, 1972). Most women accept the idea that women have to stand up for their rights, but, as the same survey indicated, some of the radical rhetoric and protest style used by women in the Movement, as well as the image that mass media have projected of it, may tend to alienate many women in all classes and races.

There are, furthermore, indications that middle class women in the Movement have in the last years focused their efforts upon organizing and politicizing different categories of working women (such as clerical women, cleaning women, waitresses) and welfare women with varying degrees of success. Usually clerical women seem to resist being organized and demanding equal types of position titles and salaries when performing the same duties and functions. Many of them are quite conservative and are reluctant to enter "protest politics" (Holden, 1972). But the signs are there that at least some of the ideals and the goals of the Women's Liberation Movement are affecting all categories of women (Hatch and Henderson, 1971). In many cases, new types of strategies, approaches, and solutions will have to be thought of for different categories of women that would be more compatible with their present values, needs, and aspirations. The middle- and upper-middle-class model of liberation and liberating social action and strategies may not be equally applicable to women in other social classes.

All discussions of problems, social changes, strategies, and social poli- cies throughout the book are mostly relevant to developed societies. There- fore, a number of questions can be raised: But what about the developing societies? How is the prevailing sexism in them to be combated and even- tually eliminated? Which of the discussed social policies, strategies, and social action programs are relevant? Who can exert pressure to adopt such policies, legislations and action programs?

For many developing nations, the liberation of women (and men) from unwanted multiple births and from the social desirability of many children (especially many sons) is a basic necessity for the further liberation of women as well as for national and economic development. All the avail- able experiences and evaluation research findings of family planning pro- grams consistently show that freedom from great numbers of births cannot result unless women and men manage to reach a higher level of "liberation" in many life sectors, both at the psychological and social level. Therefore, legal, accessible, and free-of-cost abortion (at least to low-income women) is just about the only short-range, effective means of birth control.

But who can bring about a higher level of consciousness in women and men and effectively exert pressure for necessary social changes? In most developing nations upper-middle- and upper-class women are the ones who have considerable education and most often important positions and political power. But it is doubtful that such women would initiate significant social changes to aid urban and rural women in all social classes to make some steps toward liberation. These educated and often powerful women are in many cases as sexist as the men in power.

Most probably, significant social changes could come about through the indirect intervention of international organizations through the dif- ferent assistance programs extended to developing nations. Thus, once dif- ferent program directors, because they are themselves liberated or because of pressures they receive from the major contributing nations, would be willing to initiate and support sexism-free programs and activities, the ap- propriate negotiations could take place with the governments of the devel- oping nations. In this way, for example, vocational training programs supported by the International Labor Office, different types of educational programs supported by UNESCO, and training programs for girls and women supported by different international organizations could free them- selves of the limitations of the traditional sex roles, and play an innovative and constructive role in the liberation and independence of women and men in developing nations. In other words, the stimulation for liberating social changes in most developing nations may have to come from outside, mainly through the different types of aid and intervention programs supported by developed nations or by different international organizations. The developed nations must, therefore, achieve a certain level of liberation before they might be able to stimulate strategies, programs, and social policies to aid liberation in developing nations. Innovations will tend to be relatively easy because of the organizations' prestige, particularly that attached to different UN programs, and because of their claim to scientific expertise and offers of financial aid.

With respect to projections about the future of society and man-woman relationships after liberation is achieved, all believers (including the author) tend to have idealized conceptions. An ideal image of the future is, however, a necessary motivating force for all those who put their time and energy into fighting sexism, as well as for all women and men going through the different stages of liberation. The entire transition to liberation is quite slow and painful, and there has to be a reward for undergoing traumatic experiences. All who believe in the desirability of liberation want and need to believe that eventually life, society, and all the relationships between women and men will be much more honest, open, and rewarding than they are at present.

However, it must be admitted that all is speculation. And the accuracy of the speculations is impeded by the fact that sexism and traditional sex-role appropriate values, behaviors, and beliefs have for so long permeated all aspects of our lives that it is extremely difficult to estimate all their direct and indirect effects. Because the image of liberated women and men living in a liberated society represents such a drastic change from familiar images and experiences, it is probably difficult to make accurate predictions. Probably even when we try to speculate we stick too close to the present reality, in the same way as many science fiction writers cannot imagine and describe altogether different images and realities. And we probably cannot grasp all the new complexities involved in a new model of society and interpersonal relations.

Prediction of all the possible side effects and indirect effects that liberation may have at the psychological or the social level and the complexities that might arise becomes even more difficult, because, during the same time that the battle against sexism will be taking place and liberation achieved, a number of other major social and biological changes will most probably be taking place simultaneously. Such changes as racial equality, a more egalitarian income distribution system, changes in international trade laws and international cooperation, genetic progress permitting control of inherited qualities and gender, prolongation of life expectancy, etc., could be expected to have side effects and indirect and unpredicted effects. Some changes and effects might be compatible with and reinforcing to liberation efforts and goals, others might be neutral, and others antagonistic or even mutually exclusive with liberation. In view of all these complicated and often unpredictable factors involved in speculations about the future of society and man-woman relationships, all predictions and projections offered throughout this work must be read with such limitations in mind.[2]

Finally, we could conclude that, despite the fact that the future of society and human relationships may in fact not prove to be as ideal as described in this book, there is little doubt that it will be much better than at present. At least women and men will have reached a higher level of awareness, self determination, and openness in options that they may use wisely. Their chances for happiness and self-actualization could be very good.

[2] From personal communication regarding the second draft of this book, with Jacques Dofny, November 10, 1972.

REFERENCES

Abstract of Protocol on Justice Department Matters Held Before the King in Council.
    1969   Safiero, Sweden (August 15) (mimeographed).

ADELSON, JOSEPH.
    1972   "Is Women's Lib a Passing Fad?" *The New York Times Magazine* (March 19).

Affirmative Action Plan to Improve Employment Opportunities for Minority Groups and Women.
    1972   Detroit: Detroit City Plan Commission (May 24).

"AIC Survey Shows Many Women Feel $$ Discrimination but Less So in Education; 153 Respond."
    1971   *The Chemist,* XLVIII, No. 8 (August), 204–5.

ALGRIN, KARIN.
    1969   "Eve and Martha—But What About Mary?" *Hertha,* No. 5, 64–67.

"American Nurses's Association Files Sex Discrimination Charges Against TIAA."
    1973   *Women Today,* Vol. 3, No. 6 (March 19), 2.

"American Personnel and Guidance Association Cites Vocational Test for Sex Bias."
    1972   Washington, D.C.: Association of American Colleges (June).

AMUNDSEN, KIRSTEN.
  1971 *The Silenced Majority: Women and American Democracy.*
         Englewood Cliffs, N.J.: Prentice-Hall.

ARNALDEZ, ROGER.
  1966 "Le Coran et l'Emancipation de la Femme," in *La Femme à
         la Recherche d'elle-même.* Paris-Geneva: La Palatine, pp. 38–
         54.

BADER GINSBURG, RUTH.
  1971 "Treatment of Women by the Law: Awakening Consciousness
         in the Law Schools," *Valparaiso University Law Review,* Vol.
         5, 480–88.

BANNON, JAMES.
  1973 "Institutional Sexism in the Criminal Justice System." Paper
         prepared for the Wayne State University Seminar on the
         Sociology of Women, March.

BARKER, G.R.
  1972 "La Femme en Union soviétique," *Sociologie et Societé,* Vol. 4,
         No. 2 (November), 159–91.

BARRON, NANCY.
  1971 "Sex-Typed Language: The Production of Grammatical
         Cases," *Acta Sociologica,* Vol. 14, No. 1–2 (Winter), 24–42.

BARTELL, GILBERT D.
  1971 *Group Sex.* New York: New American Library.

BART, PAULINE.
  1970a "Portnoy's Mother's Complaint," *Trans-Action,* Vol. 8, Nos.
         1/2 (Nov.–Dec.).

———.

  1970b "Divorced Men and Their Children: A Study of Emerging
         Roles," paper presented at the American Sociological Associa-
         tion Meetings, Washington, D.C.

———.

  1973 "Depression: A Sociological Theory," in Paul M. Roman and
         Harrison Trice, eds., *The Sociology of Psychotherapy.* New
         York: Science House, Inc.

BAZELL, ROBERT J.
  1970 "Sex Discrimination: Campuses Face Contract Loss Over
         HEW Demands," *Science,* Vol. 170 (November), 834–35.

BENDER, MARILYN.
  1971 "Executive Couples, Reluctance to Hire Husbands and Wives
         Is Fading," *The New York Times* (October 24).

————.

1972a "Business Discovers Women," *The New York Times* (June 9).

————.

1972b "Living with the Law on Women's Jobs," *The New York Times* (November 5).

————.

1972c "Corporate Tokenism for Women," *The New York Times* (February 20).

BERNARD, JESSIE.
1972 *The Future of Marriage*. New York: World Book.

————.

1971a *Women and the Public Interest*. Chicago: Aldine-Atherton, Inc.

————.

1971b "The Paradox of the Happy Housewife," in Vivian Gornick and Barbara K. Moran, eds., *51 Percent*. New York: Basic Books.

BERNHEIM, NICOLE.
1968 "Suedoises et Polonaises: deux examples d'intégration sociale," *Le Monde* (January).

BINGHAM, LIZA, MEREDITH GOLDEN, AND HOLLY NEWMAN.
1972 "Harvard Square Waitresses Strike," *The Second Wave*, Vol. 1, No. 4, 3–5.

BIRNBAUM, J. A.
1971 "Life Patterns, Personality Style and Self Esteem in Gifted Family-Oriented and Career Committed Women," unpublished Ph.D. dissertation, University of Michigan.

BLAKE, DAVIS, JUDITH.
1971 "Abortion and Public Opinion: The 1960–70 Decade," *Science*, Vol. 171 (February), 540–49.

BLAU, ELEANOR.
1972 "We Fell for All That," *The New York Times* (November 5).

BLEIER, RUTH.
1971 "Women and the Wisconsin Experience," paper delivered at the annual meeting of Women's Commission of Modern Languages Association (December 29).

BLOOD, ROBERT O., JR. AND DONALD M. WOLFE.
1960 *Husbands and Wives*. New York: The Free Press.

BOCK, E. WILBUR.
1967 "The Female Clergy: A Case of Professional Marginality," *American Journal of Sociology*, Vol. 72, No. 5 (March), 531–39.

BONDURANT, SUSAN.
    1972   "It's All Right Doc—I'm Only Dying," *Rough Times,* Vol. 3, No. 1 (September), 10.

BROVERMAN, INGE K., et al.
    1970   "Sex-Role Stereotypes and Clinical Judgments of Mental Health," *Journal of Consulting and Clinical Psychology,* Vol. 34, 1–7.

BUBER AGASSI, JUDITH.
    1972   "Women Who Work in Factories," *Dissent* (Winter), 233–39.

CEKALA, CYNTHIA.
    1972   "If This Be Insanity. . . ," *Rough Times,* Vol. 3, No. 1 (September), 2.

CHABAUD, JAQUELINE.
    1970   *Education et promotion de la femme.* Paris: UNESCO.

CHARZAT, GISELE.
    1972   *Les Françaises: sont-elles des citoyennes?* Paris: Denöel Gonthier.

CHEEK, FRANCES E.
    1964   "A Serendipitous Finding: Sex Roles and Schizophrenia," *Journal of Abnormal and Social Psychology,* Vol. 69, No. 4, 392–400.

CHESLER, PHYLLIS.
    1971   "Patient and the Patriarch: Women in the Psychotherapeutic Relationship," in Vivian Gornick and Barbara K. Moran, eds., *Woman in Sexist Society: Studies in Power and Powerlessness.* New York: Basic Books, Inc., Publishers.

————.
    1972   *Women and Madness.* Garden City, N.Y.: Doubleday & Company, Inc.

CHRISTENSEN, HAROLD T., AND CHRISTINA F. GREGG.
    1970   "Changing Sex Norms in America and Scandinavia," *Journal of Marriage and the Family,* Vol. 32, No. 4 (November), 616–27.

CHYLINSKA, KAMILA.
    1968   "Political Activity of Women in Eastern Europe," *The Annals of the American Academy of Political and Social Sciences,* Vol. 375 (January), 67–71.

COHEN, A. K.
    1955   *Delinquent Boys.* London: Routledge and Kegan Paul.

"Columbia Women's Liberation."
    1970   *Barnard Alumnae* (Spring), 12–18.

COMBS, ROBERT H., AND WILLIAM F. KENKEL.
 1966 "Sex Differences in Dating Aspirations and Satisfaction with Computer-Selected Partners," *Journal of Marriage and the Family,* Vol. 28, No. 1 (Feb.), 62–66.

COOK, ALICE H.
 1968 "Women and American Trade Unions," *The Annals of the American Academy of Political and Social Science,* Vol. 375, 124–32.

COOPER, DAVID.
 1971 *The Death of the Family.* New York: Pantheon Books.

"Crime Rate of Women Up Sharply Over Men's."
 1971 *The New York Times* (June 12).

CUBER, JOHN, AND PEGGY B. HARROFF.
 1965 *The Significant Americans.* New York: Appleton-Century-Crofts.

DALY, MARY.
 1970 "Women and the Catholic Church," in Robin Morgan, ed., *Sisterhood Is Powerful.* New York: Random House, pp. 124–38.

DAVID, HENRY P.
 1970 *Family Planning and Abortion in the Socialist Countries of Central and Eastern Europe.* New York: The Population Council.

DEWEY, LUCRETIA M.
 1971 "Women in Labor Unions," *Monthly Labor Review,* Vol. 94 (February), 42–48.

DIZARD, JAN.
 1968. *Social Change in the Family.* Chicago: Community and Family Study Center, University of Chicago.

"Discrimination Against Women in Physics."
 1972 *Physics Today* (July), 61–62.

"Les Disparités entre Salaires Masculins et Feminins."
 1972 *Revue Française des Affaires Sociales.*

DODGE, NORTON T.
 1966 *Women in the Soviet Economy.* Baltimore, Md.: The Johns Hopkins Press.

DOFNY, JACQUES.
 1970 "The Future of Women's Liberation as a Social Movement," unpublished manuscript, University of Montreal, Department of Sociology.

DOGAN, MATTEI, AND JACQUES NARBONNE.
 1955 *Les Françaises face à la politique.* Paris: Armand Colin.

"Don't Buy Farah Slacks for Men and Boys Says Olga M. Madar."
    1972   *Women Today,* Vol. II, No. 19 (September 18), 3.

DUFF, RAYMOND S., AND AUGUST B. HOLLINGSHEAD.
    1968   *Sickness and Society.* New York: Harper & Row.

DUGAN, GEORGE.
    1972   "Female Rabbinical Student Asks Increased 'Femininity' in
           Judaism," *The New York Times* (May 7).

DUVERGER, MAURICE.
    1955   *The Political Role of Women.* Paris: UNESCO.

DWORKING LEVERING, SUSAN.
    1972   "She Must Be Some Kind of Nut," *Rough Times,* Vol. 3, No. 1
           (Sept.), 3.

EDELMAN, JUDY.
    1970   "Unions on the Line: Myths vs. Reality," *Up From Under,*
           Vol. 1, No. 1 (May), 34–37.

EDMISTON, SUSAN.
    1972   "How to Write Your Own Marriage Contract," *Ms.* (Spring),
           66–72.

The Equal Rights Amendment and Alimony and Child Support Laws.
    1972   Washington, D.C.: Citizen's Advisory Council on the Status of
           Women.

ERB, CHARLOTTE.
    1969   "Savings and Investment Decisions in the Retirement Plans of
           Working Women," unpublished Ph.D. dissertation, Department
           of Economics, University of Wisconsin.

ETHERIDGE, CAROLYN F.
    1972   "Divide and Conquer: The Oppression of Working Class
           Women," paper presented at the annual meeting of the Society
           for the Study of Social Problems (August).

ETZIONI, AMITAI.
    1971   "On Academic Blood Tests," *Science,* Vol. 172, No. 11 (June).

————.
    1972   "The Women's Movement—Tokens vs. Objectives," *Saturday
           Review* (May 20), 31–35.

"Faculty Backlash."
    1972   *Newsweek* (December 4), 127–28.

FARRELL, WARREN.
    1970   "The Resocialization of Men's Attitudes toward Women's Role
           in Society." Paper presented at the American Political Science
           Association meetings, Los Angeles, 9 September.

————.
    1971   "Women's Liberation as Men's Liberation," mimeographed.

FASTEAU, MARC.
>   1972 "Men: Why Aren't We Talking?" *Ms.*, Vol. 1, No. 1 (July), 16.

"Father God, Mother Eve."
>   1972 *Time* (March 20), 58, 63.

"Federal Laws and Regulations Concerning Sex Discrimination in Educational Institutions."
>   1972 Washington, D.C.: Association of American Colleges.

FEDERBUSH, MARCIA.
>   1971 *Let Them Aspire*, 2nd ed. Ann Arbor, Mich.: Committee to Eliminate Sexual Discrimination in the Public Schools.

FELDMAN, HAROLD.
>   1964 *Development of the Husband–Wife Relationship, A Research Report*. Ithaca, N.Y.: New York College of Home Economics, Cornell University.

———.
>   1969 "Parent and Marriage: Myths and Realities," paper presented at the Merrill-Palmer Institute Conference on Myths and Realities About the American Family.

"Feminist Psychology Coalition Therapy Referral Service."
>   1972 *Rough Times,* Vol. 3, No. 1 (September), 14.

FILLION, EVA.
>   1972 "Report on Action Program to Change Present Sex Bias Practices in Grosse Pointe Public Schools" (November 4), mimeographed.

———.
>   1972a "Time for Change: Sex Discrimination in the Grosse Pointe Public Schools" (March 14), mimeographed.

FIRESTONE, SHULAMITH.
>   1970 *The Dialectic of Sex.* New York: William Morrow and Co.

FISKE, EDWARD B.
>   1972 "Union Theological Votes a Rise in Blacks and Women in School," *The New York Times* (June 1).

FORTNEY, JUDITH A.
>   1972 "Achievement as an Alternate Source of Emotional Gratification to Childbearing," paper presented at the Population Association of America meetings, Toronto, Canada (April).

FREDRIKSSON, INGRID.
>   1969 *Konstroller i larobocker.* Stockholm: Swedish Joint Female Labour Council.

GARLAND, T. NEAL.
    1972   "The Better Half? The Male in the Dual Profession Family,"
           in Constantina Safilios-Rothschild, ed., *Toward a Sociology of
           Women*. Lexington, Mass.: Xerox College Publishing, pp. 199–
           215.

GEHLEN, FRIEDA.
    1969   "Women in Congress," *Trans-Action,* Vol. 6 (October), 36–40.

GIBBS, JACK P.
    1966   "Conceptions of Deviant Behavior: The Old and the New,"
           Pacific Sociological Review, Vol. 9 No. 1 (Spring), 9–14.

GINSBERG, GEORGE, WILLIAM FROSCH, AND THEODORE SHAPIRO.
    1972   "The New Impotence," *Archives of General Psychiatry,* Vol.
           26 (March), 218–22.

GORE, M. S.
    1961   "The Impact of Industrialization and Urbanization on the
           Aggarwal Family in the Delhi Area," unpublished Ph.D. dis-
           sertation, Columbia University.

GOVE, WALTER R., AND JEANNETTE F. TUDOR.
    1973   "Adult Sex Roles and Mental Illness," *American Journal of
           Sociology,* Vol. 78, No. 4 (January), 812–35.

GROSSER, G. H.
    1951   "Juvenile Delinquency and Contemporary American Sex
           Roles," unpublished Ph.D. thesis, Department of Social Rela-
           tions, Harvard University.

GRUBERG, MARTIN.
    1968   *Women in American Politics.* Oshkosh, Wis.: Academia Press.

HAAVIO-MANNILA, ELINA.
    1972   "Sex Roles in Politics," in Constantina Safilios-Rothschild, ed.,
           Toward a Sociology of Women. Lexington, Mass.: Xerox Col-
           lege Publishing, pp. 154–72.

LOUIS HARRIS AND ASSOCIATES, INC.
    1972   *The 1972 Virginia Slims American Women's Opinion Poll.*

HATCH, CAROL, AND MARGARET HENDERSON.
    1971   "Fed Up: Secretaries in Academia," *The Second Wave,* Vol. 1,
           No. 2 (Summer), 18–20, 23.

HAVENS, ELIZABETH M.
    1973   "Women, Work, and Wedlock: A Note on Female Marital
           Patterns in the United States," *American Journal of Sociology,*
           Vol. 78, No. 4 (January), 975–81.

HAWLEY, ANDY.
    1969   "A Man's View," *Motive,* Vol. 29, Nos. 6–7 (March–April),
           72–75.

HEIDENSOHN, FRANCES.
    1968   "The Deviance of Women: A Critique and an Enquiry,"
            British Journal of Sociology, Vol. 19, 160–75.
HERMAN, SONDRA R.
    1972   "Sex-Roles and Sexual Attitudes in Sweden: The New Phase,"
            The Massachusetts Review, Vol. 13, Nos. 1 and 2 (Winter–
            Spring), 45–64.
HEYMANN, DANIELE.
    1972   "Jusqui'où vont-elles aller, les femmes?" *L'Express* (May 8–
            14), 39–46.
HOLDEN, CONSTANCE.
    1972   "Women in Michigan: Parlaying Rights into Power," *Science,*
            Vol. 178 (December 1), 962–65.
"The Hooker's Boswell."
    1972   *Newsweek* (December 4).
ISRAEL, JOACHIM.
    1969   *Valfardssamhallet-och darefter?* Stockholm: Aldus–Bonvier.
ISRAEL, JOACHIM, AND ROSMARI ELIASSON.
    1971   "Consumption Society, Sex Roles and Sexual Behavior," *Acta
            Sociologica,* Vol. 14, No. 1–2, 68–82.
JORDAN, JOAN.
    1972   "Local 1100 of the Retail Clerks Conducted a Militant Sit-in
            at San Francisco's Emporium," *Union W.A.G.E.,* No. 13 (Sep-
            tember–October), 5.

———.

    1972a "Red Ball Strike," *Union W.A.G.E.,* No. 13 (September–
            October), 2.
JOHNSON, RALPH E.
    1970   "Some Correlates of Extramarital Coitus," *Journal of Marriage
            and the Family,* Vol. 32, No. 3 (August), 449–56.
JOSEPH, GERI.
    1972   "Women's Influence in Legislature," *Minneapolis Tribune*
            (June 4).
KAGAN, JEROME.
    1972   "The Emergence of Sex Differences," *School Review,* (Feb-
            ruary), 217–27.
KANOWITZ, LEO.
    1969   *Women and the Law.* Albuquerque, N.M.: University of New
            Mexico Press.
KEPHART, WILLIAM M.
    1967   "Some Correlates of Romantic Love," *Journal of Marriage and
            the Family,* Vol. 29, No. 3 (August), 470–74.

KLEIN, VIOLA.
    1965   *L'Emploi des Femmes. Horaires et Responsibilités Familiales.* Paris: O.E.C.D.

KNOBLOCHOVA, J., AND F. KNOBLOCH.
    1965   *Family Psychotherapy in Aspects of Mental Health in Europe.* Geneva: World Health Organization.

KOMAROVSKY, MIRRA.
    1967   *Blue Collar Marriage.* New York: Random House.

—————.
    1973   "Cultural Contradictions and Sex Roles: The Masculine Case," *American Journal of Sociology,* Vol. 78, No. 4 (January), 873–84.

KONTOPOULOS, KYRIAKOS M.
    1972   "Women's Liberation as a Social Movement," in Constantina Safilios-Rothschild, ed., *Toward a Sociology of Women.* Lexington, Mass: Xerox College Publishing, 354–61.

KOYAMA, TAKASHI.
    1961   *The Changing Social Position of Women in Japan.* Paris: UNESCO.

LAING, R. D., AND A. ESTERTON.
    1971   *Sanity, Madness and the Family,* 2nd ed. New York: Basic Books.

LAMSON, PEGGY.
    1969   *Few Are Chosen: American Women in Political Life Today.* Boston: Houghton Mifflin.

LEIGHTON, LENNARD A., GARY E. STOLLAK, AND LUCY RAU FERGUSON.
    1971   "Patterns of Communication in Normal and Clinic Families," *Journal of Consulting and Clinical Psychology,* Vol. 36, No. 2, 252–56.

E. E. LEMASTERS.
    1970   *Parents in Modern America.* Homewood, Ill.: Dorsey Press.

LEVIN, JUDITH, AND PATRICIA VERGATA.
    1971   "Welfare Laws and Women: An Analysis of Federal Sexism." New Brunswick, N.J.: Rutgers Law School, mimeograph (available from The Center of Social Welfare Policy and Law, 401 W. 117th Street, New York, N. Y. 10027).

LEWIS, MICHAEL.
    1972   "Culture and Gender Roles: There's No Unisex in the Nursery," *Psychology Today* Vol. 5 (May), 54–57.

—————.
    1972b   "Parents and Children: Sex-Role Development," *School Report* (February), 229–40.

LINNER, BIRGITTA.

1971 "What Does Equality Between the Sexes Imply?" *American Journal of Orthopsychiatry,* Vol. 41 (October), 747–56.

LIPMAN-BLUMEN, JEAN.

1973 "Role De-Differentiation as a System Response to Crisis: Occupational and Political Roles of Women," *Sociological Inquiry,* Vol. 43, No. 1 (April).

LOPATA, HELENA Z.

1971 *Occupation Housewife.* New York: Oxford University Press.

LUCKEY, ELEANOR B., AND GILBERT D. NASS.

1969 "A Comparison of Sexual Attitudes and Behavior in an International Sample," *Journal of Marriage and the Family,* Vol. 31, No. 2 (May), 364–79.

LYTLE HOLMSTROM, LINDA.

1972 *Dual Career Couples.* Cambridge, Mass.: Schenckman.

MACCOBY, ELEANOR E., ed.

1966 *The Development of Sex Differences.* Stanford, Ca.: Stanford University Press.

MACKLIN, ELEANOR D.

1972 "Heterosexual Cohabitation Among Unmarried College Students," *The Family Coordinator,* Vol. 21, No. 4 (October), 463–72.

A Matter of Simple Justice.

1970 Washington, D.C.: Report of the President's Task Force on Women's Rights and Responsibilities.

MAUPIN, JOYCE.

1972 "Labor Heroines," *Union W.A.G.E.,* No. 13 (September–October), 2.

MAXEY, MARGARET M.

1972 "Beyond Eve and Mary," in Martin E. Marty and Dean G. Peerman, eds., *New Theology No. 9.* New York: Macmillan, pp. 207–29.

MENON, LAKSHMI N.

1968 "From Constitutional Recognition to Public Office," *Annals of the American Academy of Political and Social Sciences,* Vol. 375 (January), 34–43.

MEYER, W. J., AND G. G. THOMPSON.

1956 "Sex Differences in the Distribution of Teacher Approval and Disapproval Among Sixth Grade Children," *Journal of Educational Psychology,* Vol. 47, 385–96.

———.

1963 "Teacher Interactions with Boys as Contrasted with Girls," in

R. G. Kuhlen and G. G. Thompson, eds., *Psychological Studies of Human Development,* 2nd ed. New York: Appleton-Century-Crofts.

MILLER, GASEY, AND KATE SWIFT.
1972   "One Small Step for Genkind," *The New York Times Magazine* (April 16).

MILLER, S. M.
1972   "The Making of a Confused, Middle-Aged Husband," in Constantina Safilios-Rothschild, ed., *Toward a Sociology of Women.* Lexington, Mass.: Xerox College Publishing, pp. 245–53.

MOBERG, EVA.
1969   "Playgirl," *Hertha,* No. 5, 28–29.

MORRIS, MONICA B.
1972   "The Public Definition of a Social Movement: Women's Liberation," paper presented at the American Sociological Association meeting, New Orleans (August).

MULAWKA, EDWARD J.
1972   *Sex Role Typing in the Elementary School Classroom as Reinforcement of Sex Role Stereotypes Learned At Home.* Unpublished Ph.D. thesis, Department of Educational Sociology, Wayne State University.

MULLIGAN, LINDA W.
1969   "Structural Polygamy and Legal Monogamy," unpublished paper.

NAGEL, STUART, AND LENORE J. WEITZMAN.
1971   "Women as Litigants," *Hastings Law Journal.* Vol. 22.

————.
1972   "Double Standard of American Justice," *Trans-Action,* Vol. 9, Nos. 1–2 (March), 18–63.

NARAIN, D.
1969   "Growing Up in India," *Family Process,* Vol. 3, No. 1 (March), 127–54.

NEMY, ENID.
1972   "Young Women Challenging Their '2nd-Class Status' in Judaism," *The New York Times* (June 12).

"N.O.W. Charges WABC-TV with Blatant Sexism."
1972   *Women Today,* Vol. 11, No. 10 (May 15), 2.

OLSON, K.
1971   "For Her Own Protection: A Case Study of the Conditions of Incarceration for Female Juvenile Offenders in the State of Connecticut," unpublished paper, Yale Law School, Princeton, N. J.

PETERSON, IVER.
　1972　"College Hiring of Women Said to Slip," *The New York Times* (November 30).

PIETROFESA, JOHN K., AND NANCY K. SCHLOSSBERG.
　1972　"Counselor Bias and the Female Occupational Role," in Nona Galzer-Malbin and Helen Youngelson Waehrer, eds., *Counselor Bias and the Female Occupational Role*. Chicago: Rand McNally.

POLK, BARBARA, AND ROBERT STEIN.
　1972　"Is the Grass Greener on the other Side?" in Constantina Safilios-Rothschild, ed., *Toward a Sociology of Women*. Lexington, Mass.: Xerox College Publishing, pp. 14–23.

POLK, LON.
　1971　"Involuntary Overtime and the Liberation of Men," statement to the Michigan State House of Representatives, Committee on Labor Hearings, on legislation to abolish or limit the hours of involuntary overtime (June 25).

POLLAK, OTTO.
　1950　*The Criminality of Women*. Philadelphia: University of Pennsylvania Press.

POLOMA, MARGARET M.
　1972　"Role Conflict and the Married Professional Woman," in Constantina Safilios-Rothschild, ed., *Toward a Sociology of Women*. Lexington, Mass.: Xerox College Publishing, pp. 187–98.

POTTINGER, J. STANLEY.
　1972　Quoted in *Women Today*, Vol. II, No. 9 (May 1), 2.

POWER GOLDBERG, MARILYN
　1972　"Women in the Soviet Economy," *The Review of Radical Political Economics*, Vol. 4, No. 3 (July).

PRINCE, ALFRED JAMES, AND ANDREW R. BAGGALEY.
　1963　"Personality Variables and the Ideal Mate," *Family Life Coordinator*, Vol. 12, No. 3–4 (July–October), 93–96.

RADKE YARROW, MARIAN, et al.
　1962　"Child-Rearing in Families of Working and Nonworking Women," *Sociometry*, Vol. 25 (June), 122–40.

RAPOPORT, RHONA, AND ROBERT RAPOPORT.
　1971　*Dual Career Families*. New York: Penguin Books.

"Recent Longevity Studies."
　1972　*The Participant*, TIAA-CREF (November), 4.

Report of the Subcommittee on the Status of Academic Women on the Berkeley Campus.
　1970　University of California: Committee on Senate Policy of the

Berkeley Division of the Academic Senate of the University of California, May 19.

Report of the Task Force on Family Law and Policy.
1968   Washington, D.C.: Citizen's Advisory Council on the Status of Women.

Report of the Women's Action Program.
1972   Washington, D.C.: Department of Health, Education, and Welfare.

REYNOLDS, JANICE M.
1971   "Rape as Social Control," paper presented at the Michigan Sociological Association meeting, Detroit (November 12).

ROBERTS, BARBARA, M.D.
1972   "Psychosurgery, the Final Solution to the Woman Problem," *Rough Times,* Vol. 3, No. 1 (September), 16–17.

BOBY, PAMELA, ed.
1973   *Child Care—Who Cares?* New York: Basic Books.

ROBY, PAMELA, AND VIRGINIA KERR.
1972   "The Politics of Prostitution," *The Nation* (April 10), 463–66.

ROLLINGS, BOYD C., AND HAROLD FELDMAN.
1970   "Marital Satisfaction over the Family Life Cycle" *Journal of Marriage and the Family,* Vol. 32, No. 1 (February), 20–28.

"Room at the Top?"
1972   *Newsweek* (December 4), 96, 99.

ROSENFELD, ALBERT.
1969   "Science, Sex and Tomorrow's Morality," *Life Magazine* (June 13).

Ross, A. D.
1962   *The Hindu Family in its Urban Setting.* Toronto: Toronto University Press.

ROSSI, ALICE S.
1972   "Family Development in a Changing World," *American Journal of Psychiatry,* Vol. 128 (March), 1957–65.

SAFILIOS-ROTHSCHILD, CONSTANTINA.
1968   "The Status of Sociology in Greece," *The American Sociologist,* Vol. 3, No. 4 (November).

————.
1969   "Family Sociology or Wives' Family Sociology? A Comparison of Husbands' and Wives' Answers About Decision-Making in the Greek and American Culture," *Journal of Marriage and the Family,* Vol. 31, No. 3 (August), 290–301.

———.

1970a "Toward a Cross-Cultural Conceptualization of Modernity," *Journal of Comparative Family Studies,* Vol. 1, No. 1 (Fall), 17–25.

———.

1970b *The Sociology and Social Psychology of Disability and Rehabilitation.* New York: Random House, Inc.

SAFILIOS-ROTHSCHILD, CONSTANTINA.

1971 "A Cross-Cultural Examination of Women's Marital, Educational and Occupational Options," *Acta Sociologica,* Vol. 14, Nos. 1–2, 96–113.

———.

1972a "Companionate Marriages and Sexual Inequality: Are They Compatible?" in Constantina Safilios-Rothschild, ed., *Toward a Sociology of Women.* Lexington, Mass.: Xerox College Publishing, pp. 63–70.

———.

1972b "Discussion," Chapter 7 in *Toward a Sociology of Women.* Lexington, Mass.: Xerox College Publishing, pp. 387–92.

———.

1972c " 'Honour' Crimes in Contemporary Greece," in Constantina Safilios-Rothschild, ed., *Toward a Sociology of Women.* Lexington, Mass.: Xerox College Publishing, pp. 84–95.

———.

1972d "Men React Vindictively to Sexual Rejection . . . ," *Sexual Behavior,* Vol. 2, No. 1 (January), 60.

———.

1973a "The Dimensions of Power Distribution in the Family," in Jacob Christ and Henry Grunebaum, eds.

———

1973b "The Mother's Needs for Child Care," in Pamela Roby, ed., *Child Care—Who Cares?* New York: Basic Books, Inc., Publishers.

SAFILIOS-ROTHSCHILD, CONSTANTINA, AND JOHN GEORGIOPOULOS.

1970 "A Comparative Study of Parental and Filial Roles," *The Journal of Marriage and the Family,* Vol. 32, No. 3 (August).

SAFILIOS-ROTHSCHILD, CONSTANTINA, AND the UNICEF SECRETARIAT.

1971 *Children and Adolescents in Slums and Shanty-Towns of Developing Countries.* United Nations Economic and Social Council, UNICEF (E/ICEF/L. 1277/Add. 1).

"Sales Liberation."
    1972   *Newsweek* (July 24), 63.

SALPUKAS, AGIS
    1973   "Survey of Textbooks Detects Less Bias Against Blacks but Little to Please Feminists," *The New York Times,* (March 28).

SALPUKAS, MARY.
    1972   "Well Over 30 and Successful, They Still Join the Younger Women's Fight," *The New York Times* (December 18).

SANDLER, BERNICE.
    1972   "What Constitutes Equity for Women in Higher Education?" Address presented at Concurrent General Session I, 27th National Conference on Higher Education, Chicago (March 7).

SCHEFF, THOMAS J.
    1972   "Reevaluation Counseling: Social Implications," *Journal of Humanistic Psychology,* Vol. 12 (Spring), 58–71.

SCULLY, DIANA, AND PAULINE BART.
    1973   "A Funny Thing Happened on the Way to the Orifice: Women in Gynecology Textbooks," *American Journal of Sociology,* Vol. 78, No. 4 (January), 1945–50.

SEABURY, PAUL.
    1972   "HEW and the Universities," *Commentary* (February), 38–44.

SEEAR, B. N.
    1971   *Re-Entry of Women to the Labour Market After an Interruption in Employment.* Paris: O.E.C.D.

SHANAHAN, EILEEN.
    1972   "Women Legislators Start to Challenge Male Colleagues' Power," *The New York Times* (May 22).

SHAPLEY, DEBORAH.
    1972   "University Women's Rights: Whose Feet Are Dragging?" *Science,* Vol. 175 (January 14), 151–54.

SHERR, LYNN.
    1972   "Teaching Kit to Free Vowels from Chauvinist Consonants," *The New York Times* (February 20).

SCHLOSSBERG, NANCY K., AND JANE GOODMAN.
    1972   "Imperative for Change: Counselor Use of the Strong Vocational Blanks," *Impact,* Vol. 2, No. 1 (Fall), 26–29.

SCHNEIDER, JOSEPH W., AND SALLY L. HACKER.
    1972   "Sex Role Imagery and Use of the Generic 'Man' in Introductory Texts: A Case in the Sociology of Sociology," paper presented at the American Sociological Association meetings, New Orleans (August).

SHOSTAK, ARTHUR B.
 1969 *Blue-Collar Life.* New York: Random House, pp. 139–40.

————.

 1972 "Middle-Aged Working Class Americans at Home: Changing Expectations of Manhood," paper presented at the Eastern Sociological Society meetings, Boston (April).

Social Benefits for Part-Time Employees.
 1970 Stockholm: National Labour Market Board.

SOKOLOWSKA, MAGDALENA.
 1965 "Some Reflections on the Different Attitudes of Men and Women Toward Work," *International Labor Review,* Vol. 92 (July–December), 35–50.

SPIEGEL, IRVING.
 1972 "Paternity Leaves Offered in New City U. Contract," *The New York Times* (September 24).

STANISLAS DEVAUD, MARCELLE.
 1968 "Political Participation of Western European Women," *The Annals of the American Academy of Political and Social Sciences,* Vol. 375 (January), 61–66.

The Status of Women in Canada.
 1970 Ottawa: Report of the Royal Commission on the Status of Women in Canada.

STOLTE HEISKANEN, VERONICA.
 1971 "Sex Roles, Social Class and Political Consciousness," *Acta Sociologica,* Vol. 14, Nos. 1–2, 83–95.

The Structures of Incomes in Sweden.
 1970 Stockholm: Ministry of the Interior, Low Income Commission.

"Superficial Sex Appeal."
 1972 *The Village Voice* (June 30).

"Survey Indicates that Colleges Have Increased Hiring Women but Still Pay them Less."
 1973 *Women Today,* Vol. 3, No. 6 (March 19), 4.

TANGRI, SANDRA S.
 1969 "Role Innovation in Occupational Choice," unpublished Ph.D. dissertation, University of Michigan.

"Tennis: A Triumph for Women's Lob."
 1972 *Newsweek* (June 26), pp. 38–44.

THOMAS, ARTHUR, AND NORMAN STEWART.
 1971 "Counselor Response to Female Clients with Deviate and Conforming Career Goals," *Journal of Counseling Psychology,* Vol. 18, No. 4, 352–57.

"Toward Female Power at the Polls."
  1972   *Time* (March 20), 33–34.

U. S. DEPARTMENT OF LABOR, EMPLOYMENT STANDARDS ADMINISTRATION.
  1971   "Fact Sheet on the Earnings Gap." Washington, D.C.: Women's Bureau.

VALABRÉQUE, CATHERINE.
  1968   *La Condition Masculine.* Paris: Petite Bibliothèque Payot.

VEROFF, J., AND S. FELD.
  1970   *Marriage and Work in America.* New York: Van Nostrand Reinhold.

VINCENT, CLARK E.
  1966   "Implications of Changes in Male–Female Role Expectations for Interpreting M–F Scores," *Journal of Marriage and the Family,* Vol. 28, No. 2 (May), 196–99.

WARSHAY, DIANA W.
  1972   "Sex Differences in Language Style," in Constantina Safilios-Rothschild, ed., *Toward a Sociology of Women.* Lexington, Mass.: Xerox College Publishing.

WEAL Washington Report.
  1973   Report No. 10 (February 12).

WEINMAN LEAR, MARTHA.
  1972   "Q—If You Rape a Woman and Steal Her T.V., What Can They Get You For in New York: A—Stealing Her T.V.," *The New York Times Magazine* (January 30).

WEITZMAN, LENORE J.
  1972   "Sex Role Socialization in Picture Books for Pre-School Children," *American Journal of Sociology,* Vol. 77, No. 6 (May), 1125–50.

"Welfare Rights: The Plight of the Welfare Mothers."
  1972   *Women's Yellow Pages.* Boston: Boston Women's Collective, Inc., pp. 51–52.

WESTMAN BERG, KARIN.
  1969   "Schoolbooks and Roles of the Sexes," *Hertha,* No. 5, 48–57.

WLADIS HOFFMAN, LOIS.
  1972   "The Professional Woman as Mother," paper presented at the Conference on Successful women in Sciences, New York Academy of Sciences, New York.

WLADIS HOFFMAN, LOIS, AND FREDERICK WYATT.
  1960   "Social Change and Motivations for Having Larger Families: Some Theoretical Considerations," *The Merrill-Palmer Quarterly,* Vol. 6 (July), 235–44.

Woman in Sweden in the Light of Statistics.
    1971   Stockholm: The Joint Female Labor Council.

"Women in Michigan: Academic Sexism Under Siege."
    1972   *Science,* Vol. 178 (November 24), 841–44.

"Women in Prisons."
    1972   *Women's Yellow Pages.* Boston: Boston Women's Collective, Inc., pp. 54–55.

Women in the University of Chicago.
    1970   Chicago: Report of the Committee on University Women.

"Women M.D.'s Join the Fight."
    1970   *Medical World News* (October), reprinted in *Rough Times,* Vol. 3, No. 1 (Sept.), 10.

"A Woman Professor Replies."
    1971   *The Chemist,* XLVIII, No. 8 (August), 205–8.

"Women's Lobby to Pressure for Women's Issues."
    1972   *Women Today,* Vol. 2, No. 24 (November 27), 4.

INDEX

Abortion, 66, 71, 102-3, 166
Abstract of Protocol on Justice Department Matters Held Before the King in Council, 98, 99
Achievement
  avoidance of, 65, 84
  as male norm, 11, 73, 80, 81, 84, 85
Adelson, Joseph, 95, 162
Adoption of children, 96
Advertising, and sexism, 125
Affirmative Action Plan to Improve Employment Opportunities for Minority Groups and Women, 55
Africa, 8, 14, 44, 79. *See also* Developing nations
"AIC Survey Shows Many Women Chemists Feel $$ Discrimination But Less So in Education," 51
Algrin, Karin, 157
Alimony, replacement of, 61
Alpha One, 82
American Nurses' Association, 64
"American Nurses' Association Files Sex Discrimination Charges Against TIAA," 64
American Personnel and Guidance Association, 32
Amundsen, Kirsten, 89, 142, 143, 148, 151, 152

Aquinas, Thomas, 158
Arab societies, 8
Arnaldez, Roger, 156
Asia, 44. *See also* Developing nations
Associated Actors and Artists of America, 154
Association of American University Professors, 55

Bader Ginsburg, Ruth, 97
Baggaley, Andrew R., 67
Bannon, James, 135, 137, 139
Barker, G. R., 103
Barron, Nancy, 122
Bart, Pauline, 75, 111, 126
Bartell, Gilbert D., 107
Bazell, Robert J., 49
Behavioral sciences, 12-14
  sexism in, 123-25, 143-44
Bender, Marilyn, 55, 56, 57
Bernard, Jessie, 46, 47, 111, 126, 129
Bingham, Liza, 155
Birnbaum, J. A., 111
Birth control, 20, 66, 71, 158, 166
Black Movement, 9, 10
Black women, 153
Blake, Judith Davis, 101
Blau, Eleanor, 157, 158, 159

Nagel, Stuart, 135, 137-40
Narain, D., 110
Narbonne, Jacques, 146
Nass, Gilbert D., 66
National Center for Educational
    Statistics, 43
Nemy, Enid, 159
Nepotism, restriction of, 56-57
New Jersey, 138
Newman, Holly, 155
Newspapers, and Women's Liberation
    Movement, 162
Nigeria, 79
1972 Tax rules, 97
*The 1972 Virginia Slims American Women's
    Opinion Poll*, 144-45, 147, 153,
    161, 163
Ninety-third U.S. Congress, 150, 152
Norway, 148
NOW (National Organization of Women),
    28, 133
"N.O.W. Charges WABC-TV with Blatant
    Sexism," 125
Nuclear family, 105-7
Nursery schools, 82, 87
Nurse Training Act of 1971, 39

Oberlin University, 57
Occupations, 15-16. *See also* Equalization
    of options
  men's choice of, 78-82, 84-86
  stereotyped by sex, 35, 78-81
  women's, 35, 45, 46, 58-61, 154
Office workers, nonunionized, 154
Old age, 100-101
Olson, K., 137
Ombudswomen, 31, 41, 61
On-the-job training programs, 58
Opportunity. *See* Equalization of options
Options. *See* Equalization of options
Orgasm, feigned by women, 67, 93
Oslo, Municipal Council of, 148
Overtime work, 61, 85-86

Parental leave, for child care, 20-22
Parenthood, 19-20, 96, 99-100, 101-4.
    See also Fathers; Marriage;
    Motherhood
Part-time work, 21, 60, 84-86, 110
Pension systems, and women, 62
Personal injury awards, 139-41
Peterson, Iver, 54
Pietrofesa, John K., 32
Poland, 48, 150
Political systems, and liberation, 10-11
Politics, 141-54
  strategies to liberate, 151-54

Politics *(cont.)*
  and voting of women, 142, 146-48
  women in, 142-46, 148-54
Polk, Barbara, 33, 87, 89, 112
Polk, Lon, 111
Pollak, Otto, 136
Poloma, Margaret M., 101, 109, 128
Pompidou, Georges, election of, 147
Pope John XXIII, 157
Pottinger, J. Stanley, 50
Power, and sex stereotypes, 141-46. *See
    also* Dominance-submission;
    Politics
Power Goldberg, Marilyn, 46, 47
Preferential treatment, of women, 4-6,
    36-37, 39-40, 51-54, 141, 152-53
Pregnancy and motherhood, 20-21, 35-36
Pressure, social and political
  for men's liberation, 86, 87, 90, 95
  for women's liberation, 6, 41, 69, 70,
    161
Prince, Alfred James, 67
Prison treatment, of women, 139
Professional women. *See* Employment;
    Career women
Property, individualization of, 98-99
Prostitution, 136-37
Protest, role of, 9, 10
Psychiatry. *See* Therapy
Psychology, clinical. *See* Therapy
Psychosurgery, 129-30

Quota systems, in school admissions, 39,
    40, 141

The Radical Therapist, 132
Radke Yarrow, Marian, 19
Randall, Claire, 157
Rape, 92, 137-38
Rapoport, Rhona, 109
Rapoport, Robert, 109
Rau Ferguson, Lucy, 112, 129, 130
Rejection, sexual, 89, 90, 92, 93
Religion
  liberation of, 16, 157-59
  sexism in, 155-57
*Report of the American Task Force on
    Family Law and Policy*, 98, 108
*Report of the Subcommittee on the Status
    of Academic Women on the
    Berkeley Campus*, 38
Report of Women's Action Program, 54
Residence, legal, of married women, 108-9
Resistance, to women's liberation
  of men, 51-52, 54, 83, 95, 161
  of society, 2-5, 18-19, 49-52, 163
  of women, 49-50, 69, 161